hugo

Russian
in Three Months

Nicholas J. Brown

A Dorling Kindersley Book

A DORLING KINDERSLEY BOOK

www.dk.com

This new and enlarged edition published in Great Britain
in 1997 by Hugo's Language Books,
an imprint of Dorling Kindersley Limited,
9 Henrietta Street, London WC2E 8PS

A CIP catalogue record is available from the British Library.

ISBN 0 85285 312 2

Russian in Three Months is also available in
a pack with four cassettes, ISBN 0 85285 313 0

Written by

Nicholas J. Brown B.A. (Birmingham), Dip. Gen. Ling. (Edinburgh)
Senior Lecturer in Russian
School of Slavonic and East European Studies
University of London

Set in 10/12pt Palatino by
Samantha Borland
Printed and bound by LegoPrint, Italy

Contents

Abbreviations used in this book

acc = accusative case
adj = adjective
acc = accusative
adj = adjective
coll = colloquial
dat = dative
f = feminine
fut = future tense
gen = genitive case
i = imperfective aspect
idiom = idiomatic
imper - imperative
indecl = indeclinable

infin = infinitive
inst = instrumental
irreg = irregular
m = masculine
n = neuter
nom = nominative case
p = perfective aspect
pl = plural
pol = polite form
prep = prepositional case
pres = present tense
sing. = singular

Introduction

About Russian

Everyone ought to know some Russian. Just as educated people once felt a need to know Latin, nowadays it is Russian which we cannot afford to ignore. Whether you find Russia exciting or frightening, simply take a passing interest in that vast country, or prefer to think only of the great works of Russian nineteenth-century literature, an understanding of the language and culture of the world's largest state is undeniably important.

Is Russian difficult? It is more of a challenge for an English-speaking learner than French or German, but much easier than Japanese or Arabic. English and Russian have the same Indo-European linguistic origins, so there is a lot of grammar in common. Behind the exotic-looking alphabet, which is based on Greek, there is a simple system of pronunciation and a large number of familiar words. Try the list on page 11 as a taster.

About this book

This book is a straightforward introduction to the essentials of Russian. It is intended for those working on their own, or with a teacher one or two hours a week, and could serve as a textbook for a twenty-session evening-class course. Its main aims are communicative – how to do things in Russian – but the grammar is dealt with in detail. When you have worked through this book you should be able to make yourself understood on everyday topics (of the kind a foreign visitor to Moscow might need), hold simple conversations (particularly if you use the cassettes available) and read Russian texts with the help of a dictionary. You should also know the basic grammar of the language and have a

vocabulary of about eight hundred of the commonest Russian words.

The book is designed for those working on their own as well as those who have a teacher. So all you need is here in your hands: Russian grammar explained, useful vocabulary and phrases, and exercises with answers. The cassettes, which carry recordings by native speakers of the lesson materials, will prove a very helpful extra.

The author has tried both to give you the tools to do things in Russian (introduce yourself, find your way around, ask for assistance) and also to explain how Russian works. But you can decide for yourself what to concentrate on, whether to skim right through the book before doing any exercises, to work methodically through all the material in order, or to concentrate on some parts while ignoring others.

If you are completely new to Russian, the first hurdle is of course the Russian alphabet, so spend plenty of time on chapter 1. Once you know the letters, you can read any word: Russian spelling is much easier than English. You will need the cassettes if you want to acquire a good Russian pronunciation, but it is not difficult to make yourself understood.

After mastering the alphabet, your main task will be to learn Russian vocabulary. Don't worry if some of the grammar doesn't stick, so long as you understand the points. Concentrate instead on learning the new words as they are given. Use the technique suggested in 3.2 if it helps. Whether or not you master this book in three months will probably depend on how long it takes you to learn Russian words. Don't be put off if you find you have to keep re-learning words – most learners do. You will find that Russian vocabulary learning gets easier as you begin to recognize the pieces which make up words (once you know 'zhensheena' means 'woman', it doesn't take long to learn that 'zhena' means 'wife').

The chapter vocabularies introduce the new words used in the conversations, so you can learn them in context. If you forget words from previous chapters, all the vocabulary is listed in alphabetical order at the end of the book (pages 262–272) together with a reference to the section where it is first used.

New grammar points use as far as possible only the vocabulary already covered. Presentation of the material varies: the basic criterion is usefulness, but the author also considers that it is important both to explain grammatical points and to cover all the basic grammar of Russian.

If you are an experienced language learner and you want to go through the grammar faster, see the tables on pages 274–281.

Do the exercises as you come to them and check your answers with the key at the end (pages 243–261). As an additional exercise, try putting the English translations of the conversations back into Russian.

The conversations are based on encounters between Russians and foreigners in Moscow. You will meet secretive Jane, lovelorn Boris, straightforward Andrey, Mike the businessman, Nina the future factory director, and others.

Enjoy your journey into this important language!

Acknowledgements

The author would like to thank Olga Abramova, Alison Brown, Marcela Hajek, Ronald Overy, Kate Peters, Lina and Igor Pomeranzev, Sue Reed and Alison Russell for their comments on various drafts of this book. All the Russian has been read and revised by native speakers.

Chapter 1

- The Russian (Cyrillic) alphabet.
- The sounds of the letters.
- How to read Russian words slowly.
- Reading practice.

Russian looks difficult because of its unfamiliar alphabet, but behind the strange letters are lots of familiar words. For example,

ВЛАДИВОСТОК is simply the city of Vladivostok
V LAD I VOSTOK

You will see that some letters are the same in Russian and English, e.g. A and O and T and K. Some letters <u>look</u> like English ones but are pronounced differently, e.g. Russian **B** is English V. Some letters are new, but the pronunciation is familiar, for example, **Д** is English D. Can you now read this word?

ВОДКА

Yes, it's the word v-o-d-k-a, that well-known Russian drink.

Russian **C** is English S and **И** is pronounced like 'ee' in 'm<u>ee</u>t,' so what is this word?

ТАКСИ

It's t-a-k-s-ee, which you might recognize as our word 'taxi'.

1.1 The Russian (Cyrillic) alphabet

In this chapter we shall introduce you to the 33 letters of the Russian alphabet in four steps and show you that, once you know their English equivalents, reading Russian words is easy. In the next chapter we shall tell you more about Russian pronunciation and give you plenty of practice in reading before we tackle any grammar.

Since it is obviously very important to be able to check your own pronunciation of Russian words, particularly if you are learning without a teacher, we give an <u>imitated pronunciation</u> in English letters of all the Russian in the first five chapters. From then on we shall give imitated pronunciation from time to time so that you can check that you've remembered the letters correctly.

THE CYRILLIC ALPHABET

(1) Let's start with the five letters that are almost identical in Russian and English. Notice that most Russian small letters are simply half-size versions of the capitals.

Capital	Small	Imitated pronunciation
A	а	as in 'f<u>a</u>ther'
К	к	k as in '<u>k</u>angaroo'
М	м	m as in 'e<u>m</u>pty'
О	о	o as in 'b<u>o</u>ttle'
Т	т	t as in '<u>t</u>ent'

So you can already read the following Russian words:

КОТ	кот	kot	This word means 'cat'.
ТОМ	том	tom	'tome' or 'volume'
АТОМ	атом	atom	The same as our word 'atom'.

(2) Next we shall learn the seven letters which look like
English ones but are pronounced differently:

В	в	v as in 'very'
Е	е	ye as in 'yesterday'
Н	н	n as in 'enter'
Р	р	r as in 'error' (rolled as in Scots English)
С	с	s as in 'establish'
У	у	oo as in 'boot'
Х	х	h pronounced as the ch in Scots 'loch' or German 'ach'

Practice. Try to read the following words, slowly, covering
up the imitated pronunciation given on the right with a
piece of paper. To make the words easier to read we divide
them into syllables with hyphens.

Imitated pronunciation

нет	[nyet] ('no')
Нева	[nye-va] (the River Neva in St Petersburg)
Москва	[mosk-va] ('Moscow')
север	[sye-vyer] ('north')
сумка	[soom-ka] ('a handbag')
муха	[moo-ha] ('a fly')
вермут	[vyer-moot] (the drink 'vermouth')
совет	[so-vyet] ('a council' or 'soviet')
ресторан	[rye-sto-ran] ('restaurant')
метро	[mye-tro] ('underground', 'subway')

(3) Now we have some unfamiliar letters which however
have familiar sounds:

Б	б	b as in 'bed'. Note the difference between the capital and small forms.
Г	г	g as in 'get'. Looks like an L upside down.
Д	д	d as in 'dentist'. Like the Greek delta.
Ё	ё	yo as in 'yonder'. The letter е with two dots.
З	з	z as in 'zenith'. Looks like the figure 3.
И	и	ee as in 'meet'

Й	й	y as in 'boy'
Л	л	l as in 'people'
П	п	p as in 'pepper'. Like the Greek letter pi.
Ф	ф	f as in 'effort'
Э	э	e as in 'fed'. Looks like E backwards.
Ю	ю	yoo as in 'university'. Looks like 10 with the figures joined.
Я	я	ya as in 'yak'. Looks like R backwards.

Practice. Read the following words, slowly, syllable by syllable. Cover up the imitated pronunciation on the right, then check.

мир	meer ('peace')
да	da ('yes')
Ленинград	lye-neen-grad ('Leningrad') (renamed St. Petersburg in 1991)
футбол	foot-bol ('football')
спасибо	spa-see-bo ('thank you')
до свидания	do svee-da-nee-ya ('goodbye')
спутник	spoot-neek ('sputnik')
Владивосток	vla-dee-vo-stok ('Vladivostok')
Россия	ro-ssee-ya ('Russia')
Толстой	tol-stoy ('Tolstoy')
Достоевский	do-sto-yev-skeey ('Dostoyevsky')
Белфаст	byel-fast ('Belfast')
Юрий Гагарин	yoo-reey ga-ga-reen (cosmonaut Yury Gagarin)
уикэнд	oo-ee-kend ('weekend')
Аэрофлот	a-e-ro-flot (the airline 'Aeroflot')
ликёр	lee-kyor ('liqueur')
самолёт	sa-mo-lyot ('aeroplane')
бойкот	boy-kot ('boycott')
парк	park ('park')
киоск	kee-osk ('kiosk')
Байкал	bay-kal (Lake Baikal in Siberia)
телефон	tye-lye-fon ('telephone')

(4) The last group contains letters which take a little longer to remember:

Ж	**ж**	zh like the s in 'pleasure' (or the j in French 'je')
Ц	**ц**	ts as in 'its'
Ч	**ч**	ch as in 'check', but softer. Looks like h upside down.
Ш	**ш**	sh as in 'shall'
Щ	**щ**	shsh as in 'Welsh sheep', a longer, softer sound than the previous letter **ш**. Looks like **ш** with a small tail added.
Ъ	**ъ**	this rare letter, called the 'hard sign', has no sound of its own. It is used to separate a consonant from a following [y] sound (e.g. in the letters **ю** [yoo] or **я** [ya] or **е** [ye]). The effect is of a very brief pause, which our imitated pronunciation will show with a hyphen [-]. For example, **въехал** ('drove in') should be pronounced [v-yehal] with a slight break between the [v] and the [y].
Ы	**ы**	i as in 'bit' but with the tongue tip a little further back.
Ь	**ь**	this letter, which will be shown in the imitated pronunciation as y (as in canyon) is called the 'soft sign'. It is always pronounced simultaneously with the preceding consonant, making the consonant 'soft'. In Russian pronunciation, 'soft' means pronounced with a simultaneous [y] sound. So **нь** sounds like the ny in 'canyon', with the [n] and the [y] pronounced simultaneously. **мь** sounds like the m in 'mew'. There is more information on soft consonants in 2.6.

Practice. Try reading words using all 33 letters of the Russian alphabet:

журнал	zhoor-nal ('magazine', 'journal') [zh as in the French pronunciation of j in 'journal']
Брежнев	bryezh-nyev (former Soviet leader Brezhnev)
царевич	tsa-rye-veech ('son of a tsar')
гостиница Ритц	go-stee-nee-tsa reetts ('the Ritz Hotel')

чай	chay ('tea')
Чайковский	chay-kov-skeey (the composer Tchaikovsky)
Чехов	chye-hov (the writer Chekhov)
финиш	fee-neesh ('finish' in sport)
щи	shshee ('cabbage soup') [make the shsh a softer sound than the sh of ш]
борщ	borshsh ('beetroot soup')
шампанское	sham-pan-sko-ye ('champagne')
защищающий	za-shshee-shsha-yoo-shsheey ('defending')
Шотландия	shot-lan-dee-ya ('Scotland')
Шостакович	sho-sta-ko-veech (the composer Shostakovich)
объект	ob-yekt ('object') [the ъ is simply a slight break between the b and the y]
сын	sin ('son')
рестораны	rye-sto-ra-ni ('restaurants')
Крым	krim ('Crimea')
чёрный кофе	chyor-niy ko-fye ('black coffee')
русский язык	roo-skeey ya-zik ('Russian language')
Кремль	kryemly ('Kremlin') [ly pronounced as one sound, a 'soft' l]
царь	tsary ('tsar') [ry one sound, r and y pronounced simultaneously, a difficult combination for English speakers!]
Аэрофлот	a-e-ro-flot ('Aeroflot')

NOTE 1 Russian handwriting: You may not need to know the handwritten forms unless you want to exchange letters with Russians. For reference, Russian handwriting and a reading exercise are given at the end of the book on page 273.

NOTE 2 Russian italics: When printed in italics Russian г is *г*, д is *д*, и is *u*, й is *й*, л is *л*, п is *n*, and т is *m*, rather like the handwritten forms.

1.2 Reading Russian slowly

If you read Russian words slowly using the pronunciation of letters given above you will be understood. Although there are differences between Russian spelling and pronunciation at normal conversational speed (see chapter 2), Russian words, unlike many English ones, are comprehensible when read syllable by syllable. Read до свидания slowly as do svee-da-nee-ya and a Russian will understand that you mean 'goodbye'. Indeed, if all you need is a 'survival' pronunciation of Russian, it is sufficient to know the values of the letters as given above.

When you read, join the letters into syllables, e.g. Вла-ди-во-сток [vla-dee-vo-stok], as in the imitated pronunciation given above. A syllable is a vowel (а [a], е [ye], ё [yo], и [ee], о [o], у [oo], ы [i], э [e], ю [yoo], or я [ya]) + any preceding consonants. Consonants at the end of a word go with the last vowel. If a word contains a large or awkward group of consonants, the group can be split so that some consonants go with the preceding vowel and some with the following, e.g. Моск-ва [mosk-va]. The imitated pronunciation in this book uses hyphens [-] to divide words into syllables.

Here is an exercise to check your knowledge of the letters. The imitated pronunciation is given in the key at the back of the book.

Exercise 1

Read the following words slowly, by the syllables:

1	дача	11	пиво
2	хорошо	12	сувенир
3	доброе утро	13	Ленин
4	Владимир	14	туалет
5	Пастернак	15	аэропорт
6	Центральный Комитет	16	кофе
		17	коньяк
7	Амстердам	18	бюро
8	Нью-Йорк	19	женщина
9	автомобиль	20	человеконенавистничество
10	почта		

Exercise 2

What is the name of this drink?

Chapter 2

- More on Russian pronunciation.
- Reading Russian words at normal speed.
- Reading and pronunciation practice.

2.1 An important Russian word

здравствуйте [zdra-stvooy-tye] 'hello'

This is the commonest Russian greeting at any time of the day. <u>Notice that the first **в** is not sounded</u>. In this chapter we shall be mainly concerned with the various small differences between the way Russian is written and the way it is pronounced.

2.2 The Russian alphabet in its dictionary order

First check your Russian alphabet. In chapter 1 you learnt the sounds of the Russian letters and how to read Russian words slowly. As a check that you now know the letters, here is the Russian (Cyrillic) alphabet in its normal dictionary order. Cover up the pronunciation on the right with a piece of paper and test yourself. A shortened version of this is given at the end of the book on page 285.

1	А	а	a
2	Б	б	b
3	В	в	v
4	Г	г	g
5	Д	д	d
6	Е	е	ye as in 'yesterday'
7	Ё	ё	yo as in 'yonder'.

NOTE In most Russian publications this letter is printed without the dots, which makes it look identical to **e** (letter no. 6). However, even without the dots it must be pronounced yo. To help learners, the two dots are printed in dictionaries and books for foreigners.

8	Ж	ж	zh pronounced as the s in 'pleasure'
9	З	з	z
10	И	и	ee as in 'meet' (you may also hear yee)
11	Й	й	y as in 'boy'
12	К	к	k
13	Л	л	l as in 'people'
14	М	м	m
15	Н	н	n
16	О	о	o as in 'bottle'
17	П	п	p
18	Р	р	r as in 'error' (rolled as in Scots English)
19	С	с	s
20	Т	т	t
21	У	у	oo as in 'boot'
22	Ф	ф	f
23	Х	х	h pronounced as the ch in Scots 'loch' or German 'ach'
24	Ц	ц	ts as in 'its'
25	Ч	ч	ch as in 'check'
26	Ш	ш	sh as in 'shall'
27	Щ	щ	shsh as in 'Welsh sheep'
28	Ъ	ъ	'hard sign', a very brief pause [-]
29	Ы	ы	approximately i as in 'bit'
30	Ь	ь	'soft sign', a [y] sound which is always pronounced simultaneously with the preceding consonant, like the ny in 'canyon'
31	Э	э	e as in 'fed'
32	Ю	ю	yoo as in 'your'
33	Я	я	ya as in 'yak'

2.3 Pronunciation at normal speed

If you know the pronunciation of the letters as given above, Russians will understand you when you read words slowly. However, you will find that when Russian is spoken at normal speed there are certain regular differences between spelling and pronunciation. In this chapter the main differences will be described, in order of importance. There is no need to learn all these details now, particularly the less important ones at the end of the list (from 2.6 onwards). Study 2.4 and 2.5, glance through the rest, then refer to sections 2.6–2.11 when you are puzzled by something in the imitated pronunciation or on the cassettes.

2.4 Stress

When spoken at normal speed, Russian words are pronounced with a heavy stress on <u>one</u> of the syllables (marked in this book with ´, e.g. такси́ [tak-seé] 'taxi'). English words have stress too – compare <u>phótograph</u>, with its stress on the first syllable, and <u>photógraphy</u>, where the stress is on the second syllable – but in Russian the stress is heavier than in English. If the word has only one syllable, like нет [nyet] 'no', you cannot get the stress wrong, but if the word has more than one syllable (like такси́ [tak-seé]), you must learn which syllable is the stressed one. If you put the wrong stress on a Russian word, you may not be understood. Some examples: one of the commonest Russian male names is Влади́мир [vla-deé-meer]. This name is often mispronounced by foreigners as vlá-dee-meer, which is as bad as pronouncing <u>Belínda</u> to rhyme with <u>cálendar</u>; Бори́с [ba-reés] ('Boris') is stressed on the second syllable, and note that the <u>o</u> in the unstressed first syllable becomes an <u>a</u>. In Russian unstressed syllables are pronounced <u>much</u> less clearly than stressed ones. It isn't easy to guess where the stress falls on a Russian word and different forms of the same word may have different stresses, e.g. го́род [gó-rat] 'city' but города́ [ga-ra-dá] 'cities'. Here is one rule: if the word contains ё [yo], e.g. ликёр [lee-kyór] 'liqueur', the stress is always on the ё.

NOTE If you have to read a word whose stress you don't know, the safest thing is to read it without any stress at all, using the slow pronunciation of chapter 1.

2.5 Unstressed syllables: pronunciation of unstressed о, е, я

In Russian words of more than one syllable, there is one stressed syllable (marked ´) and all the rest are unstressed. Vowels in unstressed syllables are pronounced less distinctly than vowels in stressed syllables, but the vowel which changes most is о [o]. In unstressed syllables о is pronounced the same as Russian а. Practise the following words and listen to the cassette if you have it.

	Slow pronunciation	Normal speed	Translation
Борис	[bo-rees]	[ba-reés]	Boris
спасибо	[spa-see-bo]	[spa-seé-ba]	thank you
Толстой	[tol-stoy]	[tal-stóy]	Tolstoy
Россия	[ro-ssee-ya]	[ra-sseé-ya]	Russia
хорошо	[ho-ro-sho]	[ha-ra-shó]	good, well
доброе утро	[do-bro-ye oo-tro]	[dó-bra-ye oó-tra]	good morning
Владивосток	[vla-dee-vo-stok]	[vla-dee-va-stók]	Vladivostok

The vowel е [ye] also sounds different in unstressed syllables: in the speech of younger Russians it may sound like и [ee], so that в Ленинграде ('in Leningrad') becomes [vlee-neen-grá-dee]. For other speakers it is halfway between е [ye] and и [ee]. In our imitated pronunciation we shall always use [ye] for Russian е, but if you have the cassette you will hear the slight difference between Russian е in stressed syllables and in unstressed ones.

Unstressed **я** [ya] <u>before</u> a stressed syllable sounds like **и** [ee] or [yee]. This is important in words like **язы́к** 'language', pronounced [(y)ee-zík].

The following details (2.6–2.11) are of little importance for your own pronunciation if you are only concerned with making yourself understood. But they will help you to understand the pronunciation you will hear used by Russians.

2.6 Soft consonants = consonants with a [y] sound

A soft consonant is one pronounced with a built-in [y] sound, like the soft ny in 'ca<u>ny</u>on'. In Russian the difference between hard consonants (with no y) and soft ones is a very important feature of a 'good' accent, though if your main concern is simply to 'get by' in Russian you needn't worry about it.

In the alphabet you learnt in chapter 1 the only soft consonants are **ч**, which could be shown in English letters as [chy]) and **щ**, which could be shown as [shshy]. However, all the hard consonants in the alphabet except **ж** [zh], **ц** [ts] and **ш** [sh] become soft consonants when a letter containing a [y] sound is written after them. You already know that the function of the soft sign **ь** [y] is to make a consonant soft, but what is not obvious from the alphabet is the fact that in the pronunciation of Russian native speakers the [y] of the letters **e** [ye], **ë** [yo], **ю** [yoo] and **я** [ya] combines with the preceding consonant in exactly the same way as the [y] of the soft sign. So in the word **Ле́нин** [lyé-neen] ('Lenin') if you listen carefully to a Russian pronouncing the word, you will hear that the [l] and the [y] are pronounced as one sound, 'soft' l.

Practise pronouncing the [y] sound simultaneously with the preceding consonant:

нет	[nyet]	no
сове́т	[sa-vyét]	soviet
ликёр	[lee-kyór]	liqueur
бюро́	[byoo-ró]	office
дя́дя	[dyá-dya]	uncle
Кремль	[kryemly]	Kremlin (NB the Russian word has only one syllable. The English added 'in' to make it easier to say.)
царь	[tsary]	tsar
Нью́касл	[nyyoó-kasl]	Newcastle (NB the first [y] combines with the n, while the second [y] is a separate sound.)

If you listen carefully to Russian speakers, you will also hear that nearly all consonants become 'soft' before the vowel и [ee]. Ликёр [lee-kyór] could also be shown as [lyee-kyór].

You may also hear that stressed e [ye] before a soft consonant sounds closer to the Ya of 'Yale' than to the ye of 'yesterday'.

2.7 Three consonants ж [zh], ц [ts], ш [sh] are never soft

The letters ж [zh], ц [ts] and ш [sh] are always hard, i.e. always pronounced without a [y] sound, regardless of any following letter containing [y]. This means that if ж, ц, ш are followed by e [ye], ё [yo], ю [yoo], я [ya] or ь [y], the [y] is simply not pronounced. So

же́ны is pronounced [zhó-ni] wives
зна́ешь is pronounced [zná-yesh] you know

After ж [zh], ц [ts], ш [sh], you may also be able to hear that the letter и [ee] is always pronounced as if it were ы [i]:

жить [zhity] to live   цирк [tsirk] circus

2.8 How to read prepositions

Russian prepositions – words like 'in', 'from', 'by' – are read as if they were part of the following word. So, for example,

до свида́ния ('goodbye') sounds like [da-svee-dá-nee-ya], as if it were one word до свида́ния.
В Санкт-Петербурге ("in St. Petersburg") is pronounced [vsan-pye-tyer-boór-gye] with no break between the в and the с.

2.9 Voiced consonants are devoiced at the ends of words

At the ends of words the following six voiced consonants (pronounced with vibration of the vocal cords, like English b, d, g, v, z) are pronounced as their unvoiced equivalents (i.e. with little or no vibration of the vocal cords, e.g. English p, t, k, f, s):

Voiced	becomes	*Unvoiced*	
б [b]		[p]	You may notice that the
в [v]		[f]	six voiced consonants
г [g]		[k]	happen to be the first six
д [d]		[t]	consonants of the
ж [zh]		[sh]	Russian alphabet.
з [z]		[s]	

Practise:
Practice:

Че́хов	[chyé-haf]	Chekhov
Санкт-Петербург	[san-pye-tyer-boórg]	St. Petersburg
гриб	[greep]	mushroom
эта́ж	[e-tásh]	floor, story
четве́рг	[chyet-vyérk]	Thursday
раз	[ras]	once

2.10 Assimilation of voiced and unvoiced consonants

Within words, the same six letters as in 2.9 above (б [b], в [v], г [g], д [d], ж [zh], з [z]) become unvoiced if they stand before one of the six unvoiced consonants. To see what this means, practise the following words:

		Pronunciation	*Explanation*
вóдка	vodka	[vót-ka]	д [d] → [t] before [k]
лóжка	spoon	[lósh-ka]	ж [zh] → [sh] before [k]
в садý	in the garden	[fsa-doó]	в [v] (a preposition meaning 'in') → [f] before [s]

In the same way, the unvoiced consonants – п [p], ф [f], к [k], т [t], ш [sh], с [s] – become voiced if they stand before any of the voiced consonants (except в):

вокзáл station	[vag-zál]	к [k] →	[g] before [z]
отдáть to hand back	[ad-dáty]	т [t] →	[d] before [d]
сдать to hand in	[zdaty]	с [s] →	[z] before [d]

BUT in

свидáние meeting	[svee-dá-nee-ye]	the с [s] does not change into [z] before в [v]

2.11 Exceptions: -ого, -его

Apart from the small changes described above in 2.9 and 2.10, consonants are nearly always pronounced as written. Big differences are rare: the commonest case is the adjective endings **-ого** and **-его** in which the г is <u>always</u> pronounced в [v]. For example, **приятного аппетита** 'enjoy your meal' (lit. 'pleasant appetite') is pronounced [pree-yát-na-<u>v</u>a a-pye-teé-ta].

Other exceptions will be explained as they occur.

<u>The above sections 2.6–2.11 are for reference.</u>

2.12 Our imitated pronunciation at normal speed

From chapter 3 onwards, all the imitated pronunciation given in this book will be the pronunciation at normal speed. Nearly all differences between the pronunciation given and the values of the letters you learnt in chapter 1 should be explainable by reference to the above list 2.4 to 2.10. Any other special cases, such as the pronunciation of foreign words, will be explained when they occur.

As a checklist, here is a list of the symbols used in the imitated pronunciation together with their pronunciation. Consonants are marked C, vowels are marked V. Note that we use six two-letter symbols, each of which represents a single sound: ch, ee, oo, sh, ts, zh.

Symbol	C/V	Pronunciation
a	V	as in 'father'
b	C	as in 'bed'
ch	C	as in 'cheese'
d	C	as in 'debt'
e	V	as in 'egg'
ee	V	as in 'meet'
f	C	as in 'father'
g	C	as in 'get'
h	C	as the ch in 'loch'
i	V	as in 'it' (BUT with the tongue tip further back)
k	C	as in 'kettle'
l	C	as in 'love'
m	C	as in 'mint'
n	C	as in 'nine'
o	V	as in 'bottle'
oo	V	as in 'ooze'
p	C	as in 'pet'
r	C	as in 'error' (rolled)
s	C	as in 'sign'
sh	C	as in 'shut'
shsh	C	as in 'Welsh sheep'
t	C	as in 'tent'

ts	C	as in 'its'
v	C	as in 'yet'
y	C	(following a consonant) as in 'yet' (BUT pronounced simultaneously with the consonant)
y	C	(at the beginning of a syllable or after another y) as in 'yet'
y	Semi-vowel	(after a vowel) as in 'boy'
z	C	as in 'zone'
zh	C	as the s in 'pleasure'

- (hyphen) divides words into syllables, as an aid to pronunciation

Read the following, noting the cases (underlined) where there is a difference between slow, spelling pronunciation and pronunciation at normal speed.

	Slow speed	Normal speed	Translation
Москва́	mosk-va	ma̲sk-vá	Moscow
Достое́вский	do-sto-yev--skeey	da̲-sta̲-yéf--skee̲	Dostoyevsky (at normal speed й is inaudible after и and ы)
Че́хов	chye-hov	chyé-ha̲f	Chekhov
рубль	roobly	roobly	rouble
	(remember to pronounce [ly] as one sound)		
щи	shshee	shshee	cabbage soup
да́ча	da-cha	dá-cha	country cottage
Байка́л	bay-kal	bay-kál	Lake Baikal
война́ и мир	voy-na ee meer	va̲y-ná ee meer	war and peace
спаси́бо	spa-see-bo	spa-seé-ba̲	thank you
во́дка	vod-ka	vót-ka	vodka
до свида́ния	do svee-da--nee-ya	da̲-svee-dá--nee-ya	goodbye (lit. until meeting)
сою́з	so-yooz	sa̲-yoós	union
хорошо́	ho-ro-sho	ha̲-ra̲-shó	well, good
журна́л	zhoor-nal	zhoor-nál	magazine
до́брое у́тро	do-bro-ye oo-tro	dó-bra̲-ye oó-tra̲	good morning

Exercise 3

Read the following words slowly, then at normal speed. If you have the cassette, listen to the words and try to write down the imitated pronunciation before you look at the key at the back of the book.

1	спаси́бо	8	ёж
2	во́дка	9	рестора́ны
3	до свида́ния	10	джи́нсы
4	пи́во	11	Бори́с
5	спу́тник	12	Влади́мир
6	автомоби́ль	13	у́тро
7	маши́на	14	царь

Exercise 4

What is this brand name? How would a Russian pronounce the last letter of the name?

Chapter 3

- Reading practice.
- How to learn Russian vocabulary.
- 'am', 'is', 'are'.
- Gender.

3.1 Reading practice

Read the following useful words and phrases, noting the imitated pronunciation. Then cover the imitated pronunciation and read the words and phrases again.

	Imitated pronunciation
Здра́вствуйте. Hello/How are you? (commonest greeting at any time of day)	[zdrá-stvooy-tye] (NB first **в** not pronounced in this word)
До́брое у́тро. Good morning.	[dó-bra-ye oó-tra] (NB pronunciation of unstressed **o** as a)
Как вас зову́т? What is your name? (lit. 'How you (they) call?')	[kak vas za-voót?]
Меня́ зову́т И́горь/Андре́й/ Ни́на/Мэ́ри. I am called Igor/Andrey/ Nina/Mary. (lit. 'Me (they) call …')	[mye-nyá za-voót eé-gary/ an-dryéy/neé-na/mé-ree]
Я не понима́ю. I don't understand.	[ya nye pa-nee-má-yoo]

Говори́те ме́дленно.
Speak slowly.

[ga-va-reé-tye myé-dlye-na]
(double consonants are not
usually pronounced double;
нн is simply [n])

Пожа́луйста.
Please.

NB pronounce this [pa-zhá<u>l</u>-
-sta]

Exercise 5

Say in Russian:

1 Hello. What is your name?

2 Good morning.

3 My name is … (add your
   name)

4 I don't understand.

5 Speak slowly,
   please.

3.2 Russian vocabulary

For the majority of learners the most awkward problem in
learning Russian is the vocabulary. Everyday Russian words
are often quite different from their English equivalents
(e.g. **у́тро** [oó-tra] 'morning') which makes them harder to
learn than the basic vocabulary of, say, French or German.
In the initial stages of learning the language it is not much
consolation to know that much Russian specialist vocabulary
is easy ('mathematics' is **матема́тика** [ma-tye-má-tee-ka],
'university' is **университе́т** [oo-nee-vyer-see-tyét]) when
you are trying to learn that 'I speak' is **я говорю́** [ya ga-va-
ryoó] and 'hello' is **здра́вствуйте** [zdrá-stvooy-tye].

Many learners find it helpful to practise deliberately making
up links between the English word and the Russian word
they are trying to learn. Some links are easy to make – no-one
has difficulty thinking of a link between 'brother' and its
Russian equivalent **брат** [brat]. A word like **го́род** [gó-rat] is
easy to remember if you have heard of the Russian town
Novgorod ('new town') or notice the same three consonants

in the 'grad' of 'Volgograd' ('Volga city'). But what about
жéнщина [zhén-shshee-na] 'woman'? Make up a word link.
For example, think of a woman known as generous Sheena.
Often it will take a couple of minutes to think of a link, but
the link, once made, will help the Russian word to stick.
Here is some of the vocabulary of this chapter with suggested
linkwords and linkphrases:

мéдленно [myé-dlye-na] slowly	Imagine yourself walking slowly by the Mediterranean with Lyena.
письмó [peesy-mó] letter	Think of a letter inviting you to a Peace Congress in Moscow.
хорошó [ha-ra-shó] well/good	Think of happy Russians having a good time watching a play by Bernard Shaw.

Try reading and learning the vocabulary in the following
list. The vocabulary in this book is nearly all taken from the
commonest 2000 words of Russian. Memorize these wordlists
and you will have a good basic Russian vocabulary.

я	[ya]	I
он	[on]	he
онá	[a-ná]	she
онó	[a-nó]	it
брат	[brat]	brother
гóрод	[gó-rat]	city/town
дя́дя	[dyá-dya]	uncle
жéнщина	[zhén-shshee-na]	woman
Сибúрь	[see-béery]	Siberia
письмó	[peesy-mó]	letter
ýтро	[oó-tra]	morning
таксú	[tak-seé]	taxi
я понимáю	[ya pa-nee-má-yoo]	I understand
где	[gdye]	where
да	[da]	yes
нет	[nyet]	no

здра́вствуйте	[zdrá-stvooy-tye]	hello
	(NB first в not sounded)	
как	[kak]	how
ме́дленно	[myé-dlye-na]	slowly
не	[nye]	not
спаси́бо	[spa-seé-ba]	thank you
пожа́луйста	[pa-zhál-sta]	please/don't mention it (in reply to **спаси́бо** [spa-seé-ba])
вот	[vot]	there is/are (when pointing at something)
хорошо́	[ha-ra-shó]	well/good/OK

3.3 Some basic grammar: omission of the verb 'to be'; gender

Read the following question-and-answer drills:

A	**Где Бори́с?**	[gdye ba-reés?]	Where is Boris?
B	**Вот он.**	[vot on]	There he is.
A	**Спаси́бо.**	[spa-seé-ba]	Thank you.
B	**Пожа́луйста.**	[pa-zhál-sta]	Don't mention it.

A	**Где Ни́на?**	[gdye neé-na?]	Where is Nina?
B	**Вот она́.**	[vot a-ná]	There she is.
A	**Спаси́бо.**	[spa-seé-ba]	Thank you.
B	**Пожа́луйста.**	[pa-zhál-sta]	Don't mention it.

| *A* | **Где письмо́?** | [gdye peesy-mó?] | Where is the letter? |
| *B* | **Вот оно́.** | [vot a-nó] | There it is. |

| *A* | **Где Сиби́рь?** | [gdye see-beéry?] | Where is Siberia? |
| *B* | **Вот она́.** | [vot a-ná] | There it is. |

| *A* | **Где такси́?** | [gdye tak-seé?] | Where is the taxi? |
| *B* | **Вот оно́.** | [vot a-nó] | There it is. |

A	**Где Ва́ня?**	[gdye vá-nya?]	Where is Vanya?
B	**Вот он.**	[vot on]	There he is.
A	**Спаси́бо.**	[spa-seé-ba]	Thank you.
B	**Пожа́луйста.**	[pa-zhál-sta]	Don't mention it.

Two explanations:

(a) First, you will see that in these Russian sentences there is no word for 'is'. Russian does not require any equivalent for 'am', 'is' or 'are' (the present tense of the verb 'to be'). So what is the Russian for 'I am a woman' (see the vocabulary list above)? The answer is **Я же́нщина** [ya zhén-shshee-na].

(b) Second, Russian nouns (words like 'woman', 'week', 'meeting') all belong to one of three different categories, depending on what the last letter is. These three categories, known as 'genders', are <u>masculine</u> (m), <u>feminine</u> (f) and <u>neuter</u> (n). Most male beings are masculine, but so are tables, towns and houses; all these are referred to with the pronoun **он** [on] 'he'. Most female beings are feminine, but so are 'week', 'truth' and 'Siberia', which are all referred to as **она́** [a-ná] 'she'. The neuter category, the smallest one in Russian, includes such things as mornings, letters and taxis; they are called **оно́** [a-nó] 'it'. Gender may be familiar to you from French or German. If it is, you will be glad to know that the gender of Russian nouns is easier to learn since in most cases you can tell the gender from the ending.

Here are details and examples:

(a) Most masculine nouns end in a consonant or **й**:

го́род	брат	Ло́ндон	Бори́с	Андре́й
[gó-rat]	[brat]	[lón-dan]	[ba-reés]	[an-dryéy]
town, city	brother	London	Boris	Andrey (Andrew)

> Notice that the pronoun **он** [on] 'he' also ends with a consonant.

(b) Most feminine nouns end **-a** or **-я**:

же́нщина	во́дка	Ни́на	Москва́	неде́ля
[zhén-shshee-na]	[vót-ka]	[neéna]	[mask-vá]	[nye-dyé-lya]
woman	vodka	Nina	Moscow	week

> Notice that **она́** [a-ná] 'she' also ends **-a**.

(c) Most neuter nouns end -**о** or -**е** (cf. **онó** [a-nó] 'it'):

ýтро	**свидáние**	**письмó**
[oó-tra]	[svee-dá-nee-ye]	[peesy-mó]
morning	rendezvous	letter

(d) There is one awkward group: nouns ending with -**ь** (soft sign).

Most of these are feminine but many are masculine, so it is necessary to learn the gender with each soft sign noun. Eventually you will begin to recognize patterns – for example, all nouns ending -**чь**, -**жь**, -**шь** are feminine. But in the vocabularies the gender of soft sign nouns will always be shown as (m) or (f).

Feminine:	**мать**	**Сибúрь**	**ночь**
	[maty]	[see-béery]	[nochy]
	mother	Siberia	night
Masculine:	**царь**	**Úгорь**	**рубль**
	[tsary]	[eé-gary]	[roobly]
	tsar	Igor	rouble

(e) Nouns of foreign origin with the un-Russian endings -**и**, -**у**, -**ю** are neuter unless they denote people:

таксú [tak-seé] 'taxi' is neuter, BUT **Мэ́ри** [mé-ree] 'Mary' is feminine.

Unfortunately, it is one of the facts of language learning that most linguistic rules have exceptions. In the case of Russian gender the main exception is a logical one:

(f) Nouns ending -**а** [a] or -**я** [ya] which denote males are masculine:

дя́дя	**Вáня**	**пáпа**
[dyá-dya]	[vá-nya]	[pá-pa]
uncle	Vanya	dad

It has to be said that grammatical gender does not *mean* much (the fact that a letter is grammatically neuter and a town masculine has nothing to do with the meaning of these words), but it is generally true that nouns denoting males are masculine and nouns denoting females are feminine. Thus Russian does not normally need equivalents of Mr/Mrs/Ms to show a person's sex. The ending is enough: **А. Каре́нин** [a ka-ryé-neen] is a man, while **А. Каре́нина** [a ka-ryé-nee-na] is a woman.

But the main importance of gender is *grammatical:* how you form the plural and the various cases, and how you form the ending of accompanying adjectives (words like 'big', 'blue'), depends on which gender the given noun is. So in order to speak correctly, you have to know about gender.

Exercise 6

Translate the following and say which are called **он** *[on] 'he', which are* **она́** *[a-ná] 'she' and which are* **оно́** *[a-nó] 'it'.*

1   письмо́   4   го́род

2   Андре́й   5   Ва́ня

3   мать

Exercise 7

Read in Russian and translate:

1   Здра́вствуйте. Меня́ зову́т Ни́на.

2   Пожа́луйста, говори́те ме́дленно.

3   Я не понима́ю.

4   Где письмо́? Вот оно́.

5   Да, вот оно́. Спаси́бо.

Exercise 8

Say in Russian:

1 What is your name? My name is Andrey.

2 Hello. Where is the taxi?

3 There it is. Thank you.

4 What are you called? My name is Vladimir.

Exercise 9

Which of the actors on the right are men and which are women?

А. П. ЧЕХОВ

ДЯДЯ ВАНЯ

Сцены из деревенской жизни в 4 действиях

Действующие лица и исполнители:

Серебряков, Александр Владимирович,
   отставной профессор .... **А. П. Кторов**

Елена Андреевна, его жена .... **М. В. Анастасьева**

Софья Александровна (Соня), его дочь
   от первого брака .... **Е. А. Хромова**

                                          Т. И. Ленникова

Войницкая, Мария Васильевна,
   вдова тайного советника,
   мать первой жены профессора .... **М. А. Титова**

Войницкий, Иван Петрович, ее сын .... **М. Н. Зимин**

Астров, Михаил Львович, врач .... **Л. И. Губанов**

Телегин, Илья Ильич,
   обедневший помещик .... **М. М. Яншин**

                                          А. Н. Покровский

Chapter 4

- More reading practice.
- Talking about oneself.
- Making contact with Russians.
- Russian grammar – word endings.
- Pronouns and verbs.

4.1 Reading practice

Read the following dialogue, covering up the imitated pronunciation. After reading a section, uncover the imitated pronunciation and check your performance. If necessary, refer to chapter 2 for differences between spelling and Russian pronunciation at normal speed. Important pronunciation points are repeated in notes. Remember: exceptional pronunciation features are marked NB.

A literal translation is given below. After reading the whole dialogue through twice, try to memorize the Russian.

Me Boris, You Jane

B:	**Здра́вствуйте.**	[zdrá-stvooy-tye] (no first
	Hello.	в; oo as in b<u>oo</u>t; ty is one
		sound)
J:	**Здра́вствуйте.**	[zdrá-stvooy-tye]
	Hello.	
B:	**Прости́те, я не зна́ю,**	[pra-steé-tye, ya nye zná-
	как вас зову́т.	-yoo, kak vas za-voót]
	Excuse me, I (do) not know how you (they) call (I don't know what you are called).	

J: **Меня́ зову́т Джейн.**
Me (they) call Jane.

[mye-nyá za-voót dzheyn]
(дж is the Russian
equivalent of English j)

**И мы не зна́ем, как вас
зову́т.** And we don't know
how you (they) call.

[ee mi nye zná-yem,
kak vas za-voót]

B: **Меня́ зову́т Бори́с.**
Me (they) call Boris.

[mye-nyá za-voót ba-reés]

Вы америка́нка?
You are (an) American?

[vi a-mye-ree-kán-ka?]

J: **Нет, я англича́нка.**
No, I (am an) English-
woman.

[nyet, ya an-glee-chán-ka]

B: **Вы студе́нтка?**
You (are a) student?

[vi stoo-dyént-ka?]

J: **Нет, я учи́тельница.**
No, I (am a) teacher.

[nyet, ya oo-cheé-tyely-
-nee-tsa]

B: **Где вы рабо́таете?
В Ло́ндоне?**
Where (do) you work?
In London?

[gdye vi ra-bó-ta-ye-tye?
vlón-da-nye?] (preposition
в [v] joined to noun)

J: **Нет. Я рабо́таю в
Ливерпу́ле.**
No. I work in Liverpool.

[nyet. ya ra-bó-ta-yoo
vlee-vyer-poó-lye]

B: **А кто э́то?**
And who (is) this?

[a kto é-ta?]

J: **Э́то мой друг Марк. Он
не англича́нин. Он
америка́нец.**
This (is) my friend Mark.
He is not English.
He is an American.

[é-ta moy drook mark. on
nye an-glee-chá-neen. on
a-mye-ree-ká-nyets]

B: **Вы хорошо́ говори́те
по-ру́сски.**
You speak (in) Russian well.

[vi ha-ra-shó ga-va-reé-tye
pa-roó-skee]

J: **Спаси́бо, мой друг
говори́т, что я говорю́
по-ру́сски о́чень
ме́дленно.**
Thank you. My friend
says that I speak Russian
very slowly.

[spa-seé-ba. moy drook
ga-va-reét, shto [NB] ya
ga-va-ryoó pa-roó-skee
ó-chyeny (ny as in canyon)
myé-dlye-na]

4.2 On Russian grammar

You will see from the phrases above that Russian is an inflected language. This means that grammatical relations between words are shown by changes in the endings of words. For example, the Russian for London is Ло́ндон (Lón-dan) in the nominative case which is the form used for the subject of a sentence and the form you find in vocabulary lists and dictionaries.

Ло́ндон – го́род [Lón-dan – gó-rat]
    London is a city.

But 'in London' is в Ло́ндоне [vlón-da-nye] (this ending is dealt with in detail in 5.5–5.8).

English has endings too. For example, after 'he' and 'she' we add an 's' ('she speaks'); 'this' and 'that' have the plural forms 'these' and 'those'; 'I', 'he', 'she', 'we' have accusative forms 'me', 'him', 'her', 'us' but, compared with Russian, English has very few such variations in the forms of words.

So in order to speak correct Russian you have to learn a lot of grammatical endings. On the other hand, understanding Russian is made easier because the endings of words tell you whether you are dealing with a noun or a verb or an adjective and they also tell you about the structure of the sentence.

4.3 New vocabulary

и	[ee]	and
а	[a]	and/but (implying slight contrast, 'whereas')
америка́нец (m)	[a-mye-ree-ká-nyets]	American (man)
англича́нин (m)	[an-glee-chá-neen]	Englishman
дру́г (m)	[drook]	friend/boyfriend
Ливерпу́ль (m)	[lee-vyer-poóly]	Liverpool

Ло́ндон (m)	[lón-dan]	London
америка́нка (f)	[a-mye-ree-kán-ka]	American (woman)
англича́нка (f)	[an-glee-chán-ka]	Englishwoman
студе́нтка (f)	[stoo-dyént-ka]	(female) student
учи́тельница (f)	[oo-chée-tyely-nee-tsa]	(female) teacher
Москва́ (f)	[mask-vá]	Moscow
я рабо́таю	[ya ra-bó-ta-yoo]	I work
вы рабо́таете	[vi ra-bó-ta-ye-tye]	you work
я зна́ю	[ya zná-yoo]	I know
мы зна́ем	[mi zná-yem]	we know
кто	[kto]	who
мы	[mi]	we
они́	[a-neé]	they
о́чень	[ó-chyeny]	very
что	[shto] (NB ч = sh in this word)	that (as in 'I know that he is here'); what
э́то	[é-ta]	this (see 4.5)
мой	[moy]	my
по-ру́сски	[pa-roó-skee]	in Russian

4.4 No articles

Russian does not use equivalents of 'a' or 'the':

Я англича́нин. [ya an-glee-chá-neen]
  I am an Englishman (lit. 'I Englishman').

4.5 э́то [é-ta]

э́то [é-ta] means 'this' or 'that' or 'it' in sentences of the type 'What is this/that?', 'This/that/it is something', e.g.:

Что э́то? [shto é-ta?]
  What is this/that?

Э́то письмо́. [é-ta peesy-mó]
  This/that/it is a letter.

Э́то мой друг. [é-ta moy drook]
  This is my friend.

4.6 Personal pronouns

These are words like 'I', 'he', 'they'. You have already met six of the Russian personal pronouns. Here is the complete set of eight:

я	[ya]	I	
ты	[ti]	you	This is used to address a member of your family, a friend, or a child. We shall call it the 'familiar' (fam) form of 'you'.
он	[on]	he	
она́	[a-ná]	she	
оно́	[a-nó]	it	
мы	[mi]	we	
вы	[vi]	you	More than one person, or one person you do not know well. We shall call it the 'polite' (pol)/'plural' (pl) form of 'you'.
они́	[a-née]	they	

4.7 Present tense: verbs of Type 1 (знать [znaty] 'to know')

In the dialogue we met the verb forms 'I work', 'you work', 'I know', 'you know'. Verbs are listed in our vocabularies in the infinitive form ('to work', 'to know'), and you will find that the infinitive of nearly all Russian verbs ends -ть [ty]. Basically there are two types of Russian verb.

Type 1 verbs usually have -a- [a] before the ть. The Russian for 'to know' is знать [znaty]. To make the equivalents of the present tense 'I know', 'he knows', 'I work/am working' etc. you need, first, the right pronoun, e.g. я [ya] 'I', вы [vi] 'you', then, secondly, you take the -ть off the infinitive and add the required personal ending:

Conjugation (list of personal forms) of **знать** *[znaty] 'to know':*

я зна́<u>ю</u>	[ya zná-yoo]	I know
ты зна́<u>ешь</u>	[ti zná-yesh] (NB **ь** [y] not pronounced – 2.7)	you (fam) know
он/она́/оно́ зна́<u>ет</u>	[on/a-ná/a-nó zná-yet]	he/she/it knows
мы зна́<u>ем</u>	[mi zná-yem]	we know
вы зна́<u>ете</u>	[vi zná-ye-tye]	you (pol/pl) know
они́ зна́<u>ют</u>	[a-nee zná-yoot]	they know

NOTE **зна-** [zna-] is called the stem. The endings are **-ю** [yoo], **-ешь** [yesh], **-ет** [yet], **-ем** [yem], **-ете** [ye-tye], **-ют** [yoot].

In 3.1 we met **я не понима́ю** 'I don't understand'. 'I understand' is **я понима́ю** [ya pa-nee-má-yoo], 'to understand' is **понима́ть** [pa-nee-máty]. So you can work out the conjugation:

я понима́ю
[ya pa-nee-má-yoo]
I understand

мы понима́ем
[mi pa-nee-má-yem]
we understand

ты понима́ешь
[ti pa-nee-má-yesh]
you (fam) understand

вы понима́ете
[vi pa-nee-má-ye-tye]
you (pol/pl) understand

он понима́ет
[on pa-nee-má-yet]
he understands

они́ понима́ют
[a-nee pa-nee-má-yoot]
they understand

Exercise 10

Work out the conjugation of the verb **рабо́тать** *[ra-bó-taty]*
'to work' (Type 1).

4.8 Present tense: Type 2 (говори́ть [ga-va-rety] 'to speak')

Type 2 verbs usually end -ить [eety] in the infinitive. A good example is говори́ть [ga-va-rėety] 'to speak'. -ить [eety] is the ending and говор- [ga-var-] is the stem. Take off the -ить and add the following present tense endings: -ю [yoo], -ишь [eesh], -ит [eet], -им [eem], -ите [ee-tye], -ят [yat].

я говорю́	[ya ga-va-ryő]	I speak
ты говори́шь	[ti ga-va-re̋esh]	you (fam) speak
он/она́/оно́ говори́т	[on/a-ná/a-nó ga-va-re̋et]	he/she/it speaks
мы говори́м	[mi ga-va-re̋em]	we speak
вы говори́те	[vi ga-va-re̋e-tye]	you (pol/pl) speak
они́ говоря́т	[a-ne̋e ga-va-ryát]	they speak

NOTE There is only one Russian present, corresponding to both English presents, e.g. 'I speak/am speaking', 'he works/is working'.

4.9 Negation

'Not' is не [nye], placed in front of what is negated:

я не рабо́таю [ya nye ra-bó-ta-yoo]
   I do not work

я не понима́ю [ya nye pa-nee-má-yoo]
   I do not understand

он не понима́ет [on nye pa-nee-má-yet]
   he does not understand

он не англича́нин [on nye an-glee-chá-neen]
   he is not English

Exercise 11

Read and translate the following dialogues:

Notice that in colloquial (informal) Russian the personal pronoun (shown in brackets) can be omitted in answers to questions.

1 – **Вы зна́ете?**   [vi zná-ye-tye?]
  – **Да, (я) зна́ю.**   [da, (ya) zná-yoo]

2 – **Вы рабо́таете?**   [vi ra-bó-ta-ye-tye?]
  – **Нет, (я) не рабо́таю.**   [nyet, (ya) nye ra-bó-ta--yoo]

3 – **Вы понима́ете?**   [vi pa-nee-má-ye-tye?]
  – **Да, (я) понима́ю.**   [da, (ya) pa-nee-má-yoo]

4 – **Бори́с рабо́тает?**   [ba-reés ra-bó-ta-yet?]
  – **Да, он рабо́тает.**   [da, on ra-bó-ta-yet]

5 – **Где рабо́тает Джейн?**   [gdye ra-bó-ta-yet dzheyn?]
  – **Она́ рабо́тает в Ливерпу́ле.**   [a-ná ra-bó-ta-yet vlee-vyer-poó-lye]

6 – **Ва́ня, ты зна́ешь, где рабо́тают Джейн и Марк?**   [vá-nya, ti zná-yesh, gdye ra-bó-ta-yoot dzheyn ee mark?]
  – **Нет, (я) не зна́ю.**   [nyet, (ya) nye zná-yoo]

7 – **Я говорю́ по-ру́сски. Бори́с говори́т по-русски. Мы говори́м по-русски.**   [ya ga-va-ryoó pa-roo--skee. bareés ga-va-reét pa-roó-skee. mi ga-va--reém pa-roó-skee]
  – **Да, вы говори́те по-ру́сски.**   [da, vi ga-va-reé-tye pa-roó-skee]

8 – **Джейн и Бори́с говоря́т по-ру́сски?**   [dzheyn ee ba-reés ga-va-ryát pa-roó-skee?]
  – **Да, они́ хорошо́ говоря́т.**   [da, a-neé ha-ra-shó ga-va-ryát]

Exercise 12

Put on the correct endings:

1   **Я не зна́(   ). Я не понима́(   ).**

2   **Он рабо́та(   ) в Ло́ндоне, а они́ рабо́та(   ) в Ливерпу́ле.**

3   **Ваня, ты не понима́(   ).**

4   **Вы зна́(   ), где мы рабо́та(   ).**

5   **Я говор(   ) по-ру́сски, а они́ не говор(   ) по-ру́сски.**

6   **Мы говор(   ) по-ру́сски хорошо́.**

Exercise 13

Say in Russian:

1   I don't know. I don't understand.

2   I know and you (pol) know.

3   You (pol) don't understand.

4   I speak Russian.

5   Jane speaks Russian well.

6   They don't understand. They don't speak Russian.

Exercise 14 (general revision)

Say in Russian:

1 Hello. My name is Jane.

2 I am an Englishwoman.

3 Where is Boris? I do not know.

4 I do not understand. Speak slowly, please.

5 They speak Russian slowly.

6 The woman does not understand. She does not speak Russian.

7 You (pol/pl) are working slowly.

8 Where is my friend? Jane knows where he is.

9 What is that? It is a letter.

10 I don't know what you are called.

Exercise 15

What are Boris and Jane saying?

Борис: **Как вас зовýт** [kak vas za-voót?]

Джейн: **Марк не говорит по-рýсски.**
            [mark nye ga-va-reét pa-roó-skee]

Chapter 5

- Asking for information (questions).
- 'what', 'why', 'where'.
- Prepositional case.
- Conjugation Type 1B.

5.1 Asking for information: yes/no questions

Read these question and answer dialogues:

- **Она́ учи́тельница?** [a-ná oo-che-tyely-nee-tsa?]
  Is she a teacher?

- **Да, учи́тельница.** [da, oo-che-tyely-nee-tsa]
  Yes, (she is) a teacher.

- **Джейн говори́т по-ру́сски?** [dzheyn ga-va-reét pa-roó-skee?]
  Does Jane speak Russian?

- **Да, она́ говори́т по-ру́сски.** [da, a-ná ga-va-reét pa-roó-skee]
  Yes, she speaks Russian.

- **Прости́те, вы студе́нтка?** [pra-steé-tye, vi stoo-dyént-ka?]
  Excuse (me), are you a (female) student?

- **Нет.** [nyet]
  No.

- **Вы понима́ете?** [vi pa-nee-má-ye-tye?]
  Do you understand?

- **Нет, (я) не понима́ю.** [nyet, (ya) nye pa-nee-má-yoo]
  No, I don't understand.

In chapter 4 there were several yes/no questions like these (questions to which 'yes' or 'no' are possible answers). You probably noticed that in Russian such questions use exactly the same words as in the equivalent statement and in the same order. So

Он зна́ет [on zná-yet] means 'He knows', BUT
Он зна́ет? [on zná-yet] means 'Does he know?'

5.2 Intonation of yes/no questions

In writing, the question mark tells you which is a question, but how do you know which is which in speech? The answer is intonation. The key word (what you're asking about) in the question, usually the verb if there is one in the question, is pronounced with a sharp rise and fall of the voice on the <u>stressed</u> syllable. So

Она́ учи́тельница? ('Is she a <u>teacher</u>?') is pronounced

Она́ учи́тельница? [a-ná oo-cheé-tyely-nee-tsa?]

with a sharp <u>rise and fall</u> on the stressed syllable **чи́** [chee]. In English or American you hear a similar intonation pattern in surprised questions such as 'Oh, she's a <u>teacher</u>, is she?' with a sharp rise and fall on '<u>tea</u>'. It is obviously important to practise this intonation pattern because of the frequent need to ask this type of question and to make clear that the question is a question and not a statement. Practise:

Он говори́т по-ру́сски [on ga-va-reét pa-roó-skee?]

'Does he speak Russian?' If you pronounce it <u>without</u> the rise-fall on the [reét] of [ga-va-reét], your question will be understood as the statement 'He speaks Russian'.

This intonation pattern is the only important one you need to learn in the early stages of Russian.

Exercise 16

Read the following. Listen to the cassette. Then translate the
answers on the right into Russian.

1

Вы говори́те по-ру́сски?   Yes, I speak Russian.

[vi ga-va-reĕ-tye pa-roó-skee?]
Do you speak Russian?

2

Вы понима́ете?   Yes, I understand.

[vi pa-nee-má-ye-tye?]
Do you understand?

3

Вы зна́ете, где мой друг?   No, I don't know where he is.

[vi zná-ye-tye, gdye moy drook?]
Do you know where my friend is?

4

Вы не зна́ете, где она́ рабо́тает?   Yes, we know where
                                              she works.

[vi nye zná-ye-tye, gdye a-ná ra-bó-ta-yet?]
Do you know where she works?

NOTE Russians often use the negative form **вы не зна́ете**
[vi nye zná-ye-tye] 'Don't you know' in requests for information. This is a sign of politeness rather than pessimism.

5

Она́ рабо́тает в Ло́ндоне?   No, she works in Liverpool.

[a-ná ra-bó-ta-yet vlón-da-nye?]
Does she work in <u>London</u>?

5.3 Asking for information: 'wh-' questions

These are questions which contain question words such as 'what' **что** [shto NB], 'who' **кто** [kto], 'when' **когда́** [kag-dá], 'why' **почему́** [pa-chye-moó], 'where' **где** [gdye], 'how' **как** [kak]. There is no need to think about intonation here, because the question word makes it clear that you want information.

Что э́то?	<u>What</u> is this?
[shto é-ta?]	
Кто здесь говори́т	<u>Who</u> here speaks English?
по-англи́йски?	
[kto zdyesy ga-va-réet pa-an- -gleé-skee?]	
Как вас зову́т?	<u>What</u> (how) are you called?
[kak vas za-voót?]	
Почему́ он не зна́ет?	<u>Why</u> doesn't he know?
[pa-chye-moó on nye zná-yet?]	
Где рабо́тает Бори́с?	<u>Where</u> does Boris work?
[gdye ra-bó-ta-yet ba-reés?]	

Exercise 17

Ask in Russian:

1   Where is she?

2   Why is he working slowly?

3   Who knows where Boris is?

4   What are they saying?
    ('say' = 'speak' in Russian)

5   When do they work?

5.4 Prepositional case after в [v] 'in', на [na] 'on', о [a] 'about'

So far, most of our nouns and pronouns have been in the nominative case (**Ло́ндон** [lón-dan], **америка́нка** [a-mye-ree--kán-ka], **он** [on] etc.). The nominative case is used for the subject of the sentence (e.g. **он** in **Он зна́ет** [on zná-yet] 'He knows') and is the form given in vocabulary lists. But you have also met the examples

| **в Ло́ндоне** | [vlón-da-nye] | in London |
| **в Ливерпу́ле** | [vlee-vyer-poó-lye] | in Liverpool |

The **е** [ye] ending is the <u>prepositional</u> case (also sometimes called the <u>locative</u>). This case has no meaning; it is simply an ending which must be used after certain prepositions (hence its name). The commonest three prepositions requiring the prepositional case are:

в [v] or [f] – in
(depending on following word – see 2.8, 2.10)
на [na] – on
о [a] – about, concerning: **о Бори́се** [a-ba-reé-sye] 'about Boris'

For example, the answer to 'Where is he?' **Где он?** [gdye on?] might be 'He's in Moscow'. 'He' is **он** [on], 'in' is **в**, and 'Moscow' is **Москва́** [mask-vá]. The complete sentence is

Он в Москве́ [on vmask-<u>vyé</u> (preposition joined to noun – see 2.8)]

5.5 How to form the prepositional case

е [ye] is the prepositional ending for most nouns, whatever their gender:

Ло́ндон	[lón-dan]	London
в Ло́ндоне	[vlón-da-nye]	in London
Ливерпу́ль (m)	[lee-vyer-poóly]	Liverpool
в Ливерпу́ле	[vlee-vyer-poó-lye]	in Liverpool

The **е** [ye] replaces the soft sign **ь**.

трамва́й	[tram-váy]	tram
на трамва́е	[na-tram-vá-ye]	on the tram

The **е** [ye] replaces the nominative ending **й** [y].

музе́й	[moo-zyéy]	museum
в музе́е	[vmoo-zyé-ye]	in the museum

Москва́	[mask-vá]	Moscow
в Москве́	[vmask-vyé]	in Moscow

у́лица	[oó-lee-tsa]	street
на у́лице	[na-oó-lee-tse]	in/on the street

NOTE Russians always use **на** [na] 'on', <u>not</u> **в** [v] 'in' with the word for 'street'.

письмо́	[peesy-mó]	letter
в письме́	[fpeesy-myé: [f] not [v] – see 2.10]	in the letter

The **о** [o] nominative ending is replaced by **е** [ye].

5.6 Nouns with the prepositional ending и [ee]

Not all nouns end **е** [ye]. <u>Feminine</u> nouns ending in a soft sign **ь** replace the soft sign with **и** [ee]:

Сиби́рь (f)	[see-beéry]	Siberia
в Сиби́ри	[fsee-beé-ree]	in Siberia

And nouns ending **ия** [ee-ya] and **ие** [ee-ye] also have **и** [ee], <u>not</u> **е** [ye], in place of the final letter of the nominative:

Росси́я	[ra-sseé-ya]	Russia
в Росси́и	[vra-sseé-ee]	in Russia
упражне́ние	[oo-prazh-nyé- -nee-ye]	exercise
в упражне́нии	[voo-prazh-nyé- -nee-ee]	in the exercise

5.7 Indeclinable nouns: their endings never change

Nouns with un-Russian endings in the nominative (**-и, -у, -ю**) are indeclinable. That means their endings do not change:

такси́	[tak-seé]	taxi
на такси́	[na-tak-seé]	on a taxi (= by taxi)

NOTE Foreign <u>female</u> names (like **Джейн**) which do not end **-а, -я**, or **-ь** are also indeclinable: **о Джейн** [a-dzhéyn] 'about Jane'. (If you said **о Джейне**, a Russian would assume Jane was a man.)

Exercise 18

Translate, and put the correct endings on the nouns in brackets:

1 **Дя́дя Ва́ня в (го́род)?** [dyá-dya vá-nya v (gó-rat?]

2 **Он рабо́тает в (Москва́)?** [on ra-bó-ta-yet v (mask-vá)?]
   Нет, в (Санкт-Петербу́рг). [nyet, v (sankt-pye-tyer-boórk)]

3 **Мой друг в (Ливерпу́ль).** [moy drook v (lee-vyer-poóly)]

4 **Они́ рабо́тают в (Сиби́рь).** [a-ne ra-bó-ta-yoot f (see-beéry)]

5 **Где Джейн? В (Росси́я).** [gdye dzheyn? v (ra-sse-ya)]

5.8 Prepositional of personal pronouns

мне	[mnye]	о<u>бо</u> мне	[a-ba-mnyé]	about me (**обо** is a rare form of **о** 'about' used with **мне**)
тебе́	[tye-byé]	о тебе́	[a-tye-byé]	about you (fam)
нём	[nyom]	на нём	[na-nyóm]	on him
ней	[nyey]	о ней	[a-nyéy]	about her
нём	[nyom]	в нём	[vnyom]	in it
нас	[nas]	о нас	[a-nás]	about us
вас	[vas]	о вас	[a-vás]	about you (pol/pl)
них	[neeh]	о них	[a-neéh]	about them

5.9 More on verbs: conjugation Type 1B жить [zhity] 'to live'

Type 1 (see **знать** [znaty] 4.7) has a variant called Type 1B. The stem of 1B verbs ends in a consonant and is often hard to predict from the infinitive form. **жить** [zhity] 'to live' is a typical example: its stem is **жив-** [zhiv]. The endings of Type 1B verbs are the same as Type 1 except that they have **y** [oo] where Type 1 has **ю** [yoo], and **e** [ye] becomes **ё** [yo] when the stress falls on it.

я живу́	[ya zhi-voó]	I live (cf. **я зна́<u>ю</u>** 'I know')
ты живёшь	[ti zhi-vyósh]	you (fam) live
он живёт	[on zhi-vyót]	he lives
мы живём	[mi zhi-vyóm]	we live
вы живёте	[vi zhi-vyó-tye]	you (pol/pl) live
они́ живу́т	[a-neé zhi-voót]	they live (cf. **они́ зна́<u>ю</u>т** 'they know')

5.10 Vocabulary

Read through the vocabulary, which is in alphabetical order as in 2.1. Then use it to read the dialogue.

вас	[vas]	you (acc – see 6.1)
Вашингто́н	[va-sheeng-tón]	Washington
гости́ница	[ga-steé-nee-tsa]	hotel

жить	[zhity]	to live (5.9)
заво́д	[za-vót]	factory
на заво́де	[na-za-vó-dye]	at/in a factory
здесь	[zdyesy]	here
коне́чно	[ka-nyésh-na NB]	of course
москви́ч	[mask-véech]	Muscovite
на	[na]	on
немно́го	[nye-mnó-ga]	a little
но	[no]	but (strong contrast)
Новосиби́рск	[na-va-see-beérsk]	Novosibirsk (capital of Western Siberia)
почему́	[pa-chye-moó]	why
прия́тно	[pree-yát-na]	pleasant(ly)
проспе́кт	[pra-spyékt]	avenue
на проспе́кте	[na-pra-spyék-tye]	in/on an avenue
проспе́кт Кали́нина	[pra-spyékt ka-leé-nee-na]	Kalinin Prospekt (major avenue in central Moscow, lit. 'Prospekt of Kalinin', now renamed Но́вый Арба́т [nó-vi ar-bát])
прости́те	[pra-steé-tye]	excuse (me)
рабо́та	[ra-bó-ta]	work
ру́сский	[roó-skee] (NB й not audible)	Russian (adj)
сейча́с	[syey-chás]	at the moment, now
там	[tam]	there (opposite of 'here')
украи́нец	[oo-kra-eé-nyets]	Ukrainian
у́лица	[oó-lee-tsa]	street
у́лица Го́рького	[oó-lee-tsa góry-ka-va NB]	Gorky Street (Moscow's main street, renamed Тверска́я [tvyer-ská-ya] in 1991)
на у́лице	[na-oó-lee-tse]	in/on a street
центр	[tsentr]	centre (of city)
язы́к	[(y)ee-zík]	language

CONVERSATION

(The English version is given separately so that you can first try to translate the text yourself, using the vocabulary in the list. The key syllable in yes/no questions is underlined.)

A Westerner and a Soviet find out about each other

A: Вы говори́те по-ру́сски?
[vi ga-va-ree-tye pa-roó-skee?]

B: Да, немно́го. Вы ру́сский?
[da, nye-mnó-ga. vi roó-skee?]

A: Нет, я украи́нец, но, коне́чно, говорю́ по-ру́сски.
[nyet, ya oo-kra-eé-nyets, no, ka-nyésh-na, ga-va-ryoó pa-roó-skee]

B: Прости́те, как вас зову́т?
[pra-steé-tye, kak vas za-voót?]

A: Андре́й. А вас?
[an-dryéy. a vas?]

B: Меня́ зову́т Ба́рбара.
[mye-nyá za-voot bár-ba-ra]

A: О́чень прия́тно. Где вы живёте, Ба́рбара?
[ó-chyeny pree-yát-na. gdye vi zhi-vyó-tye, bár-ba-ra?]

B: В Вашингто́не.
[vva-sheeng-tó-nye]

A: А здесь в Москве́?
[a zdyesy vmask-vyé?]

B: В гости́нице Интури́ст на у́лице Го́рького. А вы москви́ч?
[vga-ste-nee-tse een-too-rest na-o-lee-tse góry-ka-va. a vi mask-vech?]

A: Нет, я живу́ в Сиби́ри, в Новосиби́рске.
[nyet, ya zhi-voó fsee-beé-ree, vna-va-see-beér-skye]

B: Почему́ вы в Москве́, Андре́й?
[pa-chye-moó vi vmask-vyé, an-dryéy?]

A: Здесь живёт мой дру́г Ви́ктор. Он рабо́тает на заво́де. Он сейча́с на рабо́те.
[zdyesy zhi-vyót moy drook véek-tar. on ra-bó-ta-
-yet na-za-vó-dye. on syey-chás na-ra-bó-tye]

B: Вы хоро<u>шо́</u> зна́ете Москву́?
[vi ha-ra-<u>shó</u> zná-ye-tye mask-voó?]

A: Да, о́чень хорошо́. Мой друг живёт в це́нтре, на проспе́кте Кали́нина.
[da, ó-cheny ha-ra-shó. moy drook zhi-vyót ftsén-
-trye, na-pra-spyék-tye ka-leé-nee-na]

TRANSLATION (with notes)

A: Do you speak Russian?

B: Yes, a little. Are you Russian?

A: No, I'm Ukrainian but of course I speak Russian. (Many Ukrainians speak Russian as a first or second language. Ukrainian is very similar to Russian.)

B: Excuse me, what is your name?

A: Andrey. And what's yours?

B: I'm called Barbara.

A: Pleased to meet you (a standard polite phrase, lit. 'very pleasant', short for 'It is very pleasant to meet you'). Where do you live, Barbara?

B: In Washington.

A: And (or 'but') here in Moscow?

B: In the Intourist Hotel on Gorky Street (a main street in central Moscow, lit. 'street of Gorky [a Russian writer]', now called by most Russians **Тверска́я** [tvyer-ská-ya], 'Tver Street', named after the city of Tver, north of Moscow). (And) are you a Muscovite?

A: No, I live in Siberia, in Novosibirsk (largest Siberian city).

B: Why are you in Moscow, Andrey?

A: My friend Viktor lives here ('My friend Viktor' is at the end in the Russian because the emphasis is on <u>who</u> lives in Moscow. Russian word order is very flexible; anything to be emphasized [new information] is often put at the end of the sentence). He works in a factory. He's at work now (right now).

B: Do you know Moscow (acc in Russian – see 6.2) well?

A: Yes, very well. My friend lives in the centre, on Kalinin Prospekt (Avenue) (lit. 'Avenue of Kalinin', now called by most Russians **Нóвый Арбáт** [nó-vi ar-bát] 'New Arbat').

Exercise 19

Say in Russian:

1 Do you (pol) speak Russian?

2 Do you (pol) understand?

3 Do you (pol) know where Novosibirsk is?

4 Is he Russian?

5 Do you (pol) live in <u>Moscow</u>?

6 Where is the hotel?

7 Who knows where my friend is?

8 Is this a hotel?

9 They live in Siberia.

10 Why does he work in London?

11 We are in Russia.

12 He speaks Russian very well.

13 Do you (fam) know who this is? This is Boris.

14 You (pol) are <u>Boris</u>? Pleased to meet you.

15 Barbara is American and Andrey is Ukrainian.

16 We are speaking about her, not about you (pol).

Exercise 20

What is Andrey saying to Barbara?

Вы живёте в Москве? [vi zhi-vyó-tye vmask-vyé?]

Chapter 6

- Accusative case.
- Going places.
- An exceptional verb: 'to want'.

NOTE From this chapter onwards, imitated pronunciation will be given only for new words, words and phrases with special pronunciation features, and, occasionally, for revision purposes.

Exercise 21

Read these sentences, which contain vocabulary you have already met and grammar which will be dealt with in this section. Then check your pronunciation in the Key to exercises.

1	**Он зна́ет меня́.**	He knows me.
2	**Вы понима́ете меня́?**	Do you understand me?
3	**Как вас зову́т?**	What do (they) call you?
4	**Вы хорошо́ зна́ете Москву́?**	Do you know Moscow well?
5	**Я зна́ю Ва́ню.**	I know Vanya.
6	**Мы зна́ем студе́нтку.**	We know the (female) student.
7	**Вы зна́ете Бори́са?**	Do you know Boris?
8	**Они́ зна́ют язы́к.**	They know the language.
9	**Бра́та зову́т Ива́н.**	(They) call (my) brother Ivan (My brother is called Ivan).
10	**Мы понима́ем упражне́ние.**	We understand the exercise.

6.1 Accusative case of pronouns

Just as 'me' is the accusative of 'I', so **меня́** [mye-nyá] (which we met in 3.1) is the accusative of **я**. As in English, verbs like **понима́ть** 'to understand' and **знать** 'to know' are followed by pronouns in the accusative case. We say 'He knows me', not 'He knows I.'

The full list of accusative personal pronouns is:

Nominative		*Accusative*	
я [ya]	I	**меня́** [mye-nyá]	me
ты [ti]	you (fam)	**тебя́** [tye-byá]	you (fam)
он [on]	he	**его́** [ye-vó]	him (NB **г** is [v] here)
она́ [a-ná]	she	**её** [ye-yó]	her
оно́ [a-nó]	it	**его́** [ye-vó]	it (NB **г** is [v] here)
мы [mi]	we	**нас** [nas]	us
вы [vi]	you (pol/pl)	**вас** [vas]	you (pol/pl)
они́ [a-née]	they	**их** [(y)eeh]	them

Я зна́ю вас.	I know you (pol).
Мы зна́ем его́ [ye-vó].	We know him/it.
Я не понима́ю их [(y)eeh].	I don't understand them.

NOTE Russian word order is flexible. The object (word in the accusative) can stand in front of the verb if you do not want to emphasize it:

Её (acc) **зову́т Джейн.**
> Her (they) call Jane.
> (i.e. 'She is called Jane' – emphasis on 'Jane')

Как вас зову́т?
> How you (they) call?
> (i.e. 'What is your name?')

Как зову́т вас? is also possible if you want to stress **вас** i.e. What do they call <u>you</u>?

6.2 Accusative case of nouns

English nouns do not change in the accusative ('He knows <u>Moscow</u>') and many Russian nouns do not change either. But those nouns (f or m) which end -**a** or -**я**, and masculine nouns denoting people and animals <u>do</u> have a special accusative ending:

(a) nouns ending -**a** change the **a** to **y** (Москв<u>у́</u>, Ни́н<u>у</u>)
(b) nouns ending -**я** change the **я** to **ю** (дя́д<u>ю</u> Ва́н<u>ю</u>, Росси́<u>ю</u> 'Russia').

<u>Masculine nouns which denote people or animals</u> (other than the ones ending -**a** or -**я**) add **a**, or, if the nominative ends with **й** or a soft sign, they replace the **й** or soft sign with **я**.

Э́то Ива́н. Я зна́ю Ива́н<u>а</u>.
This is Ivan (nom). I know Ivan (acc).

Э́то мой брат. Вы зна́ете бра́т<u>а</u>. Бра́т<u>а</u> зову́т Андре́й.
This is my brother (nom). You know (my) brother (acc). (They) call (my) brother (acc) Andrey.

Note that in the 'calling' construction the name is <u>not</u> an acc object of **зову́т** 'they call' and is in the nom.

Э́то И́горь. Вы зна́ете И́гор<u>я</u>?
This is Igor. Do you know Igor?

Мы не понима́ем Андре́<u>я</u>.
[mi nye pa-nee-má-yem an-dryé-ya]
We do not understand Andrey.

Э́то наш кот. [nash kot 'our cat']. **Мы лю́бим** [lyoó-beem 'love'] **кот<u>а́</u>.**
This is our cat (nom). We love the cat (acc).

Masculine nouns denoting things (not people or animals) do not change in the accusative. Nor do neuter nouns. Nor do feminine nouns ending in a soft sign. Nor do indeclinables, of course.

Я чита́ю [chee-tá-yoo 'read'] **письмо́.**	I am reading a letter.
Андре́й лю́бит Сиби́рь.	Andrey loves Siberia.
Бори́с лю́бит Джейн (indecl)?	Does Boris love Jane?

If you are in doubt when to use the accusative, as a 'rule of thumb' test whether you would say 'he' (nom) or 'him' (acc) in an equivalent English construction.

Exercise 22

Where necessary, change the form of the word in brackets:

1	Я зна́ю (Москва́).	I know Moscow.
2	Я зна́ю (вы).	I know you.
3	Я зна́ю (дя́дя Ва́ня).	I know Uncle Vanya.
4	Я зна́ю (Влади́мир).	I know Vladimir.
5	Я зна́ю (Сиби́рь).	I know Siberia.
6	Ива́н зна́ет (Росси́я).	Ivan knows Russia.
7	Ива́н зна́ет (я).	Ivan knows me.
8	Ива́н зна́ет (они́).	Ivan knows them.
9	Ива́н зна́ет (же́нщина).	Does Ivan know the woman?
10	Кто не зна́ет (царь)?	Who does not know the tsar?
11	(Мать) зову́т А́нна.	(My) mother is called Anna.
12	Мы (ты) понима́ем.	We understand you (fam).

Exercise 23

Say in Russian.

1 They call him Ivan (= His name is Ivan).

2 Do you know Boris and Vladimir?

3 This is Jane. You (pol) know her.

4 Do they understand the letter?

5 I don't understand you (pol).

6.3 The verbs 'to go' in Russian: идти and éхать

Both of these important verbs are Type 1B, like **жить** 'to live' (5.9).

(a) **идти** [ee-<u>t</u>ée NB] 'to go (on foot)', 'to walk'. The stem is **ид-** [eed] (think of Eve going on foot out of the Garden of <u>Ed</u>en).

я иду́	[ee-doó]	мы идём	[ee-dyóm]
ты идёшь	[ee-dyósh]	вы идёте	[ee-dyó-tye]
он идёт	[ee-dyót]	они́ иду́т	[ee-doót]

If you wish to stress the idea of 'on foot', add the word **пешко́м** [pyesh-kóm] 'on foot':

Мы идём пешко́м [mi ee-dyóm pyesh-kóm].
    We're going on foot.

(b) **éхать** [yé-haty] 'to go by transport'. The stem is **éд-** [yéd] (think of travelling to <u>Jedd</u>ah).

я éду	[yé-doo]	мы éдем	[yé-dyem]
ты éдешь	[yé-dyesh]	вы éдете	[yé-dye-tye]
он éдет	[yé-dyet]	они́ éдут	[yé-doot]

6.4 Going somewhere

Now that we have the verbs for 'to go', we can make further use of the accusative. The Russian for 'to (somewhere)' is translated with the same prepositions **в** and **на** that we met in 5.4 but this time with the <u>accusative</u> case:

Я иду́ в гости́ницу. [ya ee-doó vga-stée-nee-tsoo]
    I am going (on foot) to the hotel.

Compare: **Я в гости́нице.** I am <u>in</u> the hotel.

Я éду в Москву́ [ya yé-doo vmask-voó].
    I am going to Moscow.

Когда́ вы е́дете в Новосиби́рск?
When are you travelling to Novosibirsk?

Мы идём в центр. [mi ee-dyóm ftsentr].
We're walking to the centre.

You may remember that with some nouns (e.g. у́лица 'street', заво́д 'factory', проспе́кт 'avenue') 'in' or 'at' was translated **на**. So with such nouns 'to' is also **на** + acc:

Я е́ду на проспект Свобо́ды.
I am going (by vehicle) to Freedom Prospekt.

Она́ е́дет на заво́д. [a-ná yé-dyet na-za-vót].
She is going (by transport) to the factory.

Вы идёте на у́лицу? [vi ee-dyó-tye na-oó-lee-tsoo?]
Are you going into the street?/Are you going outside?

The word for 'where' with verbs of motion like 'to go' is **куда́** [koo-dá] 'whither':

Where are you going? **Куда́ вы идёте?** or **Куда́ вы е́дете?**

And the word for 'there' with verbs of motion is **туда́** [too-dá]:

He's going there on foot. **Он идёт туда́ пешко́м.**

Exercise 24

Say in Russian:

1 Where are you (pl) going (by transport)?
   We are going to town.

2 We are going to Russia (by transport).

3 She is walking to the hotel.

4 They are travelling to Moscow.

5 Are you (pol) going on foot or (**и́ли**) by transport?

NOTE Both **идти** and **éхать** mean specifically 'to go <u>in one direction</u>'. If the going involves more than one direction, e.g. 'He goes to work (and comes back home) every day' Russians use different verbs. They are in 11.9.

6.5 Exceptional verbs: хотéть 'to want'

Nearly all verbs in Russian are Type 1 (4.7), Type 2 (4.8) or Type 1B (5.9). However, there are a few awkward ones, e.g.

хотéть [ha-tyéty] 'to want', a mixture of Types 1B and 2:

я хочý [ha-choó] I want	**мы хотим** [ha-teém] we want
ты хóчешь [hó-chyesh] you want	**вы хотите** [ha-teé-tye] you want
он хóчет [hó-chyet] he wants	**они хотят** [ha-tyát] they want

Я хочý увидеть тебя.
> I want to see you.

Вы не хотите éхать в Сибирь?
> Don't you want to go to Siberia?

Они не хотят, а мы хотим.
> They don't want (to), but we do.

6.6 Vocabulary

Read the new words, then use them to translate the conversation.

дéло	[dyé-la]	matter, thing
как делá?	[kak dye-lá?]	how are things?
ничегó	[nee-chye-<u>v</u>ó NB]	not bad, all right
кудá	[koo-dá]	where (motion) – see 6.4
идти	[ee-<u>t</u>eé NB]	to go (on foot) – see 6.3

магази́н	[ma-ga-zeén]	shop, store
дру́жба	[droózh-ba]	friendship
пото́м	[pa-tóm]	next, then
на (+ acc)	[na]	to (a place – see 6.4); for (with time word)
мо́жно	[mózh-na]	it is possible; one can
метро́ (n indecl)	[mye-tró]	metro, underground, subway
на метро́	[na-mye-tró]	by metro
дава́йте	[da-váy-tye]	let's
дава́йте пое́дем	[da-váy-tye pa-yé-dyem]	let's go (by transport)
вме́сте	[vmyé-stye]	together
ста́нция	[stán-tsi-ya]	station (on metro); small railway station
недалеко́	[nye-da-lye-kó]	not far (indecl)
заче́м	[za-chyém]	for what purpose, why
пешко́м	[pyesh-kóm]	on foot
е́хать (1В)	[yé-haty]	to go (by transport) (see 6.3)
биле́т	[bee-lyét]	ticket
биле́т на (+ acc)	[bee-lyét na]	ticket for (transport)
по́езд	[pó-yest]	train
че́рез (+ acc)	[chyé-ryes]	after (with time words)
неде́ля	[nye-dyé-lya]	week
домо́й	[da-móy]	home (= to home)
А́нглия	[án-glee-ya]	England (often used for Britain)
родно́й (adj)	[rad-nóy]	native
люби́ть (2)	[lyoo-beéty]	to love, like
я люблю́	[ya lyoo-blyoó]	I love, like
ты лю́бишь	[ti lyoó-beesh]	you (fam) love, like
осо́бенно	[a-só-bye-na]	especially
надо́лго	[na-dól-ga]	for a long time
ме́сяц	[myé-syats]	month
Аме́рика	[a-myé-ree-ka]	America
обра́тно	[a-brát-na]	back
тепе́рь	[tye-pyéry]	now

хоте́ть (1В/2)	[ha-tyéty]	to want (see 6.5)
хоте́ть уви́деть	[ha-tyéty oo-vée--dyety]	to want to see
вот почему́	[vot pa-chye-moó]	that's why
наве́рно	[na-vyér-na]	probably
сли́шком	[slee-shkam]	too
бы́стро	[bí-stra]	quickly
ру́сская (adj)	[roó-ska-ya]	Russian woman

6.7 CONVERSATION

Jane and Boris meet again

Джейн: Здра́вствуйте, Бори́с.

Бори́с: Здра́вствуйте, Джейн. Как дела́?

Джейн: Ничего́. Куда́ вы иде́те?

Бори́с: Я иду́ в магази́н «Дру́жба», пото́м на рабо́ту. А куда́ вы иде́те?

Джейн: В гости́ницу «Метропо́ль».

Бори́с: Мо́жно на метро́. Дава́йте пое́дем вме́сте. Ста́нция Дзержи́нская недалеко́.

Джейн: Хорошо́. Заче́м идти́ пешко́м, когда́ мо́жно е́хать?!

Бори́с: Заче́м вы иде́те в «Метропо́ль»?

Джейн: Там мой биле́т на по́езд. Че́рез неде́лю я е́ду домо́й в А́нглию, в мой родно́й го́род Ливерпу́ль. Там живу́т мать и брат. Я их о́чень люблю́, осо́бенно бра́та.

Бори́с: А вы надо́лго е́дете?

Джейн: На ме́сяц. Пото́м я е́ду в Аме́рику на неде́лю, пото́м обра́тно в Росси́ю.

Бори́с: Заче́м вы е́дете в Аме́рику?

Джейн: Мой друг Марк тепе́рь в Аме́рике. Я хочу́ его́ уви́деть. И он хо́чет уви́деть меня́.

Бори́с: А! Вы хоти́те уви́деть Ма́рка! Вот почему́ вы е́дете в Аме́рику! Вы его́ лю́бите?

Джейн: Бори́с, вы говори́те сли́шком бы́стро, я вас не понима́ю. Говори́те ме́дленно, пожа́луйста. Я не ру́сская, а англича́нка.

Бори́с: Прости́те.

TRANSLATION

Jane: Hello, Boris.

Boris: Hello, Jane. How are things?

Jane: Not bad. Where are you going?

Boris: I'm going to the 'Druzhba' ('Friendship') store (a bookshop), then (I'm going) to work. And where are you going?

Jane: To the Metropole Hotel [where there is also a travel office].

Boris: It is possible (we can) (to go) by metro. Let's go together. 'Dzerzhinskaya' (metro) station isn't far [this station, now called Lubyanka (Лубя́нка [loo-byán-ka]) was named after Dzerzhinsky, a notorious head of the Communist secret police].

Jane: All right. Why go on foot when you can go by transport (ride)?!

Boris: Why are you going to the Metropole?

Jane: My train ticket is there. In a week's time I'm going home to England, to my home town of Liverpool. My mother and brother live there. I'm very fond of them, especially my brother.

Boris:	And are you going for long?
Jane:	For a month. Then I'm going to America for a week, then back to Russia.
Boris:	Why are you going to America?
Jane:	My friend Mark is now in America. I want to see him. And he wants to see me.
Boris:	Ah! You want to see Mark! That's why you're going to America! Do you love him?
Jane:	Boris, you are speaking too quickly, I don't understand you. Speak slowly, please. I'm not Russian, I'm English (I'm not a Russian, but an Englishwoman).
Boris:	Sorry (Excuse [me]).

Chapter 7

- Possessives: 'my', 'your' etc.
- Describing people and things using adjectives.
- The relative pronoun.

7.1 'my', 'your' etc. (possessives)

(a) Omission of possessives: You may have noticed in examples in earlier chapters that it is quite normal in Russian to omit the possessive if the possessor is clear from the context. This is particularly true of family relationships:

Мать живёт в Москве́.
　　(My) mother lives in Moscow.

Я не зна́ю, где брат.
　　I don't know where (my) brother is.

Он не зна́ет, где друг.
　　He doesn't know where (his) friend is.

(b) But in many contexts you will want to specify ownership. Here are the forms of 'my' **мой** [moy], 'your' (fam) **твой** [tvoy], 'our' **наш** [nash], 'your' (pl/pol) **ваш** [vash]:

Nom	Masculine	Feminine	Neuter
my	мой [moy]	моя́ [ma-yá]	моё [ma-yó]
your (fam)	твой [tvoy]	твоя́ [tva-yá]	твоё [tva-yó]
our	наш [nash]	на́ша [ná-sha]	на́ше [ná-she]
your (pol/pl)	ваш [vash]	ва́ша [vá-sha]	ва́ше [vá-she]

Э́то моя́ кни́га. [ma-yá knée-ga].
This is my book.

Где мое́ письмо́?
Where is my letter?

Э́то твой брат?
Is that your brother?

Где твоя́ кни́га? [tva-yá knée-ga]?
Where is your book?

Письмо́ твое́ [tva-yó].
The letter is yours.

Кто ваш брат?
Who is your brother?

Э́то ва́ше письмо́ и́ли мое́?
Is that your letter or mine?

На́ша Джейн не понима́ет вас.
Our Jane doesn't understand you.

his	= **его́**	[ye-<u>v</u>ó NB]	–	an <u>indeclinable</u> word (i.e. it has no other forms)
her	= **её**	[ye-yó]	–	indecl
its	= **его́**	[ye-<u>v</u>ó NB]	–	indecl
their	= **их**	[(y)eeh]	–	indecl

Notice that these four words look and sound the same as the accusative pronouns 'him', 'her', 'it', 'them' we met in 6.1.

Э́то её кот/письмо́/рабо́та.
This is her cat/letter/work.

Где их кот/кни́га/такси́?
Where is their cat/book/taxi?

Exercise 25

Put in the correct form of the possessive and translate:

1 Э́то (your – pol) биле́т?
2 Где (your – pol) кни́га?
3 Я не зна́ю, где (our) гости́ница.
4 (Her) мать в Москве́.
5 (Your – fam) письмо́ здесь.

7.2 Accusative forms of the possessives

Masc inanimate acc = nom	Masc animate (people, animals)	Feminine	Neuter acc = nom
мой	моего́ [ma-ye-vó]	мою́	мое́
твой	твоего́ [tva-ye-vó]	твою́	твое́
наш	на́шего [ná-she-va]	на́шу	на́ше
ваш	ва́шего [vá-she-va]	ва́шу	ва́ше
	(NB г pronounced [v])		

Я зна́ю ва́шего бра́та [vá-she-va brá-ta] и ва́шего дя́дю [vá-she-va dyá-dyoo].
   I know your brother and your uncle.

Мы не понима́ем твоего́ И́горя [tva-ye-vó ée-ga-rya].
   We don't understand your Igor.

Мы не зна́ем твою́ (ва́шу) мать и твою́ (ва́шу) сестру́ [tva-yoó (vá-shoo) sye-stroó].
   We know your mother and your sister.

Я зна́ю ваш го́род.
   I know your town.

Вы понима́ете мое́ письмо́?
   Do you understand my letter?

Его́, **её́**, and **их**, as indeclinable words, do not change:

Вы зна́ете её́ бра́та?
   Do you know her brother?

Мы зна́ем их бра́та и их дя́дю.
   We know their brother and their uncle.

Exercise 26

Say in Russian:

1   Do you (pol/fam) know my sister?

2   I know his mother.

3   She knows my brother.

4   He wants to see your (pol) friend.

7.3 Prepositional of the possessives

Nom	Prep:	m + n		f	
мой		**мое́м**	[ma-yóm]	**мое́й**	[ma-yéy]
твой		**твое́м**	[tva-yóm]	**твое́й**	[tva-yéy]
наш		**на́шем**	[ná-shem]	**на́шей**	[ná-shey]
ваш		**ва́шем**	[vá-shem]	**ва́шей**	[vá-shey]

о моём дру́ге
   about my friend

в на́шей гости́нице
   in our hotel

в твоём письме́
   in your letter

на ва́шей у́лице
   on your street

7.4 Adjectives

америка́нский	[a-mye-ree-ка́n-skee]	American
англи́йский	[an-glée-skee]	English
друго́й	[droo-góy]	different/other
кни́жный	[knéezh-ni]	book (as in 'book shop')
краси́вый	[kra-sée-vi]	beautiful/handsome
кра́сный	[krá-sni]	red
молодо́й	[ma-la-dóy]	young
но́вый	[nó-vi]	new
ру́сский	[roó-skee]	Russian
симпати́чный	[seem-pa-téech-ni]	nice (of a person)
чи́стый	[chée-sti]	clean

If you want to describe things by saying they are big, small, exciting etc., you need adjectives. All Russian adjectives in their nominative, dictionary form end in **-ый** [i] (**й** [y] not audible), **-ий** [ee] (**й** [y] not audible) or, if the ending is stressed, **-о́й** [óy]. Three typical examples are

но́в**ый** [nó-vi]	new (easy to remember – like English 'novel')
ру́сск**ий** [roó-skee]	Russian (we met this one in 5.10)
родн**о́й** [rad-nóy]	native (**родно́й язы́к** 'native language', 6.6)

Russian adjectives, like nouns, have different endings to show gender, case, singular/plural. But adjectives are easier than nouns because there are fewer rules to learn and almost no exceptions.

Take **но́вый** [nó-vi] 'new'. The stem is **нов-** [nóv] and the masculine nominative singular ending is **-ый** [i]. The equivalent feminine ending is **-ая** [a-ya] and the neuter ending is **-ое** [a-ye]

(m)	но́в**ый** дом	[nó-vi dom]	new house
(f)	но́в**ая** у́лица	[nó-va-ya oó-lee-tsa]	new street
(n)	но́в**ое** сло́во	[nó-va-ye sló-va]	new word

<u>Every</u> adjective with the ending **-ый** is like **но́вый**, e.g.
симпати́чный [seem-pa-te̐ech-ni] 'nice':

симпати́чная **же́нщина** [seem-pa-te̐ech-na-ya zhén-shshee-na]
   a nice woman

Here are the endings of **ру́сский** [roó-skee] 'Russian':

(m)	**ру́сский язы́к**	[roó-skee (y)ee-zík]	Russian language
(f)	**ру́сская же́нщина**	[roó-ska-ya zhén-shshee-na]	Russian woman
(n)	**ру́сское сло́во**	[roó-ska-ye sló-va]	Russian word

The feminine (f) and neuter (n) endings are the same as for
но́вый. And adjectives like **родно́й** [rad-nóy] 'native' and
друго́й [droo-góy] 'different, other' have the same (f) and
(n) endings, except that the ending always has the stress:

(m)	**друго́й го́род**	[droo-góy gó-rat]	another town
(f)	**друга́я же́нщина**	[droo-gá-ya zhén-shshee-na]	another woman
(n)	**друго́е сло́во**	[droo-gó-ye sló-va]	a different word

7.5 Some phrases with adjectives

Она́ зна́ет англи́йский язы́к.
   She knows the English language (= She knows English).

NOTE When talking about languages, Russians nearly
always include the word **язы́к** 'language':

Я изуча́ю [ee-zoo-chá-yoo] **ру́сский язы́к.**
   I am studying Russian.

Ру́сский язы́к краси́вый.
   Russian (language) is beautiful.

Она́ о́чень симпати́чная.
   She is very nice.

Э́то сло́во не англи́йское, а америка́нское.
   This is not an English word. It's American.

Вот Кра́сная пло́щадь.
   There is Red Square.

Джейн молода́я и краси́вая.
Jane is young and beautiful.

Э́то мой америка́нский дя́дя.
This is my American uncle.

Exercise 27

Put the adjectives in brackets into the correct Russian form:

1 **Москва́** – (beautiful) **го́род.**

2 **Ни́на** – (nice Russian) **же́нщина.**

3 **Кра́сная пло́щадь о́чень** (clean).

4 **Э́то** (is a different Russian) **сло́во.**

5 **Ваш** (English) **друг о́чень** (handsome)

7.6 Adjectives, like nouns, have case endings

Adjectives always have to be in the same case as their accompanying nouns. The forms in 7.4 are the nominative case forms of adjectives. If the noun is in another case, such as the accusative or the prepositional, the adjective has to be in that case too. Fortunately, there aren't many new forms to learn.

7.7 Prepositional of adjectives

If the accompanying noun is masculine or neuter, the ending to add to the adjective stem is **-ом** [om]:

Он живёт в но́вом [vnó-vam] **го́роде.**
He lives in a new town.

в друго́м ру́сском сло́ве [vdroo-góm roó-skam sló-vye]
in another Russian word

With feminine nouns, the adjective ending is **-ой**:

на Кра́сной пло́щади [na-krá-snay pló-shsha-dee]
    on Red Square

Мы в друго́й гости́нице [vdroo-góy ga-stee-nee-tse].
    We are in another (a different) hotel.

7.8 Accusative of adjectives

The feminine accusative adjective ending is **-ую** [oo-yoo] (easy to learn if you remember that the accusative endings for feminine nouns are the same vowels **у** or **ю** – see 6.2).

Я зна́ю краси́вую [kra-see-voo-yoo] **ру́сскую** [roó-skoo-yoo] **же́нщину.**
    I know a beautiful Russian woman.

Мы идём на Кра́сную [krá-snoo-yoo] **пло́щадь.**
    We are going to Red Square.

With masculine nouns denoting people and animals, the accusative adjective ending is **-ого** (NB the **г** is pronounced [v]):

Джейн хо́чет уви́деть америка́нского [a-mye-ree-kán-ska-va] **дру́га.**
    Jane wants to see (her) American friend.

Она́ зна́ет его́ англи́йского [an-glee-ska-va] **дя́дю.**
    She knows his English uncle.

With masculine nouns denoting things and all neuter nouns, the adjective ending is the same as the nominative:

Я зна́ю но́вое сло́во.
    I know a new word.

Мы идём в ру́сский кни́жный магази́н.
    We are going to the Russian bookshop.

Exercise 28

Add the required adjective endings and translate:

1 Вот но́в___ гости́ница.   (nom)

2 Мы живём в но́в___ гости́нице.   (prep)

3 Это Кра́сн___ пло́щадь (f 'square').   (nom)

4 Мы лю́бим Кра́сн___ пло́щадь.   (acc)

5 Это ру́сск___ кни́жн___ магази́н.   (nom)

6 Она́ рабо́тает в ру́сск___ кни́жн___ магази́не. (prep)

7 Мы лю́бим ру́сск___ язы́к.   (acc)

8 Ру́сск___ сло́во «пло́щадь» о́чень краси́в___ . (nom)

9 В Москве́ метро́ о́чень чи́ст___.   (nom)

10 Она́ е́дет на но́в___ рабо́ту.   (acc)

11 Я зна́ю её но́в___ америка́нск___ дру́га.   (acc)

12 Англи́йск___ учи́тельницу зову́т мисс Смит.   (acc)

7.9 'who'/'which': кото́рый [ka-tó-ri]

The relative pronouns 'who' and 'which', as in 'The girl <u>who</u> works there is Russian', are both translated кото́рый, which in form is an <u>adjective</u> with the same gender and case endings as но́вый.

He talks about the girl who works in the bookshop.
> **Он говори́т о де́вушке, кото́<u>рая</u> рабо́тает в кни́жном магази́не.**

Кото́рая is fem and sing because **де́вушка** is fem and sing; it is nom because it is the subject of **рабо́тает**.

The girl whom (acc) he loves works there.
> **Де́вушка, кото́рую (f sing acc) он лю́бит, рабо́тает там.**

The shop in which she works is in Gorky Street.

Магази́н, в кото́ром (m sing prep) она́ рабо́тает, на у́лице Го́рького.

Exercise 29

Put the correct ending on **кото́рый:**

1 **Вот у́лица, на котóр__ (on which) мы живём.**

2 **Я зна́ю де́вушку, котóр__ (who) живёт там.**

3 **Магази́н, в котóр__ (to which) мы идём, но́вый.**

4 **Э́то Бори́с, котóр__ (whom) вы уже́ зна́ете.**

7.10 Vocabulary

In alphabetical order. See also adjective list 7.4.

ба́бушка	[bá-boosh-ka]	grandmother
вино́	[vee-nó]	wine
во́дка	[vót-ka]	vodka
всё	[fsyo]	all, everything – see **весь**: table 4
второ́й	[fta-róy]	second
де́вушка	[dyé-voosh-ka]	girl
дере́вня	[dye-ryév-nya]	country, village
изуча́ть (1) (+ acc)	[ee-zoo-cháty]	to study (like **знать**)
и́ли	[ée-lee]	or
и́мя NB neuter!	[ée-mya]	name, first name
кварти́ра	[kvar-teéra]	flat, apartment
кни́га	[knee´-ga]	book
кот	[kot]	(tom) cat
муж	[moosh]	husband
опя́ть	[a-pyáty]	again
пе́рвый	[pyér-vi]	first
пи́во	[pee´-va]	beer
пло́щадь (f)	[pló-shshaty]	square

подру́га	[pa-droó-ga]	(girl)friend
по-мо́ему	[pa-mó-ye-moo]	in my opinion, I think
са́мый	[sá-mi]	most (with adjectives)
сестра́	[sye-strá]	sister
сла́дкий	[slát-kee]	sweet
сло́во	[sló-va]	word
ста́рый	[stá-ri]	old
то́лько	[tóly-ka]	only

7.11 CONVERSATION

Nina and Mike are looking at Nina's photographs

Майк: Это ва́ша сестра́ [sye-strá]?

Ни́на: Нет, э́то моя́ подру́га [pa-droó-ga] Ната́ша, кото́рая рабо́тает в кни́жном магази́не «Дру́жба» на у́лице Го́рького [góry-ka-va]. Это её друг Бори́с. А э́то на́ша англи́йская подру́га Джейн и её америка́нский друг.

Майк: Вы зна́ете её америка́нского дру́га [a-mye-ree-kán-ska-va droó-ga]?

Ни́на: Нет, я его́ не зна́ю. Я зна́ю то́лько, что зову́т его́ Марк и что сейча́с он в Аме́рике. Ната́ша говори́т, что он о́чень симпати́чный. Вот они́ опя́ть [a-pyáty], на Кра́сной пло́щади [na-krá-snay pló-shsha-dee].

Майк: Я хорошо́ зна́ю Кра́сную пло́щадь. Это са́мая [sá-ma-ya] краси́вая пло́щадь в Москве́. А Марк хорошо́ зна́ет ру́сский язы́к?

Ни́на: По-мо́ему, он зна́ет ру́сское сло́во «спаси́бо». И э́то всё.

Майк: Кто э́то? Ва́ша ба́бушка [bá-boosh-ka]?

Ни́на: Да. Это на́ша ба́бушка. Она́ живёт в дере́вне [dye-ryév-nye]* в ста́ром до́ме. Она́ не хо́чет жить в но́вом.

Майк: Где ва́ша сестра́? [gdye vá-sha sye-strá?]

Ни́на: Вот она́. И вот её второ́й муж. А вот краси́вая но́вая кварти́ра [kvar-tée-ra], в кото́рой они́ живу́т. А э́то её пе́рвый муж, кото́рого я не люблю́. Он о́чень лю́бит во́дку, пи́во и сла́дкое вино́.

TRANSLATION

Mike: Is that your sister?

Nina: No, that's my girlfriend Natasha who works in the Friendship bookshop in (on) Gorky Street. This is her friend Boris. And that's our English girlfriend Jane and her American friend.

Mike: Do you know her American friend?

Nina: No, I don't know him. I only know that his name is Mark and that he is in America at the moment. Natasha says that he is very nice. Here they are again, in Red Square.

Mike: I know Red Square well. It is the most beautiful square in Moscow. And does Mark know Russian well?

Nina: I think he knows the Russian word 'spaseeba'. And that's all.

Mike: Who's that? Your grandmother?

Nina: Yes. That's our grandmother. She lives in the country, in an old house. She doesn't want to live in a new (one).

Mike: Where is your sister?

Nina: Here she is. And here is her second husband. Here is the beautiful new flat (in which) they live in. And this is her first husband, whom I don't like. He is very fond of vodka, beer and sweet wine ('fortified' **креплуное** [krye-plyó-na--ye] sweet wine is for the winos who want to get drunk quickly and cheaply).

Exercise 30 (revision)

Say in Russian:

1 I do not understand you. Speak slowly please.
2 He knows English.
3 I am studying Russian.
4 Natasha is going (on foot) to the bookshop.
5 Natasha does not want to work in the bookshop.
6 We are going (on foot) to Red Square.
7 Jane and Boris do not want to go there.
8 When are you (pol) going to America?
9 Their grandmother lives in the Russian countryside.
10 Can you (pol) speak Russian? (use the structure in 4.1)
11 My girlfriend is called Nina.
12 Your (pol) flat is very clean.
13 She does not like your (fam) new husband.
14 I want to see (my) Russian friend Boris.
15 We love Russian wine and Russian vodka.
16 Where is the girl who is called (whom they call) Nina?

Chapter 8

- How to make plurals.
- A spelling rule.
- 'this' and 'that'.
- **хоро́ший** 'good' and another spelling rule.
- Fleeting vowels.

Exercise 31

Read these examples, which all contain vocabulary from chapters 1–7 and grammar which will be covered in this chapter. Then check your pronunciation from the Key.

1. **Она́ лю́бит кни́ги.** — She likes books.

2. **Вы зна́ете э́ти ру́сские слова́?** — Do you know these Russian words?

3. **Америка́нцы лю́бят краси́вые магази́ны.** — Americans like beautiful shops.

4. **В Москве́ есть гости́ницы, рестора́ны, музе́и, проспе́кты, пло́щади.** — In Moscow there are hotels, restaurants, museums, avenues (and) squares.

5. **Ва́ши бра́тья симпати́чные.** — Your brothers are nice.

8.1 Nominative plural of m/f nouns ending with a consonant or -a

If the noun ends **б, в, д, з, л, м, н, п, р, с, т, ф** or **ц**, add **ы**. If it ends with one of these consonants + **a**, replace **a** with **ы**.

Singular		*Plural*		
магази́н	shop	магази́ны	[ma-ga-zée-ni]	shops
гости́ница	hotel	гости́ницы	[ga-stée-nee-tsi]	hotels
сувени́р	souvenir	сувени́ры	[soo-vye-née-ri]	souvenirs

8.2 Plural of nouns ending with -ь (soft sign), -й or -я

Replace the **ь, й** or **я** with **и**:

вещь [vyeshshy] thing	ве́щи [vyé-shshee] things
рубль [roobly] rouble	рубли́ [roo-bleé] roubles
неде́ля [nye-dyé-lya] week	неде́ли [nye-dyé-lee] weeks
трамва́й [tram-váy] tram	трамва́и [tram-vá-ee] trams (trolleys)
ста́нция [stán-tsi-ya] station	ста́нции [stán-tsi-ee] stations

8.3 Plural of nouns ending г к х ж ш щ ч

The consonants not included in rule 8.1 are followed in the plural by **-и** (not **-ы**):

язы́к	language	языки́	[(y)ee-zi-keé]	languages
кни́га	book	кни́ги	[kneé-gee]	books
да́ча	dacha	да́чи	[dá-chee]	dachas (country cottages)

The reason for this is that Russian has a 'spelling rule' which affects the spelling of grammatical endings after the seven consonants **г, к, х, ж, ч, ш** and **щ**. This list of letters is a nuisance to learn when you first meet it, but you will find that, once learnt, it helps you to spell correctly.

8.4 Spelling rule 1

Whereas other consonants (see list in 8.1) are followed by
-ы, after the following seven consonants you <u>always</u> find
и instead:

г	To help you remember these, notice that these
к	three are all pronounced in the same place at the
х	back of the mouth
ч	These are the two consonants from the alphabet
щ	(2.6) which are always <u>soft</u>
ж	These are two of the three consonants which are
ш	always <u>hard</u> (see 2.7)

So the plural of **кни́га** has **и** (not **ы**): **кни́ги**, the plural of
да́ча is **да́чи**, the plural of **язы́к** is **языки́**.

NOTE After the same seven consonants plus **ц**, you will
always find **a** not **я**, and **y** not **ю**. This addition to spelling
rule 1 mainly affects a few Type 2 verbs, e.g. **учи́ться** (11.9).

8.5 Plural of neuter nouns

(a) Replace **o** with **a** and change the stress:

сло́во	word	**слова́**	[sla-vá]	words
вино́	wine	**ви́на**	[vée-na]	wines

(b) Replace **e** with **я**:

упражне́ние	**упражне́ния**	[oo-prazh-nyé-nee-ya]
exercise	exercises	

8.6 Exceptions

Many nouns have plurals which are exceptions to these
rules. Here is a list of the main exceptions you need to know
so far:

мать [maty] mother   **ма́тери** [má-tye-ree] mothers
дочь [dochy] daughter   **до́чери** [dó-chye-ree] daughters
(The extra **ер** makes both words look more like their English equivalents.)

англича́нин	English-man	англича́не	[an-glee--chá-nye]	English-men
брат	brother	бра́тья	[bráty-ya]	brothers
друг	friend	друзья́	[droozy-yá]	friends
дом	house	дома́	[da-má]	houses
го́род	town	города́	[ga-ra-dá]	towns
сын	son	сыновья́	[si-navy-yá]	sons

When a noun has an unpredictable plural, it will be shown in the vocabulary.

Exercise 32

Put on the correct plural endings and translate:

1 заво́д
2 же́нщина
3 англича́нка
4 дя́дя
5 музе́й
6 ба́бушка
7 ста́нция
8 подру́га
9 свида́ние
10 учи́тельница
11 пло́щадь
12 письмо́

8.7 Plural of possessives

Sing	*Pl*
мой my	**мои́** [ma-eé]
твой your (fam)	**твои́** [tva-eé]
наш our	**на́ши** [ná-shi]
ваш your (pol/pl)	**ва́ши** [vá-shi]

мои́ друзья́	my friends
ва́ши пи́сьма/кни́ги/бра́тья	your letters/books/brothers
Пи́сьма на́ши.	The letters are ours.

8.8 Plural of adjectives

Adjectives match nouns, so a plural noun needs a plural adjective. Adjectives are easy. The ending for all genders is **-ые** [i-ye]:

но́вые [nó-vi-ye] **друзья́/слова́/города́**
    new friends/words/towns

8.9 Plural of adjectives ending г к х ж ш ч щ

The only other thing to remember is the <u>spelling rule</u> (8.4), which applies to adjectives just as it applies to nouns. After the seven consonants **гкх/жш/чщ, -ые** becomes **-ие**:

ру́сские [ro-skee-ye] **слова́/же́нщины/кни́ги**
    Russian words/women/books

Exercise 33

Make the following plural and translate:

1 **краси́вая же́нщина**   5 **ва́ша кра́сная кни́га**

2 **моя́ ру́сская кни́га**   6 **друга́я гости́ница**

3 **америка́нский магази́н**   7 **твой ста́рый друг**

4 **но́вая у́лица**

8.10 Accusative plural

The accusative plural forms are the same as the nominative forms above <u>except</u> for <u>all</u> nouns (whatever the gender) denoting people and animals. We shall leave the Russian equivalents of 'I love cats and women' until 10.11. But we can now say things like:

I love Russian cities.	Я люблю́ ру́сские города́.
We know the new words.	Мы зна́ем но́вые слова́.
She loves your shops.	Она́ лю́бит ва́ши магази́ны.

8.11 хоро́ший 'good' and a second spelling rule

If you have memorized the spelling rule we met in 8.4, you will see why the ending of the important adjective **хоро́ший** [ha-ró-shi] 'good' is spelt **-ий** (and not **-ый**). Now we must point out a second spelling rule which affects adjectives ending **жий, ший, чий, щий** (note that **ж, ш, ч** and **щ** are the last four of the seven letters which participate in the first rule). After **ж, ч, ш** and **щ** you find **e** where adjectives like **но́вый** and **ру́сский** have **o**. (This rule also applies after **ц** – but there are no common adjectives ending **-цый**). So the neuter ending after these four letters is **-<u>ee</u>** (<u>not</u> **-oe**) and the prepositional endings are **-ем** (m and n) and **-ей** (f) instead of **-ом** and **-ой**:

Masculine	*Neuter*
хоро́ший good	**хоро́<u>ш</u>ее** [ha-ró-she-ye] **вино́** good wine
све́жий [svyé-zhi] fresh	**све́<u>ж</u>ее** [svyé-zhe-ye] **у́тро** fresh morning
горя́чий [ga-ryá-chee] hot	**горя́<u>ч</u>ее** [ga-ryá-chye-ye] **вино́** hot wine
сле́дующий following	**сле́дующ<u>ее</u> у́тро** following morning

Prepositional

в хоро́шей моско́вской гости́нице
в хоро́шей моско́вской гости́нице
   in a good Moscow hotel

в хоро́шем ру́сском магази́не
   in a good Russian shop

8.12 'this'/'that': э́тот

You already know the word э́то [é-ta] used in sentences like 'This/That is … (something)' (see 4.5), e.g.:

This/That is our house.   **Э́то наш дом.**

If you want to say 'this house'/'this book'/'this letter', you need the word э́тот/э́та/э́то 'this'/'that' which agrees with its noun, like an adjective:

This/That house is ours.   **Э́тот** [é-tat] **дом наш.**
This/That book is mine.   **Э́та** [é-ta] **кни́га моя́.**
This/That name is very   **Э́то** [é-ta] **и́мя** (NB neuter)
beautiful.   **о́чень краси́вое.**

The feminine accusative is э́ту [é-too]:

I know this/that woman.   **Я зна́ю э́ту же́нщину.**

The plural is э́ти for all genders:

These women/words are   **Э́ти же́нщины/слова́**
Russian.   **ру́сские.**

The other singular endings of э́тот we need are the same as for но́вый (see 7.7, 7.8).

Do you know this Englishman?
   Вы зна́ете э́того [é-ta-va] **англича́нина?**

They live in this hotel.
   Они́ живу́т в э́той гости́нице.

Exercise 34

Put on the endings:

1 **Э́то хоро́ш ____ вино́.**

2 **Мы живём в хоро́ш ____ гости́нице на э́т ____ у́лице.**

3 **Вы зна́ете э́т ____ слова́?**

4 **В э́т ____ магази́не кни́ги хоро́ш ____ .**

5 **Вы зна́ете э́т ____ америка́нку?**

8.13 Fleeting vowels

In 8.1 above we met the plural form **америка́нцы** 'Americans'. The word for 'an American' is **америка́нец** (4.3). The Russian for 'father' is <u>**отец**</u> [a-tyéts]. Now look at these two examples:

«<u>Отцы́</u> и де́ти» – хоро́шая кни́га.
 'Fathers and Children' is a good book.

Вы зна́ете э́того америка́<u>нца</u>?
 Do you know that American?

'Fathers' has the normal plural ending **-ы** (see 8.1) but the **е** of **отец** has dropped out. Similarly, in **америка́нца** (accusative of a masculine person), the **е** of **америка́нец** has dropped out. A vowel **е** or **о** which vanishes from between the last two consonants of a masculine noun <u>whenever there is an ending on the word</u> is called a <u>fleeting vowel</u>. In the vocabularies we shall show fleeting vowels in brackets:

д(е)нь	[dyeny]	day	pl **<u>дни</u>**
пода́р(о)к	[pa-dá-rak]	present	pl **пода́<u>рки</u>**

Fleeting vowels can be a nuisance when you are trying to find words in a dictionary. If you found the form **дни** 'days' in a text, you might have difficulty working out the nominative **день**. So note the fleeting vowel phenomenon and, if you can't find a noun in the dictionary, try inserting **-e-** or **-o-** between the last two consonants.

8.14 Vocabulary

Ordered as they occur in the conversation:

хоте́ть пойти́	[pay-teé]	to want to go (on foot) **пойти́** (from **идти́** 'to go') – see 12.2, 13.4
сего́дня	[sye-<u>v</u>ó-dnya NB]	today
сде́лать поку́пки	[zdyé-laty]	to do some shopping
поку́пка	[pa-koóp-ka]	purchase
покажи́те	[pa-ka-zhí-tye]	show (imper)
мне	[mnye]	to me
моско́вский	[ma-skóf-skee]	Moscow (adj)
како́й	[ka-kóy]	what (adj), what kind of
интересова́ть stem **интересу́-**	[een-tye-rye-sa-váty] (1)	to interest
пласти́нка	[pla-steén-ka]	record
сувени́р	[soo-vye-neér]	souvenir
ча́сто	[chá-sta]	often
покупа́ть stem **покупа́-** я покупа́ю, ты покупа́ешь	[pa-koo-páty] (1) + acc	to buy
есть	[yesty]	is/are (exists/exist)
зна́чит	[zná-cheet]	so (lit. '(it) means')
интере́сно	[een-tye-ryé-sna]	(that's) interesting
на́до	[ná-da]	it is necessary; one must
на́до купи́ть	[ná-da koo-peéty] + acc	it is necessary to buy (for **купи́ть** see 12.2)
пода́р(о)к	[pa-dá-rak]	present
друзья́	[droo-zyyá] (irreg pl of **друг**)	friends
тури́ст	[too-reést]	tourist

91

обы́чно	[a-bích-na]	usually
тако́й	[ta-kóy]	such (adj)
вещь (f)	[vyeshshy]	thing
Бере́зка	[bye-ryós-ka]	Beriozka (store name), lit. 'little birch tree'
брать	[braty] (1B) + acc	to take
stem бер-		
я беру́,		
ты бере́шь		
иностра́нный	[ee-na-strá-ni]	foreign
де́ньги	[dyény-gee] (pl)	money
наприме́р	[na-pree-myér]	for example
фунт	[foont]	pound (money and weight)
до́ллар	[dó-lar]	dollar
дава́йте	[da-váy-tye	let's go
пойде́м	pay-dyóm]	
подожди́те	[pa-dazh-deé-tye	wait a moment
мину́точку	mee-noó-tach-koo]	
посмотри́те	[pa-sma-treé-tye]	look (imper)
смотре́ть	[sma-tryéty] (2)	to look (at)
stem смотр-	(на + acc)	
я смотрю́,		
ты смо́тришь		
люби́мый	[lyoo-beé-mi]	favourite
стихи́	[stee-heé]	poetry, poem(s)
	(pl of стих 'line')	
до́брый	[dó-bri]	kind

8.15 CONVERSATION

Andrey and Barbara plan some shopping

Андре́й: Здра́вствуйте, Ба́рбара. Как дела́? Куда́ вы хоти́те пойти́ сего́дня?

Ба́рбара: Здра́вствуйте, Андре́й. Сего́дня я хочу́ сде́лать поку́пки. Покажи́те мне, пожа́луйста, моско́вские магази́ны.

Андре́й: Каки́е магази́ны? Что вас интересу́ет? Кни́ги, пласти́нки, сувени́ры?

Ба́рбара: Меня́ интересу́ют ру́сские кни́ги. В Вашингто́не и в Нью-Йо́рке я ча́сто покупа́ю ва́ши кни́ги. Там есть ру́сские кни́жные магази́ны.

Андре́й: Зна́чит, америка́нцы покупа́ют на́ши кни́ги. Интере́сно. Но вас интересу́ют не то́лько кни́ги.

Ба́рбара: На́до купи́ть пода́рки. Че́рез неде́лю я е́ду домо́й в Аме́рику. Мои́ друзья́ лю́бят ру́сскую во́дку.

Андре́й: Тури́сты обы́чно покупа́ют таки́е ве́щи в магази́не «Берёзка». В «Берёзке» есть о́чень краси́вые ве́щи, но там беру́т то́лько иностра́нные де́ньги, наприме́р англи́йские фу́нты, ва́ши америка́нские до́ллары. Дава́йте пойдём в кни́жный магази́н «Берёзка» – э́тот магази́н на Кропо́ткинской у́лице – пото́м в «Берёзку» в гости́нице «Росси́я».

Ба́рбара: Хорошо́.

(Andrey takes a wrapped book out of his pocket)

Андре́й: Подожди́те мину́точку. *(A pause)* Посмотри́те.

Ба́рбара: Что э́ ода́рок. Пастерна́к, мои́ люби́мые стихи́. Я зна́ю, что вы лю́бите на́ши ру́сские стихи́.

Ба́рбара: Вы о́чень до́брый, Андре́й.

Exercise 35

Translate the conversation.

Exercise 36

Say in Russian:

1   I want to do some shopping.

2   Here (they) take only Russian money.

3   In this shop there are good books.

4   My friends live in this street.

5   These Americans know where our hotel is.

Exercise 36A

What is the name of this play? Who are Dmitriy, Ivan and Alyosha?

Ф. М . ДОСТОЕВСКИЙ

БРАТЬЯ КАРАМАЗОВЫ

Пьеса Б .Н. Ливанова по одноименному роману
в 4-х действиях , 12 картинах

Действующие лица и исполнители:

Федор Павлович Карамазов . . . . **М. И. Прудкин**

Дмитрий			**Л. Ф. Золотухин**
Иван	}	его сыновья	**В. С. Давыдов**
Алеша			**Н. П. Алексеев**
			А. В. Вербицкий

Chapter 9

- Counting.
- Numbers and the genitive case.
- Quantity and the genitive case.

9.1 The Russian numerals

Read and memorize.
1 один [a-deén] (m), одна [ad-ná] (f), одно [ad-nó] (n)
   один рубль one rouble
   одна копейка [ka-pyéy-ka] one kopeck
   (1/100 of a rouble)
   одно письмо one letter
2 два [dva] with m and n nouns,
   две [dvye] with f nouns
   два рубля [roo-blyá] two roubles
   две копейки [ka-pyéy-kee] two kopecks
3 три [tree]
   три рубля three roubles
   три копейки three kopecks
4 четыре [chye-tí-rye]
   четыре рубля four roubles
   четыре копейки four kopecks
5 пять [pyaty]
   пять рублей [roo-blyéy] five roubles
   пять копеек [ka-pyé-yek] five kopecks
6 шесть [shesty]
   шесть рублей six roubles
   шесть копеек six kopecks
7 семь [syemy]
8 восемь [vó-syemy]
9 девять [dyé-vyaty]

10 **де́сять** [dyé-syaty]
11 **оди́ннадцать** [a-deé-na-tsaty NB second д not audible]
12 **двена́дцать** [dvye-ná-tsaty NB second д not audible]
13 **трина́дцать** [tree-ná-tsaty NB]
14 **четы́рнадцать** [chye-tír-na-tsaty NB]
15 **пятна́дцать** [peet-ná-tsaty NB]   NB д not
16 **шестна́дцать** [shes-ná-tsaty NB]   audible
17 **семна́дцать** [syem-ná-tsaty NB]   before ц
18 **восемна́дцать** [va-syem-ná-tsaty NB]
19 **девятна́дцать** [dye-veet-ná-tsaty NB]
20 **два́дцать** [dvá-tsaty NB]
   два́дцать рубле́й twenty roubles
21 **два́дцать оди́н** (m)/**одна́** (f)/ **одно́** (n)
   два́дцать оди́н рубль twenty-one roubles
   два́дцать одна́ копе́йка twenty-one kopecks
   два́дцать одно́ письмо́ twenty-one letters
22 **два́дцать два** (m/n)/**две** (f)
   два́дцать два рубля́ twenty-two roubles
   два́дцать две копе́йки twenty-two kopecks
23 **два́дцать три**
   два́дцать три рубля́ twenty-three roubles
   два́дцать три копе́йки twenty-three kopecks
24 **два́дцать четы́ре рубля́/копе́йки** 24 roubles/kopecks
25 **два́дцать пять** [dvá-tsaty pyaty]
   два́дцать пять рубле́й/копе́ек 25 roubles/kopecks
30 **три́дцать** [treé-tsaty NB]
31 **три́дцать оди́н** (m)/**одна́** (f)/**одно́** (n)
40 **со́рок** [só-rak]
   со́рок рубле́й/копе́ек forty roubles/kopecks
50 **пятьдеся́т** [pee-dye-syát NB]
60 **шестьдеся́т** [shez-dye-syát NB]
70 **се́мьдесят** [syém-dye-syat]
80 **во́семьдесят** [vó-syem-dye-syat]
90 **девяно́сто** [dye-vee-nó-sta]
100 **сто** [sto]
101 **сто оди́н** (m)/**одна́** (f)/**одно́** (n)
102 **сто два** (m/n)/**две** (f)
200 **две́сти** [dvyé-stee]

300	**три́ста** [tree-sta]
400	**четы́реста** [chye-tí-rye-sta]
500	**пятьсо́т** [p<u>ee</u>t-sót NB]
600	**шестьсо́т** [sh<u>es</u>-sót NB]
700	**семьсо́т** [syem-sót]
800	**восемьсо́т** [va-syem-sót]
900	**девятьсо́т** [dye-veet-sót]
1000	**ты́сяча** [tí-sya-cha]
2000	**две ты́сячи** [dvye tí-sya-chee]
5000	**пять ты́сяч** [pyaty tí-syach]
0	**ноль** [noly]

9.2 The grammar of од(и́)н 'one'

The number 1 **од(и́)н/одна́/одно́** behaves like **э́тот/э́та/э́то** 'this/that' (see 8.12) with the same endings, depending on the gender and case of the accompanying noun. Note that the **и** of **оди́н** drops out when you add an ending (a rare case of a fleeting **и**; see 8.13 for the term 'fleeting vowel').

одна́ кни́га
one book

Он зна́ет одно́ ру́сское сло́во.
He knows one Russian word.

Я зна́ю одну́ англича́нку (f acc).
I know one Englishwoman.

Я зна́ю одного́ [ad-na-vó] **англича́нина** (m acc of a person).
I know one Englishman.

The number 1 has the same endings in all numbers which end with **оди́н, одна́** or **одно́** (21, 31, 41, 101 etc.) and the accompanying noun is <u>singular</u>:

Он зна́ет два́дцать одно́ ру́сское сло́во.
He knows 21 Russian words.
(lit. 'He knows 21 Russian word.')

9.3 Other numbers take the genitive ('three of book')

All other numbers are accompanied by nouns in the genitive case (a case form which literally means 'of somebody or something' as in 'a glass of vodka' стака́н во́дки (gen) or 'the brother of Boris' брат Бори́са).

(a) After the numbers 2 (два/две), 3 (три), and 4 (четы́ре), and all numbers ending два/две, три or четы́ре, the noun is in the genitive singular.

So два рубля́ 'two roubles' = lit. 'two of rouble'. Рубля́ [roo-blyá] is gen sing of рубль (m) 'a rouble', the Russian currency unit.

Две is the form of 2 used with feminine nouns: две копе́йки 'two kopecks' (lit. 'two of kopeck'). Копе́йка 'a kopeck' is one hundredth of a rouble.

(b) The numbers from 5 up to and including 20, and all numbers which do not end with forms of оди́н (1), два (2), три (3) and четы́ре (4), are followed by the genitive plural:

пять рубле́й	five roubles	(lit. 'five of roubles')
шесть копе́ек	six kopecks	(lit. 'six of kopecks')

NOTE Apart from оди́н and одна́ (see examples above), the accusative forms of numbers are the same as the nominative:

Он зна́ет де́сять (acc) слов.
He knows ten words.

Read the following examples:

Мы зна́ем се́мьдесят слов.
We know seventy words.

Вот пять копе́ек.
Here are five kopecks.

Пожа́луйста, да́йте три рубля́.
Please give (me) three roubles.

Кни́га сто́ит четы́ре рубля́ два́дцать три копе́йки.
The book costs four roubles twenty-three kopecks.

В «Берёзке» э́та кни́га сто́ит четы́ре до́ллара.
In the 'Beriozka' this book costs four dollars.

Э́та кни́га сто́ит шесть до́лларов.
This book costs six dollars.

Во́дка сто́ит пять фу́нтов.
Vodka costs five pounds.

В э́том го́роде де́сять гости́ниц.
There are ten hotels in this city.

В гости́нице сто три́дцать оди́н тури́ст.
There are one hundred and thirty-one tourists
in the hotel.

Exercise 37

What are the following numbers?

1 **Ты́сяча две́сти со́рок оди́н**

2 **Три́ста три́дцать два**

3 **Три ты́сячи пятьсо́т шесть**

4 **Сто девяно́сто во́семь**

9.4 The genitive case

The genitive (gen) is the most useful case in Russian after
the nominative and accusative. You will need it for four
main purposes:

(1) counting (**де́сять рубле́й** 'ten (of) <u>roubles</u>')
(2) possession (**брат Ива́на** 'the brother <u>of Ivan</u>',
'<u>Ivan's</u> brother')
(3) after many prepositions (**от Ива́на** 'from Ivan')
(4) in negative constructions (**нет де́нег** 'there isn't
<u>any money</u>')

9.5 How to form the genitive singular

(a) The <u>masculine</u> and <u>neuter</u> endings are the same as the
endings you learnt for the accusative of people and
animals in 6.2, **-а** or **-я**:

(1) if the noun ends with a consonant, add **-а**;
(2) if the ending is **-о**, replace it with **-а**;
(3) if the ending is **-ь** (soft sign), **-й** or **-е**, replace it with **-я**.

Nom	*Gen*		
дом	до́ма [dó-ma]	два до́ма	two houses
брат	бра́та [brá-ta]	два бра́та	two brothers
Ива́н	Ива́на [ee-vá-na]	брат Ива́на	Ivan's brother
письмо́	письма́ [peesy-má]	два письма́	two letters
рубль	рубля́ [roo-blyá]	два рубля́	two roubles
И́горь	И́горя [ée-ga-rya]	дочь И́горя	Igor's daughter
свида́ние	свида́ния [svee-dá--nee-ya]	до свида́ния	goodbye (until meeting)

(b) All <u>feminine</u> nouns have exactly the same endings as in
the nominative plural (**-ы** or **-и** – see 8.1, 8.2):

кни́га	кни́ги [knée-gee]	две кни́ги	two books
неде́ля	неде́ли [nye-dyé-lee]	дни неде́ли	days of the week
вещь	ве́щи [vyé-shshee]	две ве́щи	two things
дочь	до́чери	три до́чери	three daughters

Exercise 38

Put the correct ending on the nouns and translate:

1 три (сестра́)   4 три (ста́нция 'station')

2 четы́ре (фунт)   5 три (трамва́й)

3 два́дцать две   6 три́ста два (сло́во)
   (пласти́нка)

9.6 The genitive plural

This is by far the most complicated ending in Russian.
We shall simplify things by giving only the main rules
and listing other forms in the vocabularies.

(a) Nouns which end **-ь** in the nominative, whether m or f,
     replace the **-ь** with **-ей**:

рубль: **пять рубле́й**   five roubles
вещь: **де́сять веще́й**   ten things

(b) Most masculine nouns ending with a consonant add **-ов**:

магази́н: **пять магази́нов**   [ma-ga-zée-naf]   five shops
го́род: **де́сять городо́в**   [ga-ra-dóf]   ten towns

(c) Feminine nouns which end **-a** and neuter nouns ending
     -o simply lose the **-a** or **-o**:

кни́га: **пять книг**   [kneek]   five books
сло́во: **де́сять слов**   [slof]   ten words

(d) Here are examples of other common but awkward
     genitive plurals:

брат (nom   **пять бра́тьев**   five brothers
pl бра́тья):   [bráty-yef]
копе́йка: **пятьдеся́т копе́ек**   fifty kopecks
                   [ka-pyé-yek]
друг (nom   **шесть друзе́й**   six friends
pl друзья́):   [droo-zyéy]

неде́ля:	де́сять неде́ль [nye-dyély]	ten weeks
ме́сяц:	семь ме́сяцев [myé-sya-tsef]	seven months
америка́нец (NB 'fleeting vowel'):	пять америка́нцев	five Americans
англича́нин (nom pl англича́не):	пять англича́н	five Englishmen

9.7 Other quantity words also take the genitive

Apart from its use with numbers, the genitive case (singular or plural, according to meaning) is used with quantity words, e.g.:

мно́го [mnó-ga] much, many
не́сколько [nyé-skaly-ka] a few
ма́ло [má-la] few, little, not many
ско́лько? [skóly-ka] how much?, how many?

не́сколько ме́сяцев [nyé-skaly-ka myé-sya-tsef]
    a few months

ско́лько до́лларов? [skóly-ka dó-la-raf?]
    how many dollars?

мно́го де́нег [mnó-ga dyé-nyek]
    a lot of money (де́нег is gen pl of the pl noun
    де́ньги money)

Exercise 39

Say in Russian.

1 Ten roubles

2 Many (a lot of) roubles

3 A few kopecks

4 Little (not much) money

5 A hundred (and) ten dollars

9.8 Vocabulary

стоя́ть (2)	[sta-yáty]	to stand
stem сто- он стои́т	[sta-eet NB stress]	he stands
о́чередь (f)	[ó-chye-ryety]	queue, line
яйцо́	[yee-tsó NB]	egg
gen pl яи́ц	[yeets]	
су́мка	[soóm-ka]	bag
gen pl су́мок	[soó-mak]	
уже́	[oo-zhé]	already
лежа́т	[lye-zhát]	(they) lie
раз	[ras]	time (as in
gen pl раз		'many times')
два ра́за	[dva rá-za]	twice
тру́дный	[troód-ni]	difficult
без + gen	[byez/byes 2.8]	without (preposition)
труд	[troot]	labour
без труда́	[byes-troo-dá]	without difficulty
мно́го (+ gen)	[mnó-ga]	many, much
са́хар	[sá-har]	sugar
я́блоко (nom pl я́блоки)	[yá-bla-ka]	apple
апельси́н	[a-pyely-seén]	orange
хлеб	[hlyep]	bread
ка́ждый	[kázh-di]	each, every
бо́льше (indecl)	[bóly-she]	more
а!	[a!]	ah! (exclamation)
поня́тно	[pa-nyát-na]	(it is) comprehensible
фо́рма	[fór-ma]	form
грамм	[gram]	gram(me)
ма́сло	[más-la]	butter
сыр	[sir]	cheese
килогра́мм	[kee-la-grám]	kilogram (kilo)
(also кило́ n indecl)	[kee-ló]	
колбаса́ (no pl)	[kal-ba-sá]	sausage (salami type, eaten cold)
тогда́	[tag-dá]	then (at that time); in that case

бутьілка	[boo-tíl-ka]	bottle
gen pl бутьілок	[boo-tí-lak]	
молоко́	[ma-la-kó]	milk
бато́н	[ba-tón]	loaf
бу́лочка	[boó-lach-ka]	bread roll
gen pl бу́лочек	[boó-la-chyek]	
сто́ить (2) stem сто́-	[stó-eety]	to cost
ско́лько сто́ит …?	[stó-eet]	how much is
different from		(costs) …?
стоя́ть to stand		
(NB stress)		
с вас	[svas]	from you (с + gen 17.7) = you owe (idiom)
да́йте	[dáy-tye]	give (imper)
возьми́те	[vazy-meé-tye]	take (imper)
сда́ча	[zdá-cha]	change (money returned)
иностра́н(е)ц	[ee-na-strá-nyets]	foreigner (male)
gen pl иностра́нцев	[ee-na-strán-tsef]	

9.9 CONVERSATIONS

Mike has difficulty buying eggs

Ни́на: Опя́ть вы сто́ите в о́череди, Майк!

Майк: Я покупа́ю я́йца.

Ни́на: Но в ва́шей су́мке уже́ лежа́т четы́ре яйца́. Заче́м стоя́ть два ра́за?

Майк: «Яйцо́» – о́чень тру́дное сло́во. Я без труда́ покупа́ю мно́го са́хара, я́блок, апельси́нов, хле́ба, но когда́ я покупа́ю я́йца, я ка́ждый раз беру́ то́лько два, три и́ли четы́ре яйца́, не бо́льше.

Ни́на: А, поня́тно! Вы не зна́ете фо́рму «пять яи́ц». Да, э́то тру́дная фо́рма.

In some old-fashioned shops you pay for goods before you receive them. This means that you have to recite a list of the things you want, and often their prices as well, to a cashier (**касси́р**) at a cashdesk (**ка́сса**) some distance from the various counters where the goods are. The cashier takes your money and gives you a set of receipts (**че́ки** [chyé-kee]). You take these **че́ки**, which show the price paid, to the various counters, where you tell the assistants (**продавцы́**) what you want and hand over the relevant **че́ки**. It's a good exercise in spoken Russian; if you don't make a written list, it's also a memory test.

Mike has learnt the genitive

Майк: Сто пятьдеся́т гра́ммов ма́сла – пятьдеся́т четы́ре копе́йки. Две́сти гра́ммов сы́ра – шестьдеся́т копе́ек. Два килогра́мма колбасы́ – четы́ре рубля́ шестьдеся́т копе́ек.

Касси́р: Колбасы́? Тогда́ не четы́ре шестьдеся́т, а пять шестьдеся́т.

Майк: Прости́те. Две буты́лки молока́ – шестьдеся́т четы́ре копе́йки. Два бато́на – два́дцать шесть копе́ек.
Де́вять бу́лочек ... Прости́те, ско́лько сто́ит бу́лочка?

Касси́р: Три копе́йки.

Майк: Де́вять бу́лочек – два́дцать семь копе́ек. Э́то всё.

Касси́р: Всё?

(She clicks the beads on her abacus)

С вас семь рубле́й девяно́сто одна́ копе́йка.

Майк: Вот де́сять рубле́й.

Кассир:	Да́йте одну́ копе́йку. Возьми́те сда́чу, два рубля́ де́сять копе́ек. Вы иностра́нец? Вы хорошо́ говори́те по-ру́сски, мно́го слов зна́ете. Наве́рно, вы зна́ете мно́го языко́в.
Майк:	Нет, то́лько два языка́, ру́сский и англи́йский. До свида́ния.
Кассир:	Возьми́те че́ки.
Майк:	Спаси́бо.
Кассир:	Пожа́луйста.

TRANSLATIONS

N: You're standing in the queue (line) again, Mike!

M: I'm buying eggs.

N: But you've already got four eggs in your bag. Why stand twice?

M: 'Eetso' is a very difficult word. I have no difficulty buying lots of sugar, apples, oranges, (and) bread, but when I buy eggs each time I take (buy) only two, three or four, not more.

N: Ah, I see. You don't know the form five 'yeets' (gen pl). Yes, it's a difficult form.

M: 150 grams of butter – 54 kopecks. 200 grams of cheese – 60 kopecks. Two kilograms of sausage – 4 roubles 60 kopecks.

C: (Of) sausage? Then not 4 (roubles) 60 (kopecks) but five sixty.

M: I beg your pardon. Two bottles of milk – 64 kopecks. Two loaves – 26 kopecks. Nine bread rolls … Excuse me, how much is a roll?

C: Three kopecks.

M: Nine rolls – 27 kopecks. That's everything.

C: Everything? That'll be 7 roubles 91 kopecks.

M: Here's ten roubles.

C: Give (me) (a) one kopeck (coin). Here's your change, two roubles ten (kopecks). Are you a foreigner? You speak Russian well, you know a lot of words. I suppose (probably) you know a lot of languages.

J: No, only two languages, Russian and English. Goodbye.

M: Take your receipts.

J: Thank you.

M: You're welcome.

Since the collapse of Communism at the beginning of the 1990s, Russia has suffered from severe price inflation. This has meant that even the most basic groceries now cost thousands of roubles. The conversation above uses the stable pre-inflation prices, which are linguistically much simpler for Russian beginners.

Exercise 40

Translate the words in brackets:

1 **Я зна́ю** (three languages).

2 **Э́то брат** (of Boris).

3 **Во́дка сто́ит** (six dollars).

4 **Я покупа́ю** (twenty-one bottles of vodka).

5 **Да́йте, пожа́луйста,** (200 grams of cheese).

6 **В гости́нице** (many Americans).

7 (How much) **сто́ит бато́н?** (Thirteen kopecks).

8 **Я здесь уже́** (two weeks).

Exercise 40A

What is the name of this play? What case is the second word of the title?

А. П. ЧЕХОВ

ТРИ СЕСТРЫ

Chapter 10

- Counting with adjectives.
- 'having' and 'not having'.
- More uses of the genitive case endings.

Exercise 41 (revision)

Say in Russian:

1 Five roubles forty kopecks

2 Twenty-four dollars

3 Bread costs thirteen kopecks.

4 How much is a kilogram of sausage?

5 Please give me five hundred grams of butter.

6 Lots of money

7 Five months

8 Three sisters

9 Goodbye

10 Ten eggs

10.1 The genitive singular of adjectives

(a) With singular masculine and neuter nouns, the adjective
    ending is **-oro** (NB г pronounced [v]) or **-ero** [ye-<u>vo</u>]
    after the spelling rule letters ж, ч, ш, щ and ц (8.11).

This is the same ending as the masculine accusative with people and animals you learnt in 7.8.

килогра́мм хоро́шего ру́сского [roó-ska-va] **сы́ра**
  a kilo of good Russian cheese

и́мя америка́нского [a-mye-ree-kán-ska-va] **тури́ста**
  the name of the American tourist
  (= the American tourist's name)

(b) With feminines, the ending is **-ой** (**-ей** after **ж, ч, ш, щ** and **ц**), the same as the prepositional adjective endings (see 7.7):

килогра́мм ру́сской [roó-skay] **колбасы́**
  a kilo of Russian sausage

и́мя краси́вой молодо́й америка́нской [kra-seé-vay ma-la-dóy a-mye-ree-kán-skay] **студе́нтки**
  the name of the beautiful young American student

10.2 The genitive plural of adjectives

The ending for <u>all genders</u> is **-ых** (or **-их**, if the last letter of the stem is one of the seven spelling rule letters – see 8.4):

килогра́мм краси́вых све́жих америка́нских
[a-mye-ree-kán-skeeh] **я́блок**
  a kilo of beautiful fresh American apples

10.3 Adjectives with numbers

As you would expect, when the noun is gen pl (after **пять** 'five' etc.), the adjective is also gen pl:

Мы зна́ем сто ру́сских [roó-skeeh] (gen pl) **слов** (gen pl).
  We know a hundred Russian words.

Два́дцать шесть америка́нских [a-mye-ree-kán-skeeh] (gen pl) **тури́стов** (gen pl).
  Twenty-six American tourists.

But it is a peculiarity of Russian numbers that after **два/две**, **три** and **четы́ре**, adjectives are also put in the gen <u>plural</u>, even though nouns are gen <u>singular</u>.

В э́том го́роде три кни́жн<u>ых</u> [kneezh-nih] (gen pl) **магази́н<u>а</u>** (gen sing).
In this town there are three bookshops.

Мы зна́ем сто два́дцать [dvá-tsaty] **два ру́сск<u>их</u>** [roo-skeeh] (gen pl) **сло́ва** (gen sing).
We know one hundred and twenty-two Russian words.

Пожа́луйста, да́йте э́ти (acc pl) **четы́ре кра́сн<u>ых</u>** [krá-snih] (gen pl) **я́блок<u>а</u>** (gen sing).
Please give (me) these four red apples.

Exercise 42

Add the genitive endings and translate:

1   **Джейн – учи́тельница ру́сск___ языка́.**

2   **Вы зна́ете и́мя краси́в___ молод___ англича́нки?**

3   **Де́сять хоро́ш___ ру́сск___ друзе́й.**

4   **Я зна́ю три иностра́нн___ языка́.**

10.4 Genitive of the possessives and э́тот 'this'

(a)   **мой, твой, наш, ваш** have the same genitive endings as **хоро́ший**. So in the singular, their endings are **-его** (m and n) or **-ей** [yey] (f), and in the plural **-их** (all genders).

и́мя мо<u>его́</u> [ma-ye-vó NB stress] **дру́га**
the name of my (male) friend (= my friend's name)

и́мя твое́й [tva-yéy] **подру́ги**
the name of your (girl) friend (= your girlfriend's name)

у́лицы на́ших [ná-shih] **городо́в**
the streets of our cities

кварти́ра ва́ших [vá-shih] **ру́сских друзе́й**
the flat of your Russian friends (= your Russian friends' flat)

(b) **э́тот** has the singular genitive forms **э́того** [é-ta-va] (m and n) and **э́той** [é-tay] (f) 'of this':

и́мя э́того [é-ta-va] **америка́нца**
the name of this American

But in the genitive plural the ending is **-их**: **э́тих** [é-teeh] 'of these':

э́тих америка́нцев
'of these Americans'.

Exercise 43

Put the correct endings on the possessives and adjectives:

1 **Где кварти́ра ва́ш___ ру́сск___ дру́га?**

2 **Э́то дом мо___ хоро́ш___ друзе́й.**

3 **И́мя мо___ англи́йск___ подру́ги – Джейн.**

4 **Мы хоти́м купи́ть килогра́мм э́т___ кра́сн___ я́блок.**

10.5 Genitive with prepositions

Many Russian prepositions are followed by the genitive case. Here are four of the commonest:

для [dlya] for

для [dlya] for
   пода́рок <u>для</u> мо<u>его́</u> дру́<u>га</u> a present for my friend

у [oo] by, near
   у в<u>а́шего</u> до́<u>ма</u> by (near) your house

из [eez/ees] out of, from (the opposite of в + acc 'to, into')
   тури́сты <u>из</u> А́нгл<u>ии</u> [eez-án-glee-ee] tourists from England

без [byez/byes] without
   ко́фе <u>без</u> молок<u>а́</u> coffee without milk, black coffee
   (молоко́ milk)

10.6 Genitive of pronouns

The genitive forms of the personal pronouns are the same as the accusative forms (see 6.1):

я	меня́	of me	мы	нас	of us
ты	тебя́	of you	вы	вас	of you
он	его́ [NB ye-<u>v</u>ó]	of him	они́	их	of them
она́	её [ye-yó]	of her			
оно́	его́ [ye-<u>v</u>ó]	of it			

для тебя́ for you   без нас without us

NOTE When его́, её or их is preceded by a preposition, the letter **н** is added to the pronoun, so его́, её, их become <u>н</u>его́, <u>н</u>её, <u>н</u>их:

для <u>н</u>его́ for him/it   у <u>н</u>их by them
без <u>н</u>её without her   из <u>н</u>его́ out of it

10.7 How to say 'I have five roubles'

In English we have a common verb 'to have' to express possession. Russian does not. To say 'I have five roubles', Russian has a quite different construction which literally translates as 'By me is five roubles':

У меня́ есть пять рубле́й [oo mye-nyá yesty pyaty roo-blyéy].

есть means 'is' or 'are' (in the sense of 'exist'). So the construction for 'someone has something' is у + gen of the person + есть + noun in the nom:

У	моего брáта (gen)	есть	дéньги (nom pl).
By	my brother	is (exists)	money.

= My brother has money.

He has a son.	У негó [nye-vó] есть сын.
She has a son.	У неё [nye-yó] есть сын.
They have a son.	У них [neeh] есть сын.

'Do you have X?' in Russian is **У вас есть X** (nom)?
The rise-fall question intonation is always on the **есть**.

– У вас есть сын? [oo-vás yesty sin?]
   Do you have a son? (lit. 'By you exists son?')

– Да, у меня есть сын. [da, oo-mye-nyá yesty sin]
   Yes, I have a son.
   (lit. 'Yes, by me exists son')

Or you can answer more colloquially and simply:
– **Да, есть.** [da, yesty] Yes, I do. (lit. 'Yes, exists')

Exercise 44

Translate the dialogue (It's called 'Little hope for Boris here'):

Борúс: – У вас есть муж?

Мэ́ри: – Да, есть.

Борúс: – У вас есть дéти?

Мэ́ри: – Да, дочь и два сы́на.

Борúс: – У вáшего [vá-she-va NB] мýжа есть дéньги?

Мэ́ри: – Да, есть.

10.8 'there is'/'there are'/'there exists': есть

In 10.7 we met **есть** meaning 'is', 'are' ('exist') in the construction 'I have a son' ('By me is son'). **Есть** is the word to use to translate 'there is …'/'there are …' in sentences such as 'In this street there is a restaurant'.

На э́той у́лице есть рестора́н.
There is a restaurant in this street.

Здесь есть америка́нцы.
There are Americans here.

В Москве́ есть краси́вые па́рки.
There are beautiful parks in Moscow.

Есть америка́нцы и в на́шей гости́нице.
There are Americans in our hotel too.
(**и** 'and' can also mean 'too', 'also')

10.9 'there isn't'/'there aren't': another use of the genitive

The opposite of **есть** 'there is/are' is **нет** 'there isn't/aren't'
(a quite different use of **нет** from its meaning 'no'). In this
meaning **нет** <u>is followed by the genitive case</u> (sing or pl).

Здесь нет рестора́<u>на</u> (gen sing).
There is no restaurant here.
(lit. 'Here is not of a restaurant')

Нет рестора́<u>нов</u> (gen pl).
There are no restaurants.

В на́шей гости́нице нет америка́<u>нцев</u> (gen pl).
There aren't any Americans in our hotel.
(lit. 'In our hotel is not of Americans')

Сего́дня в магази́не нет апельси́<u>нов</u> (gen pl).
There are no oranges in the shop today.

10.10 'I don't have'

If 'I have a son' is **У меня́ есть сын** can you guess the
Russian for 'I don't have a son'? The opposite of **есть** + the
nominative is **нет** + the genitive, so 'I don't have a son' is
У меня́ нет сы́на (lit. 'By me is not of son').

У моего брата нет денег.
My brother has no money/My brother hasn't (got) any money.

У моих друзей нет детей.
My friends have no children.

У её мужа нет друзей.
Her husband has no friends.

Exercise 45

Give negative answers to the questions using **нет** + *gen:*

1 **Здесь есть магазин?**

2 **В бутылке есть молоко?**

3 **У вас есть рубль?**

4 **У вас есть один доллар?**

5 **У вас есть доллары?**

6 **У них есть яйца?**

7 **У вашего брата есть квартира?**

8 **У вас есть новые книги?**

10.11 People and animals: acc plural = gen plural

You know that masculine nouns denoting people and animals have the same ending **-а/-я** in both the acc and gen singular:

Я знаю вашего брата (acc).   I know your brother.
Это книга вашего брата (gen).   This is your brother's book.

In the accusative plural, all nouns (of whatever gender) denoting people and animals have the same ending as the genitive plural:

Я зна́ю ва́ших бра́тьев.		I know your brothers. (ва́ших бра́тьев can also mean 'of your brothers')
Я зна́ю э́тих же́нщин.		I know these women.
Я люблю́ кото́в.		I love cats. (кото́в = gen pl of кот)

10.12 Vocabulary

де́вушка	[dyé-voosh-ka]	girl, miss (addressing a young woman)
продав(е́)ц	[pra-da-vyéts]	sales assistant (NB fleeting vowel)
экземпля́р	[eg-zyem-plyár]	copy (of book)
для + gen	[dlya]	for
бе́лый	[byé-li]	white (same endings as но́вый)
Столи́чная (f adj)	[sta-leéch-na-ya]	Stolichnaya ('Capital'), a well-known Russian vodka
большо́й -ая (f), -ое (n), -и́е (pl)	[baly-shóy]	big, large
ма́ленький -ая (f), -ое (n), -ие (pl)	[má-lyeny-kee]	small
литр	[leetr]	litre
пол-ли́тра	[pól-leé-tra]	half a litre (from полови́на ли́тра 'half of a litre')
сестра́ nom pl сёстры, gen pl сестёр	[sye-strá]	sister (7.10)
грузи́нский	[groo-zeén-skee]	Georgian (from the former Soviet republic of Georgia in the Caucasus)
де́ти pl gen pl дете́й	[dyé-tee] [dye-tyéy]	children
матрёшка gen pl матрёшек	[ma-tryósh-ka]	matryoshka (the wooden dolls which fit inside each other)

ещё	[ye-shshyó]	yet, still
ещё оди́н	one more	
игру́шка	[ee-groósh-ka]	toy
gen pl игру́шек		
совсе́м	[sa-fsyém]	completely, totally
шту́ка	[shtoó-ka]	thing (a colloquial word, useful when you don't know the word for something or when counting things)
роди́тели pl	[ra-deé-tye-lee]	parents
sing роди́тель (m),		
gen pl роди́телей		
до́ма	[dó-ma]	at home
почти́	[pach-teé]	almost
му́зыка	[moó-zi-ka]	music
цент	[tsent]	cent

You should now have a Russian vocabulary of about 300 words.

10.13 CONVERSATION

Andrey and Barbara are shopping

Андре́й: **Де́вушка! У вас есть кни́ги о Москве́?**
Miss! Do you have any books about Moscow?

Продаве́ц: **Есть. Но но́вых нет.**
We do. But there aren't any new ones.

Ба́рбара: **Покажи́те, пожа́луйста. Вот э́та краси́вая кни́га у меня́ у́же есть, а э́той кни́ги нет. Да́йте, пожа́луйста, четы́ре экземпля́ра.**
Show (me), please. This attractive one I've already got, but I don't have this one. Give me four copies please.

Андре́й: **Заче́м так мно́го экземпля́ров?**
Why so many copies?

Бáрбара: Э́то подáрки для моúх друзéй. А в э́том магазúне есть вóдка и винó?
They're presents for my friends. Does this shop have vodka and wine?

Андрéй: По-мóему, крáсного винá нет, но есть бéлое. И вóдка есть.
I think there's no red wine, but there is white. And there's vodka.

Бáрбара: Хорошó. Пожáлуйста, три бутýлки Столúчной. Дáйте однý большýю и две мáленьких. Скóлько в них грáммов?
Good. Three bottles of Stolichnaya (vodka), please. Give me one big (bottle) and two small ones. How much do they hold? (How many grams [of vodka] in them? Russians measure vodka in grams, treating a litre as equal to 1000 grams; '100 grams' is a generous glassful.)

Продавéц: В большóй литр, а в мáленькой пóл-лúтра.
The big one holds a litre and the small one half a litre.

Бáрбара: Литр для мýжа моéй сестрý. И дáйте однý бутýлку бéлого винá, грузúнского.
The litre is for my sister's husband. And give (me) one bottle of white wine, (of) Georgian.

Андрéй: У вáшей сестрý есть дéти?
Does your sister have any children?

Бáрбара: Есть. Два мáленьких сýна, Скотт и Джейк.
Yes. Two small sons, Scott and Jake.

Андрéй: Вот красúвый подáрок для них: рýсские матрёшки.
Here's a nice present for them: Russian matryoshkas.

Бáрбара: Да, у них такúх игрýшек нет. Скóлько их?
Yes, they don't have any toys like that. How many of them (are there)?

Андрей: **Две матрёшки, три, четы́ре, пять матрёшек, шесть, семь, вот ещё одна́, совсе́м ма́ленькая – во́семь штук.**
Two matryoshkas, three, four, five matryoshkas, six, seven, here's another one, really small – eight of them.

Ба́рбара: **Хорошо́. А для мои́х роди́телей я беру́ пять пласти́нок. У нас до́ма почти́ нет ру́сской му́зыки. Ско́лько с нас?**
OK. And for my parents I'm taking five records. We have hardly any Russian music at home. How much do we owe?

Продаве́ц: **Каки́е у вас де́ньги? До́ллары? Шестьдеся́т до́лларов три́дцать пять це́нтов.**
What kind of money do you have? Dollars? Sixty dollars thirty-five cents.

Exercise 46 (revision)

Say in Russian (see the section references to check points):

1   Hello (2.1). What's your name (3.1)?
    Mine is Jane (3.1).

2   Hello. I'm Boris. Are you American (4.1)?

3   No, I'm English. I'm a teacher (4.1).

4   Are you working in Moscow (5.1, 5.2, 5.4)?

5   Yes, but I'm going (6.3) home to England (6.4) in ('after' 6.6) three months (9.3).

6   You speak Russian very well (4.1) and you understand everything.

7   I understand everything when you speak slowly.

8   Excuse (me), where are you going (on foot).

120

9   I'm going to the Russian bookshop (7.8).

10 Let's go together (6.6). I'm very fond of bookshops (7.9, 8.10).

11 OK. I often buy Russian books. I like Russian poetry (8.15).

12 I like American books (8.3). But our shops aren't very good.

13 Let's go to the centre (5.10). I need to buy (8.14) presents (8.13).

14 This shop has very few (9.7) foreign (10.2) books (9.6). (Say: In this shop very few foreign books.)

15 Foreigners have (10.7) dollars, so (поэтому) they buy good wine (8.11).

16 I have no dollars (10.10). You too (тоже) have no foreign money.

17 I know these Americans (10.11). They have money.

18 The vodka costs twenty dollars (9.1, 9.3) and the books twenty-three dollars.

19 Are you buying those bottles of vodka for your husband (10.12)?

20 I don't have a husband (10.10) but I have many (9.7) good (10.2) friends (9.6).

Chapter 11

More on verbs:
- talking about past events (past tense).
- reflexive verbs.
- learning new verbs.

11.1 Talking about the past

Up till now we have used only the present tense ('I am doing', 'I do'). To talk about past time we need the past tense – forms such as 'I did', 'He was doing'. Russian has only one past tense, and it is easy to form. Simply remove the **-ть** of the infinitive and replace it with the ending **-л**:

рабо́та/ть to work	Бори́с рабо́та**л**.	Boris worked/was working.
бы/ть to be	Бори́с бы**л** до́ма.	Boris was at home.

If the subject is feminine, you must add **а** to the **л**:

Ни́на рабо́тал<u>а</u>.   Nina worked/was working.

If the subject is neuter, add **о** to the **л**:

Письмо́ бы<u>ло</u> там.   The letter was there.

If the subject is plural, add **и** to the **л**:

Ни́на и Бори́с рабо́тал<u>и</u>.   Nina and Boris worked/ were working.

So a man says: **Я рабо́та<u>л</u>.** I worked/was working.

But a woman says: **Я рабо́тал<u>а</u>.** I worked/was working.

122

It doesn't matter if the verb has an irregular stem in the present tense; the past tense is regular. So the past of **хоте́ть** 'to want', a difficult verb in the pres tense (see 6.5), is straightforward:

Singular
я хоте́л (m)/я хоте́ла (f)
ты хоте́л (m)/ты хоте́ла (f)
он хоте́л
она́ хоте́ла

оно́ хоте́ло

Plural
мы хоте́ли
вы хоте́ли (**вы** always has the plural ending, even when you're talking to one person)
они́ хоте́ли

Exercise 47

Put in the past tense and translate:

1 **Ива́н (чита́ть).**

2 **Мы (жить) в Москве́.**

3 **Вы (говори́ть) по-ру́сски?**

4 **Я** (woman) **(знать), что вы англича́нин.**

5 **Он (е́хать) в Москву́.**

6 **Майк и Ни́на (стоя́ть) в о́череди.**

7 **Они́ не (понима́ть), когда́ я** (woman) **(говори́ть).**

Note that **быть** 'to be', usually omitted in the present tense (e.g. **Я в Москве́** 'I (am) in Moscow'), has a normal past tense: **был** (m), **была́** (f) (NB stress), **бы́ло** (n), **бы́ли** (pl) 'was/were'.

Я был в Москве́.
   I was in Moscow. (*man* speaking)

Я была́ в Москве́.
   I was in Moscow. (*woman* speaking)

Фильм был интере́сный.
   The film was interesting.

Вино́ бы́ло хоро́шее.
  The wine was good.

Мы бы́ли в Москве́.
  We were in Moscow.

11.2 Stress of the past tense

The stress of the masculine, neuter and plural forms is the same as the infinitive (with a few exceptions). But in the case of short (one syllable) verbs (e.g. **быть**) the stress of the <u>feminine</u> form is usually on the **-ла́**:

быть (to be): **он был, оно́ бы́ло, они́ бы́ли**
BUT **она́ была́** was/were
жить (to live): **он жил, оно́ жи́ло, они́ жи́ли**
BUT **она́ жила́** lived

Exception: 'she knew' is **она́ зна́ла**.

11.3 Past tense of идти́

Those few verbs which do not end **-ть** in the infinitive have exceptional past tense forms. For example, **идти́** 'to go (on foot)' has the forms:

он шёл [shol], **она́ шла** [shla], **оно́ шло** [shlo], **они́ шли** [shlee]

Бори́с шёл домо́й.
  Boris was going home.

Ни́на шла в магази́н.
  Nina was going to the shop.

The past tense of such verbs will be given as we meet them.

11.4 'there was'/'there were'

To say 'there was' or 'there were' you use the past tense of **быть**:

There were Russian books in the shop.
В магазине были (pl agreeing with 'books') **русские книги.**

There was an American woman here.
Здесь была американка.

11.5 'I had'

The past of **У меня есть** ('I have' 10.7) is **У меня был/была/было/были** depending on the gender of the subject:

У меня была бутылка водки.
I had a bottle of vodka.

У него были доллары.
He had dollars.

11.6 'there wasn't/weren't': не было + gen

The past of **нет** (meaning 'there wasn't/there weren't') is **не было** [nyé-bi-la], stressed on the **не**, and followed by the gen:

Не было автобусов.
There weren't any buses.

У нас не было денег.
We had no money. (lit. 'By us was not of money.')

Там не было книжного магазина.
There was no bookshop there.

Exercise 48

Say in Russian:

1 I had one dollar.

2 I didn't have a dollar.

3 There was a kilogram of sausage in the bag.

4 There was no sausage in the shop.

5 We had friends in Moscow.

6 We had no friends in St. Petersburg.

11.7 Reflexive verbs

Russian has many verbs which end **-ться** (NB pronounced [tsa]). The **-ть** is the normal infinitive ending and the reflexive ending **-ся** means 'self':

одева́ться [a-dye-vá-tsa] 'to dress oneself'
(or 'to get dressed')
This is a Type 1 verb like **знать** (4.7). <u>Present tense</u>:

я одева́юсь	[a-dye-vá-yoosy]	I dress myself
ты одева́ешься	[a-dye-vá-yesh-sya]	you (fam) dress yourself
он одева́ется	[a-dye-vá-ye-<u>tsa</u> NB]	he dresses himself
мы одева́емся	[a-dye-vá-yem-sya]	we dress ourselves
вы одева́етесь	[a-dye-vá-ye-tyesy]	you (pol/pl) dress yourself/yourselves
они́ одева́ются	[a-dye-vá-yoo-<u>tsa</u> NB]	they dress themselves

So 'myself', 'yourself' etc. all translate as **-ся** or **-сь**, which is joined to the verb ending. You find **-ся** after consonants and **-сь** after vowels. The same rule works for the <u>past tense</u>:

я одева́лся	[a-dye-vál-sya]	I dressed myself (*man* speaking)
я одева́лась	[a-dye-vá-lasy]	I dressed myself (*woman* speaking)
мы одева́лись	[a-dye-vá-leesy]	we dressed ourselves

NOTE Many verbs with the -ся ending are not reflexive in meaning, e.g. улыбáться [oo-li-bá-tsa] 'to smile' (Type 1) (there is no verb улыбáть):

я улыбáюсь	[oo-li-bá-yoosy]	I smile
ты улыбáешься	[oo-li-bá-yesh-sya]	you (fam) smile
онá улыбáлась	[oo-li-bá-lasy]	she smiled

родúться   [ra-dée-tsa]   'to be born':

Я родúлся в Вашингтóне.
    I (male) was born in Washington.

Я родилáсь в Санкт-Петтербурге.
    I (female) was born in St. Petersburg.

Где вы родúлись [ra-de-léesy]?
    Where were you born?

Exercise 49

Use the past tense of the reflexive verbs and translate:

1 Еѐ дочь (родúться) в Москвé.

2 Почемý они (улыбáться)?

3 Онá (одевáться) красúво.

4 Я (учúться) (to study) в э́той шкóле (school).

11.8 Verbs in the vocabularies: how to make the present tense

Each new verb is shown with its present tense conjugation pattern (1), (1B) or (2), i.e. Type 1 (like знать 'to know' – see 4.7), Type 1B (like жить 'to live' – see 5.9) or Type 2 (like говорúть 'to speak' see 4.8). To show you the stem (the part to which the endings are added) and the stress pattern, two of the personal forms are given: the 'I' (я) form (which in many Type 1B and Type 2 verbs has a slightly different stem from the other forms) and the 'you' (fam) (ты) form. If you have these two forms you can predict the other four, because the stem and stress of the он, мы, вы and они forms are always the same as in the ты form. Take the important verb видеть [vee-dyety] 'to see' (Type 2): 'I see' is я вижу and 'you (fam) see' is ты видишь, so the stem of the other four forms is вид- and the stress is on the stem.

видеть to see:	я вижу	мы видим
	ты видишь	вы видите
	он/она́/оно́ видит	они́ видят

Another Type 2 verb люби́ть 'to love': 'I love' is я люблю́ (note the extra л), 'you (fam) love' is ты лю́бишь, so the other four forms must be он лю́бит, мы лю́бим, вы лю́бите, они́ лю́бят.

Now the verb ждать [zhdaty] (1B) 'to wait', which has the stem жд-: 'I wait': я жду; 'you (fam) wait': ты ждёшь. So the other forms must be он ждёт, мы ждём, вы ждёте, они́ ждут.

NOTE When **e** in a verb ending is stressed, it always turns into **ё**.

Exercise 50

Work out the underlined form from the information given:

1 писа́ть (1B) 'to write' я пишу́, ты пи́шешь:
   you (pol) write

2 стоя́ть (2) 'to stand' я стою́, ты стои́шь:
   they are standing

3 смотре́ть (2) 'to look' я смотрю́, ты смо́тришь:
   we look

4 де́лать (1) 'to do' я де́лаю, ты де́лаешь: they do

11.9 Vocabulary

сно́ва [snó-va] — again (like опя́ть)

прия́тный [pree-yát-ni] — pleasant

сюрпри́з [syoor-preés] — surprise

ожида́ть [a-zhi-dáty] (1) — to expect
  я ожида́ю, ты
  ожида́ешь + gen/acc

до́лго [dól-ga] — for a long time

ждать [zhdaty] (1B) + acc — to wait for
  stem жд- я жду, ты ждёшь

недо́лго [nye-dól-ga] — not long

самолёт [sa-ma-lyót] — aeroplane

опа́здывать [a-páz-di-vaty] (1) — to be late
  я опа́здываю, ты
  опа́здываешь

всего́ [fsye-vó NB] — only (particularly with numbers)

ну [noo] — well (to show hesitation or a pause)

расска́зывайте [ras-ská-zi--vay-tye] — tell (imper)

ма́ма [má-ma] — mother, mum (fam)

ведь [vyety] — you know (a word that shows that you expect the other person to agree or to know the information already)

учи́ться [oo-cheé-tsa] (2) — to study (somewhere, e.g. at school: Он у́чится в шко́ле, а я учу́сь в университе́те. 'He's (studying) at school but I'm at university.')
  я учу́сь (NB spelling), ты
  у́чишься; the они́ form is
  у́чатся (NB spelling – see 8.4
  note)

университе́т [oo-nee-vyer--see-tyét] — university

вре́мя [vryé-mya] NB neuter — time
  gen sing вре́мени

ходи́ть [ha-deéty] (2)	to go somewhere (on
я хожу́, ты хо́дишь	foot) and return;
	to walk about
кино́ [kee-nó] n indecl	cinema
писа́ть [pee-sáty] (1B)	to write
я пишу́, ты пи́шешь	
за [za] + acc	for (in return for)
спаси́бо за + acc	thank you for
интере́сный [een-tye-ryés-ni]	interesting
смея́ться [smye-yá-tsa] (1)	to laugh
я смею́сь, ты смеёшься	
снача́ла [sna-chá-la]	at first
быть в гостя́х у + gen [bity	to visit (someone)
vga-styáh oo]	(lit. 'to be in guests by
	someone')
не́сколько [nyé-skaly-ka] + gen	a few
свобо́дный [sva-bód-ni]	free
д(е)нь [dyeny] (m) gen pl **дней**	day
е́здить [yéz-deety] (2)	to travel somewhere
я е́зжу, ты е́здишь	and return; to travel
	around
дава́й [da-váy]	let's (fam)
дава́й бу́дем на «ты» [da-váy	let's use 'ti' to each
boó-dyem na-tí]	other
друг дру́га [droog-droó-ga]	each other
договори́лись [da-ga-va-reé-leesy]	that's agreed
	(idiomatic expression)
дава́йте поговори́м [da-váy-tye	let's talk
pa-ga-va-reém]	
смотре́ть [sma-tryéty] (2) + acc	to watch (also 'to
я смотрю́, ты смо́тришь	look' – see 8.14)

11.10 CONVERSATION

Boris goes to Sheremetyevo

Шереме́тьево *is Moscow's international airport, where all flights from the West arrive.*

Бори́с: Джейн, здра́вствуйте! Как хорошо́, что вы сно́ва в Москве́! Как бы́ло в Ливерпу́ле? Что вы де́лали в Аме́рике? Вы ви́дели Ма́рка?

Джейн: Бори́с! Како́й прия́тный сюрпри́з! Я не ожида́ла. Вы до́лго жда́ли?

Бори́с: Нет, недо́лго. Говори́ли, что твой – прости́те, ваш самолёт опа́здывает, но я ждал всего́ три́дцать мину́т. Ну, расска́зывайте.

Джейн: В Ливерпу́ле всё бы́ло хорошо́. Я ви́дела ма́му и бра́та. Пото́м я была́ в Ло́ндоне три дня, ви́дела друзе́й. У меня́ там мно́го друзе́й, ведь я там учи́лась в университе́те. А вы, наве́рно, всё вре́мя рабо́тали.

Бори́с: Ну, не всё вре́мя, коне́чно. Я ходи́л в кино́ не́сколько раз, чита́л кни́ги, писа́л пи́сьма.

Джейн: Да, спаси́бо за интере́сное письмо́. Вы о́чень хорошо́ пи́шете. Я смея́лась.

Бори́с: Оно́ шло до́лго?

Джейн: Дней де́сять.

Бори́с: А где ты была́ – прости́те, где вы бы́ли в Аме́рике?

Джейн: Снача́ла я была́ в Нью-Йо́рке, пото́м я была́ в гостя́х у друзе́й мои́х роди́телей в Филаде́льфии. У них бы́ло не́сколько свобо́дных дней, мы е́здили в Вашингто́н. А вы …

Борис:	Джейн, давай будем на «ты». Ведь мы знаем друг друга уже два месяца.
Джейн:	Ну, я не знаю. Если хотите …
Борис:	Договорились! А ты видела этого Марка, твоего друга?
Джейн:	Видела.
Борис:	Что вы делали? Вы долго были вместе? Ты его любишь?
Джейн:	Почему вы хотите всё знать? Я не хочу говорить о Марке. Давайте поговорим о другом. Какие фильмы вы смотрели в кино?

TRANSLATION

B: Jane, hello! How good (it is) that you're back in Moscow. How was Liverpool? What did you do in America? Did you see Mark?

J: Boris! What a nice surprise! How unexpected. Did you wait (Have you waited) long?

B: No, not long. They said that your (fam) – I'm sorry, your (pol) plane was late, but I waited only thirty minutes. Well, tell me about it.

J: In Liverpool everything was fine. I saw my mother and my brother. Then I was in London for three days and saw my friends. I have many friends there, as you know I was at university there. But you no doubt worked all the time.

B: Well, not all the time, of course. I went to the cinema several times, read books and wrote letters.

J: Yes, thanks for the interesting letter. You write well. I laughed.

B: Did it take long to reach you? (lit. 'did it go long?'; **шло:** past of **идти́** – Russian letters go on foot.)

J: About ten days (inversion of the noun and number means 'approximately').

B: And where were you (fam), I'm sorry, where were you (pol) in America? (= Where did you go in America?)

J: First I was in New York, then I visited friends of my parents in Philadelphia. They had a few free days and we went to Washington. And you ...

B: Jane, let's use 'ti'. After all, we've known each other for two months now.

J: Well, I don't know ... If you (pol) want ...

B: That's agreed, then! And did you (fam) see that Mark, your friend?

J: Yes, I saw him.

B: What did you (pl) do? Were you together for long? Do you love him?

J: Why do you (pol) want to know everything? I don't want to talk about Mark. Let's talk about something else ('about other' from **другой** 'other'). What films did you see ('watch') at the cinema?

Exercise 51

Translate into English:

1 Письма из Москвы идут медленно.

2 Джейн ездила в Америку.

3 Борис ходил в кино.

4 Борис и Джейн уже на «ты».

5 Он ждал минут тридцать.

Chapter 12

- Making arrangements and plans: Talking about the future.
- Aspect and the future tense.
- Dative pronouns.

12.1 The future

'I shall write a letter' is **Я напишу** [na-pee-shoó] **письмо́**.

In 11.9 we met the verb **писа́ть** 'to write' (**я пишу́, ты пи́шешь**). In the example above, you can see that 'I shall write' (**я напишу́**) has the same ending as 'I am writing' (**я пишу́**). To form the future tense, you use <u>the same set of endings</u> as you learnt for the present tense (4.7, 4.8) but these endings are added to a different infinitive. If you look up any verb, e.g. 'to write', in an English–Russian dictionary, you will generally find <u>a pair</u> of equivalent Russian verbs. 'To write' is in Russian both **писа́ть** and **написа́ть**. **Писа́ть** is called the <u>imperfective (non-completed) aspect</u> of this verb, and **написа́ть** is called the <u>perfective (completed) aspect</u>. We shall go into more detail on the distinction between the aspects in chapter 13. The main thing to remember now is that the present tense is ALWAYS formed from the <u>imperfective aspect</u> (and all the infinitives we have met so far have been imperfective), while the future tense is most often (though not always – 14.2) formed from the <u>perfective</u> aspect.

12.2 Imperfective and perfective pairs

Here are some examples of imperfective/perfective pairs, using imperfectives we have already met:

Imperfective (i)

понима́ть (1)　　to understand
　я понима́ю, ты понима́ешь
смотре́ть (2)　　to watch

　я смотрю́, ты смо́тришь

брать (1В)　　to take
　я беру́, ты берёшь

говори́ть (2)　　to speak/say
　я говорю́, ты говори́шь
идти́ (1В)　　to go (on foot)
　я иду́, ты идёшь
е́хать (1В)　　to go (ride)
　я е́ду, ты е́дешь
ви́деть (2)　　to see
　я ви́жу, ты ви́дишь
улыба́ться (1)　to smile

　я улыба́юсь, ты улыба́ешься

де́лать (1)　　to do
　я де́лаю, ты де́лаешь
покупа́ть (1)　to buy
　я покупа́ю, ты покупа́ешь

Perfective (p)

поня́ть [pa-nyáty] (1В)
　я пойму́, ты поймёшь
посмотре́ть
[pa-sma-tryéty] (2)
　я посмотрю́, ты
　посмо́тришь
взять [vzyaty] (1В)
　я возьму́ [vazy-moó],
　ты возьмёшь
сказа́ть [ska-záty] (1В)
　я скажу́, ты ска́жешь
пойти́ [pay-teé] (1В)
　я пойду́, ты пойдёшь
пое́хать [pa-yé-haty] (1В)
　я пое́ду, ты пое́дешь
уви́деть [oo-vée-dyety] (2)
　я уви́жу, ты уви́дишь
улыбну́ться
[oo-lib-noó-tsa] (1В)
　я улыбну́сь,
　ты улыбнёшься
сде́лать [zdyé-laty] (1)
　я сде́лаю, ты сде́лаешь
купи́ть [koo-peéty] (2)
　я куплю́ [koo-plyoó],
　ты у́пишь

Мы смо́трим фильм. (i)
　We are watching a film.
Мы посмо́трим фильм. (p)
　We'll watch a film.

Я беру́ э́ту кни́гу. (i)
　I'm taking this book.
Я возьму́ э́ту кни́гу. (p)
　I shall take this book.

Он не понима́ет. (i)
He doesn't understand.
Он не пойме́т. (p)
He won't understand.

Мы идём на Кра́сную пло́щадь. (i)
We're going to Red Square.
Мы пойдём на Кра́сную пло́щадь. (p)
We'll go to Red Square.

Вы ви́дите Бори́са? (i)
Do you see Boris?
Вы уви́дите Бори́са? (p)
Will you see Boris?

The conjugation of perfectives follows exactly the same rules as for imperfectives (see 11.8). You will see that many perfectives are formed by adding a prefix to the imperfective (e.g. **писа́ть/написа́ть**); in these cases, the conjugation (stem and endings) are always exactly the same as for the imperfective. That means that if you know how to conjugate **писа́ть**, you automatically know how to conjugate **написа́ть**.

Exercise 52

Put the perfective verbs in the future form and translate:

1 **Вы (купи́ть) э́ту кни́гу?**

2 **Я (сде́лать) э́то че́рез неде́лю.**

3 **Он не (пое́хать) в Санкт-Петербу́рге.**

4 **Когда́ Джейн (поня́ть), что он её лю́бит?**

5 **Она́ не (сказа́ть), что она́ его́ не лю́бит.**

At the moment, perfective forms are simply new vocabulary items to be learnt, but with practice you will discover that it is often possible to guess what the perfective of an imperfective verb will be and that it is usually possible to tell immediately whether a new verb is perfective or imperfective.

12.3 More pairs of useful verbs

Imperfective (i)

встреча́ть (1) [fstrye-cháty]
  я встреча́ю, ты встреча́ешь
звони́ть (2)
  я звоню́, ты звони́шь
отвеча́ть (1)
  я отвеча́ю, ты отвеча́ешь
открыва́ть
  я открыва́ю,
  ты открыва́ешь
приходи́ть (2)
  я прихожу́, ты прихо́дишь
приезжа́ть (1) [pree-ye-
-zháty NB]
  я приезжа́ю,
  ты приезжа́ешь
расска́зывать (1)

  я расска́зываю,
  ты расска́зываешь
чита́ть (1)
  я чита́ю, ты чита́ешь

возвраща́ться (1)
  я возвраща́юсь,
  ты возвраща́ешься

Perfective (p)

встре́тить (2) to meet
  я встре́чу, ты встре́тишь
позвони́ть (2) to telephone
  я позвоню́, ты позвони́шь
отве́тить (2) to answer
  я отве́чу, ты отве́тишь
откры́ть (1) to open
  я откро́ю, ты откро́ешь

прийти́ (1B) to arrive (foot)
  я приду́, ты придёшь
прие́хать (1B) to arrive
(transport)
  я прие́ду, ты прие́дешь

рассказа́ть (1B) to tell,
relate
  я расскажу́,
  ты расска́жешь
прочита́ть (1) to read
  я прочита́ю, ты
  прочита́ешь
верну́ться (1B) to return
  я верну́сь, ты вернёшься

Exercise 53

Say in Russian:

1 I am reading a book.

2 I shall read this book.

3 Why doesn't he answer?

4 He won't answer.

5 Will you (pol) phone?

6 Yes, I'll phone.

7 Barbara is coming back to Moscow.

8 When will Barbara come back?

9 When will they arrive (by transport)?

12.4 The irregular but important verb мочь/смочь 'to be able'

Imperfective (i)

Perfective (p)

мочь [moch] 'to be able' (1B)

смочь [smoch] (1B)

я могу́	I can	**я смогу́**	I'll be able
ты мо́жешь	you (fam) can	**ты смо́жешь**	you'll be able
он мо́жет	he can	**он смо́жет**	he'll be able
мы мо́жем	we can	**мы смо́жем**	we'll be able
вы мо́жете	you (pol/pl) can	**вы смо́жете**	you'll be able
они́ мо́гут	they can NB	**они́ смо́гут** NB	they'll be able

This verb is followed by an infinitive (perfective for single events, imperfective for processes):

Я могу́ (i) **прийти́** (p) **за́втра.**	I can (am able to) come tomorrow.
Они́ не мо́гут (i) **прийти́** (p).	They can't (aren't able to) come.

Она́ не смо́жет (p) **позвони́ть** (p).　　She won't be able to phone.

Мы не мо́жем (i) **ждать** (i).　　We can't wait.

Since **мочь** ends **-чь**, it has an unpredictable past tense:

я мог [mok]　　　　　　　I was able/I could (man speaking)
я могла́ [mag-lá]　　　　　I was able (woman speaking)
оно́ могло́ [mag-ló]　　　　it was able (n)
мы могли́ [mag-leé]　　　　we were able (pl)

Она́ не могла́ прийти́.　　She couldn't come.

Exercise 54

Translate the words in brackets using the correct form of
мочь/смочь:

1　**Мы** (can) **прийти́.**

2　**Она́** (cannot) **прочита́ть э́то письмо́.**

3　**У меня́ нет де́нег. Я** (cannot) **купи́ть пода́рки.**

4　(Will you [pol] be able) **прийти́ за́втра?**

12.5 Present referring to the future

Note that in Russian, just as in English, the pres tense can be used for future events which are regarded as definite, e.g. **За́втра** ('tomorrow') **я е́ду** (present tense) **в Москву́.** 'I'm going (present tense) to Moscow tomorrow.'

12.6 Dative of pronouns

The primary meaning of the dative case is <u>to</u> a person, with verbs like 'give', 'show', 'say', 'telephone'.

мне [mnye]　　　　　　　　　　　　　to me
тебе́ [tye-byé]　　　　　　　　　　　to you (fam)

ему́	[ye-moó]	(**н**ему́ after prepositions)	to him
ей	[yey]	(**н**ей after prepositions)	to her
ему́	[ye-moó]	(**н**ему́ after prepositions)	to it
нам	[nam]		to us
вам	[vam]		to you (pol/pl)
им	[(y)eem]	(**н**им after prepositions)	to them

See examples with prepositions in 14.9.

12.7 Verbs with the dative

The main verbs which take the dative of the person ('the indirect object') <u>to</u> whom something is given or shown or said are:

говори́ть/сказа́ть (see 12.2)	to speak/say
звони́ть/позвони́ть (see 12.3)	to telephone
отвеча́ть/отве́тить (see 12.3)	to answer, reply
пока́зывать/показа́ть (1B)	to show
я покажу́, ты пока́жешь	
расска́зывать/рассказа́ть (see 12.3)	to tell, relate
дава́ть/дать (see below, 12.8)	to give

Put the dative pronoun in front of the verb unless you want to emphasize it. The thing given or shown or said ('the direct object') is in the accusative case.

Notice that 'to' is often not used in English, e.g. we can say 'I shall give the book <u>to him</u>' or 'I shall give <u>him</u> the book'.

Что вы ей ска́жете?	What will you say to her?
Я вам скажу́ три сло́ва.	I shall say three words to you.
Я вам позвоню́.	I'll telephone (to) you.
Я позвоню́ тебе́.	I'll telephone <u>you</u>.
Он нам пока́жет Москву́.	He'll show Moscow to us/ He'll show us Moscow.
Когда́ вы нам позвони́те?	When will you phone (to) us?

Exercise 55

Say in Russian:

1   He'll tell you (pol).

2   I won't tell her.

3   She telephones me.

4   I shall phone them.

5   Nina is showing him Red Square.

6   They will show us Moscow.

12.8 The irregular verb дава́ть/дать 'to give'

Imperfective

дава́ть [da-váty] (Type 1) stem да-, stress on ending

я даю́ I give	мы даём
ты даёшь	вы даёте
он даёт	они́ даю́т

Perfective

дать [daty] (unique verb)

я дам I shall give	мы дади́м
ты дашь	вы дади́те
он даст	они́ даду́т

Она́ даёт/даст мне три рубля́.
She gives/will give me three roubles.

Exercise 56

Use the correct form of дать:

1   Я (shall give) вам пять рубле́й.

2   Они́ (will give) ей де́ньги.

3   Кому́ [= to whom] ты (will give) э́тот биле́т?

12.9 Vocabulary

See also verbs in 12.2 and 12.3

давно́	[dav-nó]	long ago, since long ago
гру́стный	[groó-sni NB]	sad
вид	[veet]	expression, view
за́втра	[záf-tra]	tomorrow
уе́хать (p) (1B) я уе́ду, ты уе́дешь	[oo-yé-haty]	to leave (by transport)
бо́льше не	[bóly-she nye]	no longer, no more
гру́стно	[groó-sna NB]	(it is) sad; sadly
мо́жет быть	[mó-zhet bity]	perhaps, maybe
рожде́ние	[razh-dyé-nee-ye]	birth
день рожде́ния		birthday
обяза́тельно	[a-bee-zá-tyely-na]	definitely, without fail
е́сли	[yé-slee]	if

позво́лить (p) (2)
  я позво́лю, ты
  позво́лишь + dat
	[pa-zvó-leety]	to permit

вокза́л	[vag-zál]	(main) station (terminus)
оди́н (m)/одна́ (f)	[a-deén] [ad-ná]	alone (also means 'one')
спу́тник	[spoót-neek]	travelling companion
вопро́с	[va-prós]	question

задава́ть (i) (1)
  я задаю́, ты
  задаёшь + dat
	[za-da-váty]	to set (a task), ask (a question)

зада́ть (p)
  like дать: я зада́м,
  ты зада́шь
	[za-dáty]	(p of задава́ть)

прости́	[pra-steé]	excuse me, sorry (fam)

спеши́ть (i) (2)
  я спешу́,
  ты спеши́шь
	[spye-shíty]	to hurry

а то	[a to]	or else

опозда́ть (p) (1)	[a-paz-dáty]	to be late
я опозда́ю,		
ты опозда́ешь		
стра́нный	[strán-ni]	strange
никогда́ не	[nee-kag-dá nye]	never

12.10 CONVERSATIONS

Ни́на: Здра́вствуй, Андре́й, я тебя́ давно́ не ви́дела. Почему́ у тебя́ тако́й гру́стный вид?

Андре́й: Я тебе́ всё расскажу́. У меня́ есть подру́га Ба́рбара. Она́ америка́нка. Мы зна́ем друг дру́га всего́ две неде́ли. Но за́втра она́ уе́дет, и я её бо́льше не уви́жу. Ведь в Аме́рику я пое́хать не могу́.

Ни́на: Да, гру́стно. Но, мо́жет быть она́ верне́тся.

Бори́с: За́втра у Ната́ши день рожде́ния. Ты придёшь?

Джейн: Я не зна́ю. За́втра я е́ду в Заго́рск. Я не зна́ю, когда́ я верну́сь. Когда́ я прие́ду домо́й, я вам
… я тебе́ позвоню́.

Бори́с: Заче́м ты е́дешь в Заго́рск?

Джейн: Я тебе́ скажу́ за́втра.

Бори́с: Ты обяза́тельно позвони́шь?

Джейн: Обяза́тельно.

Бори́с: Е́сли ты позво́лишь, я тебя́ встре́чу на вокза́ле.

Джейн: Не на́до. Я не зна́ю, когда́ мы прие́дем.

Бори́с:	Мы? Ты прие́дешь из Заго́рска не одна́? Кто твой спу́тник?
Джейн:	Я не отве́чу на э́тот вопро́с. Ты задаёшь мне сли́шком мно́го вопро́сов.
Бори́с:	Но я ...
Джейн:	Прости́ меня́. Мне на́до спеши́ть, а то опозда́ю.
Бори́с:	Куда́ ты опа́здываешь?
	(She rushes off)
	Стра́нная де́вушка. Никогда́ не пойму́ её.

TRANSLATIONS

N: Hello, Andrey, I haven't seen you for a long time. Why are you looking so sad?

A: I'll tell you everything. I have a friend called Barbara. She's an American. We've known each other for only two weeks. But tomorrow she will leave and I won't see her any more. You know I can't go to America.

N: Yes, it's sad. But perhaps she will come back.

B: It's Natasha's birthday tomorrow. Will you (fam) come?

J: I don't know. I'm going to Zagorsk (historic town and religious centre north of Moscow recently renamed **Се́ргиев Поса́д**). I don't know when I'll return. When I get home I'll call you (she hesitates between the polite and familiar forms).

B: Why are you going to Zagorsk?

J: I'll tell you tomorrow.

B: Will you definitely phone (call)?

J: Of course.

B: If you'll permit, I'll meet you at the station.

J: It's not necessary (Don't). I don't know when we'll arrive.

B: We? You'll come back from Zagorsk with someone else (lit. 'not one' = 'not alone'). Who's your travelling companion?

J: I won't answer that question. You ask me too many questions.

B: But I ...

J: Excuse me. I have ('to me it is necessary') to hurry or else I'll be late.

B: What ('to where') are you late for? Strange girl. I'll never understand her.

Chapter 13

- Completed and uncompleted events in the past.
- More on the imperfective (i) and perfective (p) aspects.

13.1 Perfective (p) verbs in the past

In chapter 12 we met a number of perfective verbs and used them to form the future. But all these perfective verbs have another use too: we can form a past tense from them, using exactly the same rules as we learnt in 11.1 (the endings **-л, -ла, -ло, -ли**).

Taking the verb **писа́ть** (i)/**написа́ть** (p) 'to write', we have the <u>imperfective</u> past:

я писа́л, я писа́ла etc. I wrote/I was writing

and the <u>perfective</u> past:

я написа́л, я написа́ла etc. I wrote (and finished what I wrote)

So the perfective past has an extra element of meaning which is not present in the imperfective past form: the idea of an action thought of as a completed whole (the Russian word for 'perfective' **соверше́нный** literally means 'completed').

If you say **Я <u>писа́л</u>** (i) **письмо́** 'I wrote/was writing a letter' your hearer doesn't know whether you finished the letter or not, but if you say **Я <u>написа́л</u>** (p) **письмо́** you mean that you wrote and finished the letter.

If you have learned French, you will see some similarities with the use of the imparfait (imperfect), e.g. j'écrivais, and the parfait (perfect), e.g. j'ai écrit.

The full details of when to use perfective verbs and when to use imperfective verbs in the past tense are complex and subtle, but fortunately a wrong choice is unlikely to cause misunderstanding.

In 13.2 and 13.3 we give some rules of thumb for the choice of aspect in the past tense.

13.2 Use of imperfective (i)

1 Unfinished actions are always imperfective:

She was writing.	Она́ писа́ла (i).
She was walking to the shop.	Она́ шла (i) в магази́н.

The English past continuous 'was/were (verb)ing' always corresponds to the imperfective.

2 Actions repeated an indefinite number of times are always imperfective:

She wrote me a letter every day.	Она́ писа́ла (i) мне письмо́ ка́ждый день.
She wrote interesting letters.	Она́ писа́ла (i) интере́сные пи́сьма.

3 Verbs denoting states and processes rather than actions are normally imperfective (and many such verbs do not have perfective forms).

She was in Moscow.	Она́ была́ (i) в Москве́.
She lived in Siberia.	Она́ жила́ (i) в Сиби́ри.
They stood in the queue.	Они́ стоя́ли (i) в о́череди.

4 Time expressions of duration (often with 'for' in English) require the imperfective:

We wrote for a long time.	Мы до́лго писа́ли (i).
She wrote for three hours.	Она́ писа́ла (i) три часа́.
We watched television all day.	Мы смотре́ли (i) телеви́зор весь день.

5 If there was no action, usually the imperfective is used:

She didn't write to me.	Она́ мне не писа́ла (i).
I haven't seen (watched) that film.	Я не смотре́л (i) э́тот фильм.
We didn't telephone her.	Мы ей не звони́ли (i).

6 Actions attempted but without result are imperfective:

| I telephoned you (but didn't get through or you weren't in). | Я вам звони́л (i). |

What all these examples have in common is emphasis on the process rather than the result.

13.3 Use of perfective (p)

1 The perfective form emphasizes completion and result:

She wrote a letter (and finished it) or She has written a letter (and here it is).	Она́ написа́ла (p) письмо́.
She read the book (all of it).	Она́ прочита́ла (p) кни́гу.
She has taken my book (and has it now).	Она́ взяла́ (p) мою́ кни́гу.

2 Sequences of actions (except when they are repeated actions – see 2 above) are perfective, because each action must be finished before the next one can take place:

| She bought my book, read it and then wrote me a letter. | Она́ купи́ла (p) мою́ кни́гу, прочита́ла (p) её, пото́м написа́ла (p) мне письмо́. |

3 With negation (**не**) the perfective is used to mean failure to do something.

 She didn't (failed to) understand. **Она́ не поняла́** (p).

So the perfective describes an action as a completed whole and emphasizes its result.

Note the contrast between the perfective and the imperfective in such examples as:

She telephoned (completed action) when (while) I was writing (action in process) a letter.
Она́ позвони́ла (p), **когда́ я писа́л** (i) **письмо́.**

Exercise 57

Explain the aspect of the verbs in this text:

Ба́рбара уе́хала (p) **в Аме́рику. Андре́й писа́л** (i) **ей ка́ждую неде́лю. Он ждал** (i), **но Ба́рбара не писа́ла** (i), **не звони́ла** (i). **У него́ был** (i) **о́чень гру́стный вид. Но вчера́** ('yesterday'), **когда́ он писа́л** (i) **ей письмо́, она́ позвони́ла** (p) **из Вашингто́на и сказа́ла** (p), **что она́ получи́ла** (p) **его́ пе́рвое письмо́ и уже́ давно́ отве́тила** (p) **на него́.**

– Ты не получи́л (p) **моё письмо́? – спроси́ла** (p) ('asked') **она́.**

– Нет, – отве́тил (p) **он.**

Её письмо́ шло (i) **о́чень до́лго, три неде́ли. Оно́ пришло́** (p) **сего́дня.**

13.4 Aspect of the infinitive

You also have to choose between the aspects in sentences such as 'I want <u>to read</u> this book: **Я хочу́ чита́ть** (i)/ **прочита́ть** (p) **э́ту кни́гу.** If you mean 'read without

necessarily reading all of it', choose the imperfective **читáть**.
If you mean 'read and finish it', use the perfective **прочитáть**.
In many situations the choice will seem tricky, and it will
take a bit of practice and reading to acquire a feel for
Russian usage. Fortunately, it makes little communicative
difference if you pick the wrong one.

13.5 How to recognize imperfectives and perfectives

Though you have to learn perfective and imperfective
forms, you may find it useful to have some clues to help
you to work out the aspect of a verb and remember it.

(a) If a verb contains **-ыва-** it is almost certainly
    <u>im</u>perfective, and the equivalent perfective is the same
    verb without the **-ыв-**.

> Examples:
> **расскáзывать** (i), **рассказáть** (p)   to tell, recount
> **опáздывать** (i), **опоздáть** (p)   to be late

(b) If a verb is short (one or two syllables) and has no
    prefix, it is likely to be <u>im</u>perfective. The equivalent
    perfective will probably have a prefix (**по-**, which is the
    commonest one, or **на-**, **про-**, **за-** etc.).

> Examples:
> **писáть** (i), **написáть** (p)   to write
> **читáть** (i), **прочитáть** (p)   to read

(c) It follows from (a) and (b) that if a verb has a prefix and
    doesn't contain **-ыва-**, it is almost certainly perfective;
    the imperfective will either be the same verb without
    the prefix or the same verb with **-ыва-**.

Exceptions to (b) are plentiful: e.g. **взять** 'to take' and
купи́ть 'to buy' are both perfective.

Exercise 58

What is the aspect of each verb and why?

1 **Вчера́ я <u>чита́ла</u> э́ту кни́гу.** Yesterday I read/was reading this book.

2 **Вчера́ я <u>прочита́ла</u> э́ту кни́гу.** Yesterday I read this book.

3 **Бори́с <u>звони́л</u> ей ча́сто.** Boris telephoned her often.

4 **Когда́ Бори́с <u>верну́лся</u>, я <u>чита́ла</u> письмо́.** When Boris returned, I was reading a letter.

5 **Ни́на <u>купи́ла</u> буты́лку, <u>верну́лась</u> домо́й и <u>дала́</u> её мне.** Nina bought a bottle, returned home and gave it to me.

6 **Ка́ждое у́тро она́ <u>открыва́ла</u> окно́.** Every morning she opened the window.

7 **Вчера́ Джейн не <u>приходи́ла</u> и не <u>звони́ла</u>.** Yesterday Jane didn't come and didn't telephone.

8 **Она́ <u>написа́ла</u> три письма́.** She wrote three letters.

9 **Мы <u>покупа́ли</u> «Пра́вду» ка́ждый день.** We bought 'Pravda' every day.

10 **Сего́дня мы <u>купи́ли</u> «Пра́вду».** Today we bought 'Pravda'.

11 **Он <u>говори́л</u> ме́дленно.** He spoke slowly.

12 **Он <u>сказа́л</u> не́сколько слов.** He said a few words.

13 **Мы <u>понима́ли</u>, когда́ она́ <u>говори́ла</u>.** We understood when(ever) she spoke.

14 **Мы <u>по́няли</u>, что она́ <u>говори́т</u> по-англи́йски.** We realized (came to understand) that she is (was) speaking English.

Exercise 59

Translate into Russian explaining your choice of aspect:

1 We were buying books.

2 I wrote to her every week.

3 I arrived in Moscow, went to the hotel, then telephoned him.

4 I want to buy this book.

5 Have you written the letter?

13.6 Vocabulary

окно́ [ak-nó] gen pl о́кон	window (ex. 58)
ко́мната [kóm-na-ta]	room (ex. 58)
телеви́зор [tye-lye-vée-zar]	television (ex. 59)
прожи́ть (p of жить) (1B)	to live (for a specified period)
перее́хать [pye-rye-yé-haty]	to move house (p) (1B)
Калифо́рния	California
око́нчить (p) (2) + acc	to graduate, finish
я око́нчу, ты око́нчишь	
наза́д [na-zát]	ago; back
доучи́ться [da-oo-chée-tsa] (p) (2)	to complete one's studies
случи́ться [sloo-chée-tsa] (p) (2)	to happen
про́сто	simply
надое́сть [na-da-yésty] (p) + dat	to bore
past: надое́л, надое́ла, надое́ло	
он мне надое́л	he has bored me (= I'm tired of him)
реши́ть [rye-shíty] (p) (2)	to decide
я решу́, ты реши́шь, они́ реша́т	
зараба́тывать (i) (1)	to earn
же	(emphasizes previous word)
узна́ть (p) (1)	to find out
я узна́ю, ты узна́ешь	

153

плати́ть (i) (2)	to pay
я плачу́, ты пла́тишь	
кра́йний -яя (f), -ее (f), -ие (pl)	extreme
се́вер	north
Кра́йний Се́вер	Far North (of Russia), where conditions are harsh and pay is generally higher than in the south
хо́лодно	(it is) cold; coldly
пое́хать (p of е́хать) (1B)	to go (by transport, one direction)
стро́йка	construction site
понра́виться (p) + dat of person	to please
мне понра́вился фильм	I liked the film
замеча́тельный	remarkable
лю́ди pl (acc/gen pl люде́й)	people
приро́да	nature
великоле́пный	magnificent
приве́т	greeting, hi!
ко́шка (gen pl ко́шек)	cat (female)
верне́е	more accurately, rather
вот как!	ah!, so that's how it is!
ду́мать (i) (1)	to think
я ду́маю, ты ду́маешь	
живо́тное [zhi-vót-na-ye] (n adj)	animal
наоборо́т [na-a-ba-rót]	on the contrary
весь [vyesy] (m), вся (f), всё (n)	all (see table 4 for declension)
и́ли … и́ли	either … or
соба́ка	dog
назва́ть (p) (1B)	to call, give a name
я назову́, ты назовёшь	
свой [svoy] (endings like мой)	own (belonging to the subject of the verb – translate as 'my', 'his' etc. according to context)
смешно́	(it's) funny; comically
приду́мать (p) (1)	to think up, invent
ничего́ [nee-che-<u>v</u>ó NB]	nothing
смешно́й	funny, comic
честь (f)	honour

в честь + gen	in honour of, after somebody
недáвно	recently
получи́ть (p) (2)	to receive
я получу́, ты полу́чишь, они́ полу́чат (8.4)	
приз [prees]	prize
вы́ставка [ví-staf-ka]	exhibition
на вы́ставке	at an exhibition
обрáдоваться (p) (1)	to be pleased
stem обрáду-	
кáжется [ká-zhe-tsa]	it seems
вчерá [fchye-rá]	yesterday
срáзу	immediately
полюби́ть (p) (2) + acc	to fall in love with
и … и	both … and
кстáти	by the way
спроси́ть (p) (2) + acc	to ask (someone)
я спрошу́, ты спрóсишь	
предложи́ть [pryed-la-zhíty] (p)	to offer
я предложу́, ты предлóжишь, они́ предлóжат (+ acc + dat)	(something to someone)
преподавáть (i) (1) (+ acc + dat)	to teach (something to somebody)
я преподаю́, ты преподаёшь	
захотéть (p of хотéть)	to want, conceive a desire
мнóгие (pl adj)	many (people)
крóме тогó [kró-mye ta-vó NB]	furthermore, also
ошибáться (i) (1) [a-shi-bá-tsa]	to make a mistake
скýчно [skoósh-na NB]	(it is) boring
ромáн	romance, love affair
что вы! [shto vi!]	come now! don't be silly!
серьёзный [sye-ryyóz-ni]	serious

CONVERSATION

Бáрбара: Где вы роди́лись, Андрéй?

Андрéй: В Одéссе. А вы?

Бáрбара: Я родила́сь в Нью-Йóрке. И прожила́ там двена́дцать лет. Потóм мы переéхали в Вашингтóн.

Андрéй: А где вы учи́лись?

Бáрбара: В Калифóрнии. Окóнчила там университéт три гóда наза́д.

Андрéй: Я тóже учи́лся в университéте, но не доучи́лся.

Бáрбара: Почему́? Что случи́лось?

Андрéй: Мне прóсто надоéло учи́ться. Я реши́л пойти́ рабóтать. Я хотéл зараба́тывать дéньги.

Бáрбара: Где же вы рабóтали?

Андрéй: Я узна́л, что пла́тят óчень хорошó на Кра́йнем Сéвере, где óчень хóлодно. Я поéхал в Яку́тск рабóтать на стрóйке.

Бáрбара: Вам понра́вилось там?

Андрéй: Бы́ло óчень интерéсно. В Сиби́ри живу́т замеча́тельные лю́ди, и приро́да там великолéпная.

TRANSLATION

B: Where were you born, Andrey?

A: In Odessa (Black Sea port in the Ukraine).
What about you?

B: I was born in New York. And I lived there for
twelve years. Then we moved to Washington.

A: And where did you study?

B: In California. I graduated from college there
three years ago.

A: I was at university too, but I didn't graduate.

B: Why? What happened?

A: I simply got tired of studying. I decided to get a
job. I wanted to earn money.

B: And where did you work?

A: I found out that they pay very well in the Far
North, where it is very cold, and I went to Yakutsk
(capital of the Republic of Yakutia, locally called
Sakha, a huge area in the Russian Far East) to
work on a construction site.

B: Did you like it there?

A: It was very interesting. Wonderful people live
in Siberia, and nature (the scenery) there is
magnificent.

Exercise 60

Translate:

Майк: Привéт, Ни́на, что у вас нóвого?

Ни́на: Я купи́ла кóшку, и́ли, вернéе, котá.

Майк: Вот как! А я дýмал, что рýсские не лю́бят живóтных.

Ни́на: Наоборóт. У всех мои́х друзéй есть и́ли кóшка, и́ли собáка.

Майк: Как вы назвáли своегó котá?

Ни́на: Ливерпýль.

Майк: Прости́те, я не пóнял. Как вы сказáли?

Ни́на: Я сказáла: Ливерпýль. Почемý вы улыбнýлись?

Майк: Но ведь э́то смешнó. Кто придýмал?

Ни́на: Ничегó смешнóго здесь нет. Мы егó назвáли в честь óчень краси́вого котá, котóрый недáвно получи́л пéрвый приз на москóвской вы́ставке.

Майк: Джейн обрáдуется, когдá узнáет. Кáжется, Ливерпýль её роднóй гóрод.

Ни́на: Онá узнáла вчерá, когдá онá былá у меня́ в гостя́х. Онá егó срáзу полюби́ла.

Майк: Зна́чит, онá тепéрь лю́бит и Ливерпýль и Ливерпýля. Кстáти, о Джейн. Я хотéл вас спроси́ть, когдá онá приéхала в Москвý?

Нина: Она́ прие́хала ме́сяцев шесть наза́д. Ей предложи́ли рабо́ту в шко́ле.

Майк: Где она́ рабо́тала в А́нглии?

Нина: Она́ преподава́ла ру́сский язы́к в Ливерпу́ле. Она́ вернётся туда́ неде́ль че́рез во́семь-де́вять.

Майк: Почему́ она́ захоте́ла жить и рабо́тать в Москве́?

Нина: В Москве́ интере́сно. Мно́гие иностра́нцы о́чень лю́бят ру́сских люде́й. Кро́ме того́, Джейн лю́бит ру́сский язы́к.

Майк: По-мо́ему, вы ошиба́етесь. Я ду́маю, что в Ливерпу́ле ей бы́ло ску́чно. Мо́жет быть, у неё здесь рома́н?

Нина: Что вы! Она́ де́вушка о́чень серьёзная.

Chapter 14

- Imperfective future.
- Feelings and states.
- Dative case and uses of the dative.

14.1 The future of быть (i) 'to be'

Just as **быть** has a past tense (**был, была́** etc.), it also has a future:

я бу́ду	I'll be/I will be
ты бу́дешь	you'll be/you will be
он/она́/оно́ бу́дет	he, she, it'll be/will be
мы бу́дем	we'll be/we will be
вы бу́дете	you'll be/you will be
они́ бу́дут	they'll be/they will be

Я бу́ду в Москве́ три дня.
　　I'll be in Moscow for three days.

Вы бу́дете до́ма?
　　Will you be at home?

Где она́ бу́дет за́втра?
　　Where will she be tomorrow?

14.2 Future of imperfective verbs

In chapter 13 we met the choice between the imperfective and the perfective in the past tense. There is also a choice to be made in the future. If you wish to show that an action or state in the future will be repeated or unfinished, you need the <u>imperfective</u> future. This relatively rare verb form consists of the future of the verb **быть** 'to be' (see above 14.1) + the <u>imperfective</u> infinitive. So **Я бу́ду чита́ть** means 'I shall be reading' or 'I shall read (without finishing or an indefinite number of times)'.

я бу́ду рабо́тать	I shall be working
ты бу́дешь рабо́тать	you (fam) will be working
он/она́/оно́ бу́дет рабо́тать	he/she/it will be working
мы бу́дем рабо́тать	we shall be working
вы бу́дете рабо́тать	you (pol/pl) will be working
они́ бу́дут рабо́тать	they will be working

As mentioned above, this form is used for future unfinished and repeated actions and states. In other situations use the perfective future we met in chapter 12.

Он бу́дет чита́ть весь ве́чер.
He will be reading all evening.

Ка́ждый день мы бу́дем встава́ть в семь часо́в.
Every day we will get up at seven.

Я бу́ду писа́ть ча́сто.
I shall write often.

14.3 Differences between English and Russian use of tenses

(a) In English, when someone's words are reported with a phrase such as 'He said that ...', 'He asked if ...' we change the tense of the actual words:

Boris's actual words: 'I am a Ukrainian'. **Я украи́нец.**
Report of Boris's words: 'Boris said that he <u>was</u> a Ukrainian'.

When Russians report what someone said, they keep the tense of the actual words:

Бори́с сказа́л, что он украи́нец.
Boris said that he was a Ukrainian. (lit. 'Boris said that he is a Ukrainian.')

Джейн: Я позвоню́ (fut p) ве́чером.
Jane: I shall ring in the evening.

Джейн сказа́ла, что она́ позвони́т (fut p) ве́чером.
Jane said that she would ring in the evening.
(lit. 'Jane said that she <u>will ring</u> in the evening')

(b) In English, after the conjunctions 'when', 'if', 'until', 'while' etc. we use only the present tense, even when the meaning is <u>future</u>. For example, we say 'When they come, I shall phone you' using the present tense after 'when' even though 'when they come' here means 'when they will come'. In Russian, after such conjunctions as когда́ 'when', е́сли 'if', пока́ 'while', пока́ ... не 'until', if the meaning is future you must use the future tense:

Когда́ они́ приду́т (fut p), я тебе́ позвоню́.
When they (will) come, I shall phone you.

Когда́ я бу́ду (fut) в Москве́, я бу́ду говори́ть то́лько по-ру́сски.
When I am (lit. 'will be') in Moscow, I shall speak only in Russian.

Е́сли я уви́жу (fut p) её, я ей скажу́.
If I (will) see her, I'll tell her.

Я бу́ду чита́ть (fut i), пока́ они́ не приду́т (fut p).
I shall read until they (will) come.

Exercise 61

Translate the dialogue with special attention to the verb forms:

Нина: Завтра я бу́ду (fut) у Ната́ши ('at Natasha's place'). Ты придёшь (p)? Мы бу́дем танцева́ть ('to dance') (i fut).

Майк: Коне́чно, приду́ (p fut). А Джейн бу́дет (fut) там?

Нина: Она́ сказа́ла (p past), что она́ бу́дет (fut) весь день ('all day') в Заго́рске. Когда́ она́ вернётся (p fut) в Москву́, она́ позвони́т (p fut).

Майк: Что она́ бу́дет де́лать (i fut) в Заго́рске?

Нина: Она́ сказа́ла (p past), что хо́чет (pres) пойти́ в монасты́рь ('monastery').

Майк: А Бори́с?

Нина: Он сказа́л, что придёт (p fut) обяза́тельно.

Exercise 62

Say in Russian, choosing the perfective or imperfective future as required:

1   We will be working tomorrow.

2   He will live in a hotel.

3   When will the train arrive?

4   When we arrive in Moscow, we shall go to the hotel 'Intourist'.

5   If you give him five dollars, he'll give you the book.

14.4 Dative case of nouns

The dative is the least common case of nouns, but the forms are easy to learn. Here is the dative singular (for the plural see 18.10).

(a) Masculine and neuter nouns ending with a consonant or -**o** have -**y**:

Я дал до́ллар Ива́ну.
    I gave the dollar to Ivan.

Masculine and neuter nouns ending -**ь**, -**й**, -**e** have -**ю**:

Мы пока́жем Андре́ю го́род.
    We shall show (to) Andrey the city.

(b) All feminine nouns have the same ending as in the prepositional (see 5.5, 5.6):

Она́ дала́ сестре́ пять рубле́й.
    She gave to (her) sister five roubles.

14.5 Dative of adjectives and possessives

Take the prepositional form (see 7.3, 7.7, 8.11). If it is masculine or neuter (i.e. if it ends -**ом** or -**ем**), add -**y** to the -**ом** or -**ем**:

ва́шему ру́сскому дру́гу
    to your (male) Russian friend

The feminine ending is the same as the prepositional -**ой** or -**ей**:

ва́шей ру́сской подру́ге
    to your (female) Russian friend

14.6 The dative with indeclinable words describing states

The Russian for 'I am cold' is literally 'to me it is cold':
мне хо́лодно [hó-lad-na].

There are many words like **хо́лодно** ('it is cold') denoting states. We have met several already, for example,

гру́стно [groós-na]   it is sad (12.9)
мо́жно [mózh-na]   it is possible/permitted; one may (6.6)
на́до   it is necessary (8.14)
ску́чно [skoósh-na]   it is boring (13.6)

These words are all indeclinable. If you wish to specify the person involved, use the dative.

Нам на́до идти́.   We must go. (lit. 'To us it is necessary to go.')

If you want to ask for permission to do something use **мо́жно** [mózh-na] 'it is possible/permitted' + the infin, e.g.

May I smoke? **Мо́жно кури́ть?** or **Мо́жно мне кури́ть?**

NOTE You don't have to translate the 'I' (**мне** 'to me') if it is obvious that you are asking for permission for yourself.

May my wife smoke? **Мое́й жене́ мо́жно кури́ть?**

The answer may be **мо́жно** ('you may', lit. 'it is permitted') or **пожа́луйста** ('please do') or **нельзя́** ('it is not permitted').

Мо́жно мне войти́?
     May I come in? (lit. 'To me it is possible to come in?')

Мо́жно or **Вам мо́жно.**
     You may.

Мне на́до позвони́ть.
     I must make a telephone call.

NOTE **не на́до** corresponds to 'one shouldn't':

Не на́до говори́ть так гро́мко.
     You shouldn't speak so loudly.

ну́жно, like **на́до**, means 'it is necessary':

Ей ну́жно рабо́тать сего́дня.
     She has to (must) work today.

нельзя [nyely-zyá] 'it is not possible/permitted, one must not':

Здесь нельзя курить.
   One is not allowed to smoke here.

Ему нельзя курить.
   He must not smoke.

14.7 Other states/situations

интере́сно	it is interesting (8.14)
Ему́ интере́сно.	He is interested.
жа́рко [zhár-ka]	it is hot
Мне жа́рко.	I am hot.
тепло́ [tye-pló]	it is warm
Здесь тепло́.	It's warm here.

Вам здесь ску́чно?
   Do you find it boring here? (lit. 'To you here it is boring?')

Нет, мне здесь о́чень интере́сно.
   No, I find it very interesting here.

14.8 Past and future of words expressing states

To make any of these indeclinable 'state' words past tense, simply add **бы́ло** (usually after the state word):

Нам на́до бы́ло идти́.	We had to go.
Ему́ бы́ло хо́лодно.	He was cold.
(or **Ему́ хо́лодно бы́ло.**)	
Нельзя́ бы́ло.	It was not allowed.
Мне на́до бы́ло позвони́ть.	I had to make a phone call.

To make the state future, just add **бу́дет** ('will be', 3rd person sing fut of **быть** – see above, 14.1):

Нам на́до бу́дет купи́ть три биле́та.
   We'll have to buy three tickets.

Éсли вы откро́ете окно́, нам бу́дет хо́лодно.
If you open the window we'll be cold.

Бу́дет ску́чно.
It will be boring.

Exercise 63

Express the following in Russian:

1   I am cold.

2   Is your friend (m) bored?

3   We must go (i).

4   You must speak (i) Russian.

5   I had to speak (i) Russian.

6   They had to work (i).

7   She will have to speak (i) slowly.

8   It is necessary to take (p) (**взять**) a taxi.

9   May we ask (p) how much you earn?

10   You may not smoke here.

11   It was not possible to find (p) (**найти́**) a taxi.

12   It was cold in Moscow.

13   May I smoke?

14   May I open (p) (**откры́ть**) the window?

15   May I buy (p) that book?

16   May I ask (p) where you bought (p) that map
(**план**) of the city?

14.9 Dative with the prepositions к and по

Two common prepositions take the dative case:

к	towards:	к до́му/ко (NB) мне	towards the house/me
		к нему́/к нам	towards him (12.6)/us
по	along:	по у́лице	along the street

Apart from this basic meaning, по – the vaguest of all Russian prepositions – can translate as 'about', 'according to', 'across', 'in' and other ways according to context:

рабо́та по до́му	housework (work about the house)
экза́мен по ру́сскому языку́	Russian exam (exam in/ about Russian)
е́здить по Росси́и	to travel about/around Russia
по моему́ мне́нию = по-мо́ему (7.10)	in my opinion (мне́ние 'opinion')

14.10 Vocabulary

с днём рожде́ния [zdnyom razh--dyé-nee-ya]	happy birthday
поцелова́ть (р) (1) stem поцелу́- я поцелу́ю, ты поцелу́ешь	to kiss
как дела́?	how are things?
поздравля́ю с днём рожде́ния!	congratulations on your birthday
шампа́нское (n adj)	(Russian) champagne
все (pl of весь – see table 4)	everybody, all
вы́пить (р) (1) за + acc я вы́пью, ты вы́пьешь	to drink (to)
здоро́вье	health
ой!	oh! (surprise)
ве́чер (nom pl вечера́)	evening
пить (i) (1) stem пь- я пью, ты пьёшь	to drink
ве́село	(it is) merry; merrily
нельзя́	(it is) not possible/not allowed; one must not
немно́жко [nye-mnósh-ka] from немно́го	a little

открь́ть (p) (1) stem **откро́-**   to open
  я откро́ю, ты откро́ешь
жа́рко   (it is) hot
звон(о́)к   ring, telephone call
волнова́ться (i) (1) stem **волну́-** to worry
  я волну́юсь, ты волну́ешься
дава́й потанцу́ем!   let's dance!

14.11 CONVERSATIONS

At Natasha's party

Бори́с: С днём рожде́ния, Ната́ша! Мо́жно тебя́ поцелова́ть?

Ната́ша: Мо́жно.

Бори́с: Как дела́? Тебе́ не ску́чно рабо́тать в магази́не?

Ната́ша: Нет, коне́чно. В «Дру́жбе» о́чень интере́сно.

Майк: Поздравля́ю с днём рожде́ния! Вот вам шесть буты́лок шампа́нского. Мы все вы́пьем за ва́ше здоро́вье.

Ната́ша: Ой, спаси́бо. Но не на́до бы́ло покупа́ть так мно́го.

Майк: Весь ве́чер бу́дем пить шампа́нское! Бу́дет ве́село!

Ната́ша: Мне нельзя́ пить. И Ни́не то́же.

Майк: Что вы говори́те? Сего́дня у вас день рожде́ния, на́до вы́пить.

Ната́ша: Ну, немно́жко.

→

Борис: Мо́жно откры́ть окно́? Жа́рко.

Ната́ша: Пожа́луйста. Мне то́же жа́рко.

Борис: Джейн не звони́ла? Она́ сказа́ла, что позвони́т, когда́ прие́дет из Заго́рска.

Ната́ша: Нет, не звони́ла.

Борис: Я сказа́л, что бу́ду ждать её звонка́.

Ната́ша: Не на́до волнова́ться. Éсли она́ сказа́ла, что позвони́т, зна́чит, обяза́тельно позвони́т. Тебе́ без неё ску́чно?

Борис: Нет, коне́чно! Дава́й потанцу́ем!

TRANSLATIONS

B: Happy birthday (lit. [I congratulate you] with birthday – inst, 16.2), Natasha. May I give you a kiss?

N: You may.

B: How are things? Don't you find it boring working in a shop?

N: Of course not. It's very interesting (to work) in the 'Friendship' (bookshop).

M: Congratulations on your birthday (lit. 'I congratulate with birthday'). Here are six bottles of champagne for you (lit. 'to you'). (In Russia [Russian] sparkling wine is readily available.) We'll all drink to your health.

N: Oh, thank you. But you shouldn't have bought so much.

M: We shall drink (shall be drinking) champagne all evening! We'll have a good time (it will be merry).

N: I mustn't drink. And Nina shouldn't either.

M: What are you saying? It's your birthday today, you've got to have a drink.

N: Well, a little.

B: May I open the window? It's hot.

N: Please do. I'm hot too.

B: Has Jane rung? (Jane didn't ring?) She said she would (will) ring when she got back (will arrive) from Zagorsk.

N: No, she hasn't rung.

B: I told her I would be waiting (will be waiting) for her call (gen sometimes used after **ждать**).

N: There's no need to worry. If she said she would (will) ring, that means she will definitely ring. Are you bored without her?

B: Of course not! How about a dance?

Exercise 64

What messages do these convey?

У НАС
НЕ КУРЯТ

С днем рождения!

Chapter 15

- Asking people to do things.
- Imperative.

15.1 Imperative

When asking people to do things in English, we tend to use such polite constructions as 'Would you pass me the butter?' Russians make such requests with a form of the verb called the <u>imperative</u> (as in 'Pass the bread', 'Come here', 'Please repeat') + the word **пожа́луйста** 'please' [pa-zhál-sta]. 'Give me that book please' sounds abrupt in English, but its literal equivalent **Да́йте мне э́ту кни́гу, пожа́луйста** is normal usage in Russian.

We have already met forms such as **возьми́те** (9.8) 'take', **подожди́те** (8.14) 'wait', **дава́й** and **дава́йте** (11.7) 'let's', **говори́те ме́дленно** (3.1) 'speak slowly', **прости́те** (4.1) 'excuse me', **расска́зывайте** (11.9) 'tell', **покажи́те** (8.14) 'show'. These imperatives are formed from both perfective and imperfective verbs.

15.2 Formation of the imperative

There are three possible endings for the imperative: **-йте**, **-и́те** and **-ьте** – if you are speaking to someone you call **вы**. If you are speaking to someone you call **ты**, leave off the **-те**.

(a) **-й(те)** is the ending if the stem of the verb ends with a vowel (for 'stem' see chapter 4.7); e.g.:

чита́ть (i), stem чита́-, so imper is чита́й(те) 'read'.
прочита́ть (p), stem прочита́-, imper: прочита́й(те) 'read'.
откры́ть (p), stem откро́-, imper: откро́й(те) 'open'.

Ва́ня, чита́й, пожа́луйста!	Vanya, read, please.
Ва́ня и А́ня, чита́йте, пожа́луйста!	Vanya and Anya, read, please.
Ва́ня, прочита́й э́то сло́во, пожа́луйста.	Vanya, please read this word.
Де́ти, прочита́йте э́ти слова́.	Children, read these words.

More examples:

слу́шайте (i) listen	Слу́шайте меня́. Listen to me.
да́йте (p) give	Да́йте мне рубль. Give me a rouble.
узна́йте (p) find out	Узна́йте, где бар. Find out where the bar is.
переда́йте (p) pass	Переда́йте хлеб. Pass the bread.
откро́йте (p) open	Откро́йте окно́. Open the window.

NOTE You may now have spotted that **Здра́вствуй(те)** ('Hello') is an imperative. It comes from the rare verb **здра́вствовать** (i) 'to be healthy' (**я здра́вствую, ты здра́вствуешь**), so the greeting literally means 'Be healthy!'

(b) The commonest ending is **-й(те)**. Use it if the stem of the verb ends in a consonant and the first person singular (the **я** ['I'] form) is stressed on the end. NOTE: if the stems of the **я** and **ты** forms are different, the imperative is formed from the **ты** stem, e.g.:

приходи́ть (я прихожу́, ты прихо́дишь), the stem is прихо́д- and the **я** form is stressed on the ending **-у́**, so the imper is **приходи́(те)**.

Ва́ня, приходи́ за́втра.	Vanya, come tomorrow.
Пожа́луйста, приходи́те в на́шу гости́ницу.	Please come to our hotel.
скажи́те (p) say	Скажи́те ей. Tell her.
возьми́те (p) take	Возьми́те мой телефо́н. Take my phone number.

иди́те (i) go	**Иди́те туда́.** Go over there.
поверни́те (p) turn	**Поверни́те напра́во.** Turn right.
уходи́те (i) go away	**Уходи́те, пожа́луйста.** Please go away.
посмотри́те (p) look	**Посмотри́те на план.** Look at the map.
купи́те (p) buy	**Купи́те две буты́лки.** Buy two bottles.
покажи́те (p) show	**Покажи́те э́ту кни́гу.** Show (me) that book.
подожди́те (p) wait	**Подожди́те меня́ здесь.** Wait for me here.
говори́те (i) speak	**Говори́те ме́дленно.** Speak slowly.
прости́те (p) excuse	**Прости́те, я не хоте́л.** Sorry, I didn't mean to.
пиши́те (i) write	**Пиши́те нам.** Write to us.
позвони́те (p) phone	**Позвони́те мне за́втра.** Call me tomorrow.
расскажи́те (p) tell	**Расскажи́те мне о ней.** Tell me about her.
разреши́те (p) allow	**Разреши́те мне пройти́.** Please let me pass.
принеси́те (p) bring	**Принеси́те два стака́на.** Bring two glasses.
входи́те (i) come in	**Входи́те, пожа́луйста.** Please come in.
помоги́те (p) help	**Помоги́те нам.** Help us.

(c) The rarest ending is **-ь(те)**. This is the ending for verbs whose stems, like the verbs in (b), end in a consonant but have the stress on the stem of the **я** ('I') form, e.g.:

забы́ть (p) 'to forget': (**я забу́ду, ты забу́дешь**), stem **забу́д-**, stress **забу́ду**, so the imperative is **забу́дьте** 'forget':

Не забу́дьте! Don't forget. (This is a common warning.)

отве́тьте (p) answer	**Отве́тьте на вопро́с.** Answer the question.
позво́льте (p) permit	**Позво́льте мне уйти́.** Permit me to leave.

174

быть, which has no pres tense, forms its imperative from the fut forms **я бу́ду, ты бу́дешь**, stem **бу́д-** (14.1). Since the stress is on the stem, the imperative is **бу́дьте**:

Бу́дьте здоро́вы! Be healthy!
(Russians use the phrase when someone sneezes, like 'Bless you')

NOTE If the verb is reflexive, add **-ся** after **-й** and **-ь**, and add **-сь** after **-и** and **-те**:

Улыба́йся!/Улыба́йтесь!	Smile! → улыба́ться (i) (ты улыба́ешься) to smile
Сади́сь/Сади́тесь!	Have a seat/Sit down → сади́ться (i) (я сажу́сь, ты сади́шься) to sit down

15.3 Choice of aspect in the imperative

Requests (perfective)

Скажи́те (р), **пожа́луйста, где здесь кино́.**	Could you tell me where the cinema is? (lit. 'Say please where here is the cinema')
Принеси́те (р), **пожа́луйста, ко́фе.**	Please bring me some coffee.
Переда́йте (р), **пожа́луйста, хлеб.**	Would you pass the bread?
Возьми́те (р) **э́тот биле́т.**	Take this ticket.
Переда́й (р), **пожа́луйста, са́хар.**	Please pass (fam) the sugar.

In Russian shops you are often not allowed to examine an item (e.g. a book in a bookshop) without first asking an assistant to show it to you:

Покажи́те (р) [pa-ka-zhí-tye], **пожа́луйста, э́ту кни́гу.**
Please show me that book.

Negative commands (imperfective)

Не говори́те (i) **ей об э́том.**	Don't tell her about this.
Не покупа́йте (i) **э́то вино́.**	Don't buy that wine.
Не уходи́те (i)**.**	Don't go away.

NOTE **Не забу́дьте** (<u>perfective</u>) ('Don't forget') is a warning that something might happen rather than a command. Compare English 'Mind you don't forget'. Such warnings (in which you could use 'Mind …' in English) are perfective in Russian.

Invitations (imperfective)

Входи́те (i)**, пожа́луйста.**	Do come in, please.
Сади́тесь (i)**.**	Do take a seat.

Repeated actions (imperfective)

Пиши́те (i) **мне ка́ждый день.**	Write to me every day.

Exercise 65

Translate these imperative sentences into English:

1 **Приходи́те** (i) **к нам за́втра.**

2 **Скажи́те** (p)**, пожа́луйста, где здесь ка́сса** (cash desk)**?**

3 **Не волну́йтесь** (i) (14.10)**, она́ обяза́тельно позвони́т.**

4 **Пожа́луйста, помоги́те** (p) **мне найти́ моего́ дру́га.**

5 **Позвони́** (p) **нам за́втра.**

15.4 Exceptional imperative forms

пить (i)/**вы́пить** (p) 'to drink' (14.9): imper **пе́йте** (i)/**вы́пейте** (p)

Verbs ending -ава́ть keep the -ав- (missing in the pres stem), so дава́ть (i) 'to give' (я даю́) (12.8) has дава́йте 'give', 'let's'. See also вы́йдите 'go out' and поезжа́йте 'go' in 15.6.

15.5 'let's': дава́й(те)

The imperative дава́й/дава́йте is used in the construction 'let's do something' with the 1st person pl perfective future, e.g.:

Дава́йте пойдём.
Let's go.

Дава́йте забу́дем об э́том.
Let's forget about that.

Дава́йте ку́пим три биле́та.
Let's buy three tickets.

Дава́йте вы́пьем за мир.
Let's drink to peace.

Exercise 66

Say in Russian using the imperative forms given above:

1 Would you give (p) me these books, please?

2 Show (fam) (p) me the photographs, please.

3 Bring (p) me a coffee, please.

4 Could you tell (p) us where Anna Ivanovna lives?

5 Please help (p). I don't know where my hotel is.

6 Don't go away (i).

7 Do sit down (i).

8 Please buy (p) me (to me) 'Pravda'.

9 Bless you (Be healthy) (pol/pl).

10 Let's drink to her health.

Optional exercise 67
(If you've learnt the rules in 15.2)

Form the imperatives from the following verbs (12.2, 12.3):

1	**(Улыбну́ться)** (p)!	Smile!
2	**(Поня́ть)** (p) меня́ пра́вильно.	Understand me correctly. (Don't misunderstand me)
3	**(Сде́лать)** (p) э́то, пожа́луйста.	Do this please.
4	**(Верну́ться)** (p)!	Come back!
5	Не **(задава́ть)** (i) таки́е вопро́сы.	Don't ask such questions.

15.6 Vocabulary

находи́ться [na-ha-de'e-tsa] (i) (2) я нахожу́сь, ты нахо́дишься	to be, be located
вы́йти (p) (1B) (из + gen) я вы́йду, ты вы́йдешь (imper вы́йдите)	to go out (of)
поверну́ть (p) (1B) я поверну́, ты повернёшь	to turn
напра́во	to the right
у́г(о)л prep углу́	corner
вход [fhot]	entrance
записа́ть (p) (1B) я запишу́, ты запи́шешь	to note down
поезжа́йте (i)/(p) [pa-ye-zháy-tye]	go (travel) (used as imper of both е́хать and пое́хать)
до (+ gen)	as far as, until
остано́вка [a-sta-nóf-ka]	stop
вы́ход [ví-hat]	exit
спра́ва	on the right
пря́мо	straight, straight on

успева́ть (i) (1) (+ p infin)	to have time (to do something)
после́дний, -яя (f), -ее (n), -ие (pl) (adjectives ending -ний all have these endings)	last (see table 5)
фра́за	phrase
по + dat	along
сле́ва	on the left
бу́дьте внима́тельны (special adj called a short adjective)	be careful/pay attention (set phrase)
заме́тить (p) (2)	to notice
я заме́чу, ты заме́тишь	
совреме́нный	modern
рома́н	novel (also 'love affair' 13.6)
слова́рь (m)	dictionary
найти́ (p) (1B)	to find
я найду́, ты найдёшь	
иска́ть (i) (1B) stem ищ- + acc/gen	to look for
я ищу́, ты и́щешь (imper ищи́те)	
обы́чный	usual
исчеза́ть (i) (1)	to disappear
я исчеза́ю, ты исчеза́ешь	
как то́лько	as soon as
попада́ть (i) (1)	to get (somewhere) (coll)
я попада́ю, ты попада́ешь	
прила́в(о)к	counter

CONVERSATION

Майк: Я хочу́ пойти́ в кни́жный магази́н «Берёзка». Пожа́луйста, покажи́те мне на пла́не, где он нахо́дится.

Ни́на: Смотри́те. Ва́ша гости́ница здесь, на у́лице Го́рького. Вы́йдите из гости́ницы, поверни́те напра́во, пото́м на углу́ вы уви́дите вход в метро́ Проспе́кт Ма́ркса.

Майк: Подожди́те мину́точку. Я хочу́ всё э́то записа́ть.

Ни́на: Поезжа́йте на метро́ до остано́вки Кропо́ткинская. Там найди́те вы́ход на пло́щадь. Спра́ва вы уви́дите Кропо́ткинскую у́лицу. Иди́те пря́мо …

Майк: Пожа́луйста, не говори́те так бы́стро. Я не успева́ю. Повтори́те после́днюю фра́зу.

Ни́на: Извини́те. Вы уви́дите Кропо́ткинскую у́лицу. Иди́те пря́мо по э́той у́лице. Сле́ва вы уви́дите магази́н «Берёзка». Бу́дьте внима́тельны, э́то ма́ленький магази́н. Мо́жно его́ не заме́тить.

Майк: Я хочу́ купи́ть совреме́нные рома́ны и хоро́шие словари́. Мне сказа́ли, что о́чень тру́дно найти́ таки́е кни́ги в моско́вских магази́нах.

Ни́на: Да, не ищи́те их в обы́чных кни́жных магази́нах. Хоро́шие кни́ги исчеза́ют, как то́лько попада́ют на прила́вок. Но э́тот магази́н то́лько для иностра́нцев. Там всё есть.

Nina and Mike were talking before the name changes of the early 1990s. **У́лица Го́рького** is now **Тверска́я**; the metro station **Проспе́кт Ма́ркса** is now **Охо́тный ряд**; **Кропо́ткинская у́лица** is now **Пречи́стенка**.

TRANSLATION

M: I want to go to the 'Beriozka' bookshop. Would you show me on the map where it is?

N: Look. Your hotel is here, in Gorky Street. Go out of the hotel, turn right, then at the corner you'll see the entrance to the metro station 'Marx Prospekt'.

M: Wait a moment. I want to note all this down.

N: Take (lit. 'Go on') the metro as far as the stop called 'Kropotkinskaya'. There find the exit to the square. On the right you'll see Kropotkinskaya Street. Go straight on ...

M: Please don't speak so quickly. I can't keep up. Would you repeat the last phrase?

N: I'm sorry. You'll see Kropotkinskaya Street. Go straight on along this street. On the left you'll see the 'Beriozka' shop. Be careful (set phrase), it's a small shop. You can miss it (fail to notice it).

M: I want to buy modern novels and good dictionaries. I've been told that it is very difficult to find such books in Moscow shops (prep pl – see 18.10, 18.11).

N: Yes, don't look for them in the ordinary bookshops (i.e. where Soviet citizens shopped with roubles) (книжных магазинах is prep pl – see 18.10). Good books disappear as soon as they reach the shops (lit. 'get onto the counter'). But that shop is only for foreigners. It has everything.

Exercise 68

Using the structures in the conversation, give the following directions in Russian.

1 Go out of the shop.

2 Turn right.

3 Go straight on, then turn left.

4 Take the metro to the station Kitay-gorod [kee-tay-gó-rat] ('China-town').

5 Find the exit onto the square.

6 Go straight on along Kitaysky Prospekt (**Китáйский проспéкт**).

7 On the right you will see the Hotel Russia.

Chapter 16

- Instrumental case.
- Russian names.
- Forms of address.

16.1 Instrumental case

The last case we have to deal with is a very distinctive one. Its primary meaning is 'by means of' – it is the case form for the <u>instrument</u> used to do something, as in

She wrote <u>with (by means of) a pencil</u>. **Она́ писа́ла карандашо́м** [ka-ran-da-shóm].
Here the **-ом** on **каранда́ш** 'pencil' means 'by means of'.

16.2 Other uses of the instrumental

The instrumental has three other main uses which are not connected with the primary meaning:

(a) after six prepositions

с with (don't confuse it with **с** + gen, meaning 'from')
за behind
ме́жду between
над above
пе́ред in front of, before
под under

Познако́мьтесь <u>с</u> Ната́шей.
    Meet (become acquainted with) Natasha.

(b) with parts of the day and the seasons of the year to mean 'in' or 'during'

у́тром in the morning → у́тро morning
днём in the afternoon день (m) day
ве́чером in the evening ве́чер evening
но́чью during the night ночь (f) night
весно́й in spring весна́ spring
ле́том in summer ле́то summer
о́сенью in autumn о́сень (f) autumn
зимо́й in winter зима́ winter

(c) after a number of verbs of which the commonest are

быть (i) to be
стать (p) (1B) to become: я ста́ну, ты ста́нешь
  (see 16.4b)
занима́ться (i) (1) to occupy oneself with, to study:
  я занима́юсь, ты занима́ешься

16.3 Instrumental of the personal pronouns

Nom Instrumental

я мной [mnoy]
ты тобо́й [ta-bóy]
он им [(y)eem] (ним [neem] after prepositions)
она́ ей [yey] (ней [nyey] after prepositions)
оно́ им [(y)eem] (ним [neem] after prepositions)
мы на́ми [ná-mee]
вы ва́ми [vá-mee]
они́ и́ми [(y)eé-mee] (ни́ми [neé-mee] after prepositions)

с ним with him
ме́жду на́ми between us
пе́ред ва́ми in front of you

16.4 Formation of the instrumental singular of nouns

(a) Masculine and neuter nouns ending with a consonant or -о in the nom have -ом in the instrumental:

каранда́ш pencil   карандашо́м with (by means of) a pencil
у́тро morning   у́тром in the morning

(b) Masculine nouns ending with -ь or -й and neuter nouns ending -e replace the -ь, -й or -e with -ем (-ём if stressed):

учи́тель teacher   Он стал учи́телем. He became a teacher.
д(е)нь day   днём during the day/during the afternoon
мо́ре sea   мо́рем by sea

(c) All nouns (m or f) ending -a have -ой in the instrumental:

зима́ winter   зимо́й in winter
Ни́на Nina   за Ни́ной behind/after Nina

(d) All nouns (m or f) ending -я have -ей (-е́й if stressed):

О́ля Olya   с О́лей with Olya
семья́ family   с её семьёй with her family

(e) Feminine nouns ending with a soft sign add ю:

о́сень autumn   о́сенью in autumn

NOTE Remember that the second 'spelling rule' (8.11) will affect the endings of nouns whose last consonant is ж, ц, ч, ш or щ. When the ending is unstressed, -ом becomes -ем and -ой becomes -ей:

муж husband   с му́жем with a husband
Са́ша Sasha   с Са́шей with Sasha
америка́н(е)ц an American   с америка́нцем with an American

Exercise 69

Say in Russian:

1   I was writing with a pencil.

2   He is with us.

3   She works in the evening.

4   Between the hotel and the square.

5   She became a teacher.

16.5 Instrumental plural

There are only two endings for all genders:

(a) **-ами**, if the nom sing ends in a consonant, **-а** or **-о** and the nom pl does <u>not</u> end **-я**.

Sing	Nom pl	Inst pl	
дом	дома́	дома́ми	ме́жду дома́ми between the houses
кни́га	кни́ги	кни́гами	под кни́гами under the books
письмо́	пи́сьма	пи́сьмами	с пи́сьмами with letters

(b) **-ями**, if the nom sing ends in **-ь**, **-я** or **-е**, or if the noun has an irregular <u>nominative plural</u> ending **-я** (8.6), in which case **ями** replaces the **я** of the plural ending:

Sing	Nom pl	Inst pl	
мо́ре	моря́	моря́ми	за моря́ми beyond the seas
брат	бра́тья	бра́тьями	с его́ бра́тьями with his brothers
друг	друзья́	друзья́ми	стать друзья́ми to become friends

Exceptions: three common nouns whose inst pl ends **-ьми́**:

дочь daughter	**до́чери**	**с дочерьми́**	with daughters
ребёнок child	**де́ти**	**с детьми́**	with children
челове́к person	**лю́ди**	**с людьми́**	with people

16.6 Instrumental of adjectives and possessives

If the nominative adjective ends **-ый** or **-о́й**, the masculine and neuter inst is **-ым**. If it ends **-ий,** the inst is **-им**. Feminine adjectives have **-ой** or **-ей**, exactly the same endings as in the sing of the gen, dat and prepositional.

In the plural, all genders have **-ыми** or, for adjectives spelt with **-ий** in the nom sing, **-ими**.

мой, твой etc. (table 6) all have **-им** (m and n sing), **-ей** (f sing), **-ими** (pl).
э́тот has m/n **э́тим**, f **э́той**, pl **э́тими**.

встре́ча с интере́сным челове́ком
 a meeting with an interesting person

Познако́мьтесь с мои́м бра́том и с его́ но́вой жено́й.
 Meet (become acquainted with) my brother and
 his new wife.

За́втра бу́дет встре́ча с интере́сными ру́сскими студе́нтами.
 Tomorrow there will be a meeting with interesting
 Russian students.

Я писа́ла э́тим кра́сным карандашо́м.
 I was writing with this red pencil.

Бори́с стал хоро́шим инжене́ром.
 Boris became a good engineer.

Мы занима́емся ру́сским языко́м.
 We are studying Russian.

Ни́на рабо́тает с ма́ленькими детьми́.
 Nina works with small children.

Exercise 70

Translate the sentences and fill in the gaps with the required forms of the instrumental:

1 **За́втра бу́дет встре́ча с на́ш(   ) но́в(   ) учи́тельниц(   ).** [sing, NB 8.11]

2 **Познако́мьтесь с мо(́) ру́сск(   ) (друг   ).** [pl]

3 **Мно́гие ру́сские же́нщины ста́ли хоро́ш(   ) инжене́р(   ).** [pl]

4 **Вы пойду́те с (де́ти   ) в кино́?** [pl]

5 **Вы говори́ли с э́т(   ) (лю́ди   )?** [pl]

16.7 Russian names

If you have read Russian novels in English translation, you will know that a Russian's name tends to turn up in a confusing variety of forms. A Russian's birth certificate shows <u>three</u> names (no more, no less). The first is a <u>given name</u> (**и́мя** [n]) which for men ends in a consonant, soft sign or **й** (**Ива́н, Влади́мир** [one of the commonest], **Бори́с, Никола́й, И́горь**) and for women in **-а, -я** or a soft sign (**Татья́на** [currently very popular], **О́льга, Ната́лья, Любо́вь**). The second is the <u>father's name</u> plus **-ович** (**-евич** from names ending **-ь** or **-й**) for sons and **-овна** (**-евна**) for daughters. This name is called **о́тчество** [ó-<u>chye</u>-stva] 'patronymic'.

Ива́нович	[ee-vá-na-veech *or* ee-vá-nich] son of **Ива́н**
Никола́евич	[nee-ka-lá-ye-veech *or* nee-ka-lá-eech] son of **Никола́й**
Петро́вна	[pye-tróv-na] daughter of **Пётр**
Серге́евна	[syer-gyé-(ye)-vna] daughter of **Серге́й**

NOTE Patronymics are often shortened in speech: see the examples above.

The third name is the <u>family name</u> (фами́лия), normally ending -ов, -ев, -ёв, -ин, or -ын for men (Ивано́в, Бре́жнев, Горбачёв, Ле́нин, Голи́цын) and -ова, -ева, -ёва, -ина, or -ына for women (Ивано́ва, Цвета́ева, Каре́нина). Some Russian surnames are adjectives, e.g. Достое́вский, so the feminine form ends -ая (e.g. Достое́вская). Thus in a list of surnames the ending will normally reveal who is male and who is female. Non-Russian names such as Черне́нко (Ukrainian) or Смит (English) do not have feminine forms; the only clue to sex here is the grammar: women's names ending in a consonant do not decline (5.7). So письмо́ от Д. Сми́та (gen after от 'from') is 'a letter from Mr D. Smith', while письмо́ от Д. Смит is 'a letter from Mrs/Miss/Ms D. Smith'.

Russians who call each other вы generally address each other with the first name and patronymic. So if Бори́с Петро́вич Ивано́в meets his acquaintance Ната́лья Влади́мировна Попо́ва, the conversation begins

– Здра́вствуйте, Ната́лья Влади́мировна.
– Здра́вствуйте, Бори́с Петро́вич.

The use of the first name and patronymic is a mark of respect. A younger person will use them to older people (e.g. to friends' parents), though older people may use just the first name in reply.

When you are introduced to someone with whom you are likely to have repeated dealings, you should ask for the person's и́мя 'first name' and о́тчество 'patronymic' (Как ва́ше и́мя и о́тчество?) and use them at subsequent meetings.

When Russians move on to ты terms, they use the first name without the patronymic, but in these circumstances the first name is usually converted into one of its so-called 'diminutive' or 'intimate' forms (like Bill or Billy from William, or Maggie from Margaret, but there are far more of these forms in Russian and every name has several). Here are some typical examples:

MALE FIRST NAMES		FEMALE FIRST NAMES	
Full form	*Diminutive*	*Full form*	*Diminutive*
	(= intimate)		
Алекса́ндр	Са́ша	Алекса́ндра	Са́ша
Алексе́й	Алёша	Еле́на	Ле́на
Бори́с	Бо́ря	Ири́на	Йра
Влади́мир	Воло́дя	Ната́лья	Ната́ша
Ива́н	Ва́ня	О́льга	О́ля
Никола́й	Ко́ля	Татья́на	Та́ня

Note that both male and female diminutives end in **-а** or **-я** and are declined as feminine nouns (**Я зна́ю Ва́ню**). But of course male diminutives take masculine adjective and verb agreements (**Наш Ко́ля роди́лся в Ту́ле** 'Our Kolya was born in Tula').

In addition to these 'standard' diminutive forms, used by everyone who is intimate enough to use the first name, there are large numbers of other possible diminutive forms of each name. These forms are more intimate and will be used by family members and very close friends. For example, in addition to the standard diminutive form **О́ля** from **О́льга** there are also **Лёля**, **О́ленька**, **О́лечка**, **Ольгу́нечка**, **Ольгу́нчик**, **Ольгу́ня**, **Ольгу́ша**, **Ольгу́шка**, **О́лька** (a form to use when you're cross with her), and about another forty variants, most of them rare.

16.8 Russians and foreigners

Russians addressing foreigners will often use the title associated with the foreigner's language. So British and Americans are **ми́стер**, **ми́ссис** or **мисс**, the French are **мосье́** or **мада́м**, Germans are **герр**, **фрау** etc. The foreigner addressing Russians has more of a problem, since the Russians do not have any generally used equivalents of Mr/Mrs/Miss. Since the Russians themselves address acquaintances (people they call **вы**) with the first name and patronymic (e.g. **Ива́н Петро́вич** – see 16.7), your politeness and effort will be appreciated if you take the trouble to remember and pronounce these double names – which can be something of a tongue-twister if the patronymic is a long one like **Все́володович** [fsyé-va-la-da-veech]. However, if you do not know the first name and patronymic, it is permissible for foreigners to use the pre-revolutionary term **господи́н** ('gentleman') for 'Mr' and **госпожа́** ('lady') for Mrs or Miss; occasionally Russians use these words to address foreigners (**госпожа́ Тэ́тчер** 'Mrs Thatcher').

16.9 Vocabulary

познако́мить (p) **я познако́млю,** **ты познако́мишь** + acc + **с** + inst	[pa-zna-kó-meety]	to introduce someone to someone
с + inst		with
познако́миться (p)	[NB -<u>tsa</u>] **с** + inst	to become acquainted
кем (inst of **кто**)	[kyem]	by whom (here 'as whom')
а́нгло- **америка́нский**	[án-gla-a-mye …]	Anglo- American
шко́ла	[shkó-la]	school
уговори́ть (2) (p) **я уговорю́,** **ты уговори́шь** (+ acc)	[oo-ga-va-reéty]	to persuade (someone)
стать (1B) (p)	[staty] (+ inst)	to become (something)
инжене́р	[een-zhe-nyér]	engineer
счита́ть (1) (i) **я счита́ю,** **ты счита́ешь** (+ acc + inst)	[shshee-táty]	to count, consider (something to be something)
маши́на	[ma-shí-na]	machine, car
ску́чный	[skoósh-ni NB]	boring
я дово́лен (m)	[da-vó-lyen] (+ inst)	I am satisfied (with)
я дово́льна (f)	[da-vóly-na]	I am satisfied (set phrases)
не пра́вда ли?	[nye práv-da lee?]	isn't it?
я согла́сен (m)	[sa-glá-syen] **с** + inst	I agree (with someone)

я согла́сна (f)	[sa-glá-sna]	I agree (set phrases)
ма́мочка	[má-mach-ka]	intimate form of 'mother'
разреши́те (p)	[raz-rye-shí-tye]	permit (imper)
предста́виться (p)	[pryet-stá-vee-tsa]	to introduce oneself
фами́лия	[fa-mée-lee-ya]	surname
о́тчество	[ó-chyest-va]	patronymic
познако́мьтесь (p) с + inst	[pa-zna-kómy--tyesy]	meet; become acquainted (imper) with
жена́ (pl жёны)	[zhe-ná] [zhó-ni]	wife
дочь (f)	[dochy]	daughter

adds **-ep-** before endings: pl до́чери (see 8.6)

ско́лько тебе́ лет?	[skóly-ka]	how old are you (fam)?

CONVERSATION

Бори́с: Джейн, я хочу́ познако́мить тебя́ со свое́й ма́мой. Ма́ма, э́то Джейн. Мы с ней познако́мились почти́ четы́ре ме́сяца наза́д.

Джейн: О́чень прия́тно с ва́ми познако́миться. Как ва́ше и́мя и о́тчество?

Ма́ма: Кла́ра Миха́йловна. Ка́жется, вы прие́хали в Москву́ о́сенью? Кем вы рабо́таете, Джейн?

Джейн: Я рабо́таю учи́тельницей в а́нгло-америка́нской шко́ле.

Ма́ма: Да, Бо́ря то́же хоте́л стать учи́телем, но мы с му́жем уговори́ли его́ стать инжене́ром. Снача́ла он счита́л рабо́ту с маши́нами ску́чной, но тепе́рь он дово́лен свое́й рабо́той, не пра́вда ли, Бо́ренька?

Бори́с: Да, тепе́рь я с тобо́й согла́сен, ма́мочка.

TRANSLATION

B: Jane, I want to introduce you to (acquaint you with) my mother. Mother, this is Jane. We met (became acquainted) almost four months ago.

J: Pleased to meet you (It is very pleasant with you to become acquainted). What (how) are your first name and patronymic?

M: Klara Mikhaylovna. I think (it seems) you came to Moscow in the autumn. What do you do (As whom do you work), Jane?

J: I'm a teacher at the Anglo-American school.

M: Yes, Boris also wanted to become a teacher, but my husband and I (we with husband) persuaded him to become an engineer. At first he thought working with machines was boring (he considered work with machines boring) but now he is satisfied with (by) his job, aren't you (is it not truth), Borenka (intimate diminutive form)?

B: Yes, now I agree with you, mother.

Exercise 71

Translate the two dialogues:

K: Здра́вствуйте.

C: Здра́вствуйте.

K: Разреши́те предста́виться. Моя́ фами́лия – Кузнецо́в.

C: О́чень прия́тно. Меня́ зову́т Майкл Смит. А как ва́ше и́мя и о́тчество?

K: Бори́с Петро́вич.

C: Здра́вствуйте, Бори́с Петро́вич.

K: Здра́вствуйте, ми́стер Смит. Познако́мьтесь с мое́й жено́й. Э́то Ната́лья Алекса́ндровна. А э́то моя́ дочь Ле́на.

C: Здра́вствуйте, Ната́лья Алекса́ндровна. Здра́вствуй, Ле́на. Ско́лько тебе́ лет?

Д: Здра́вствуйте. Мне шесть.

Exercise 71A

Work out the first name of the father of each of the following:

1   Алекса́ндр Влади́мирович Серебряко́в

2   Еле́на Андре́евна Серебряко́ва

3   О́льга Алекса́ндровна Смит

4   Лев Васи́льевич Бро́дский

5   Илья́ Петро́вич Смирно́в

6   Татья́на Льво́вна Попо́ва

7   Влади́мир Ильи́ч Ле́нин

Chapter 17

- Ordinal numbers.
- The time.
- Dates.

17.1 Ordinal numbers (adjectives)

Revise the numbers and the grammar of numbers in chapter 9, then learn the ordinal (adjective) number words:

пе́рвый	first
второ́й [fta-róy]	second
тре́тий [tryé-tee]	third
An exceptional adj: the forms you need to know are тре́тья (f), тре́тье (n) and тре́тьего (m + n gen)	
четвёртый [chyet-vyór-ti]	fourth
пя́тый	fifth
шесто́й	sixth
седьмо́й [syedy-móy]	seventh
восьмо́й [vasy-móy]	eighth
девя́тый	ninth
деся́тый	tenth
оди́ннадцатый [a-dée-na-tsa-ti]	eleventh
двена́дцатый [dvye-ná-tsa-ti]	twelfth
трина́дцатый [tree-ná-tsa-ti]	thirteenth
четы́рнадцатый [chye-tír-na-tsa-ti]	fourteenth
пятна́дцатый [peet-ná-tsa-ti]	fifteenth
шестна́дцатый [shest-ná-tsa-ti]	sixteenth
семна́дцатый [syem-ná-tsa-ti]	seventeenth
восемна́дцатый [va-syem-ná-tsa-ti]	eighteenth
девятна́дцатый [dye-veet-ná-tsa-ti]	nineteenth
двадца́тый [dva-tsá-ti]	twentieth

два́дцать пе́рвый	twenty-first
тридца́тый [tree-tsá-ti]	thirtieth
сороково́й [sa-ra-ka-vóy]	fortieth
пятидеся́тый [pee-tee-dye-syá-ti]	fiftieth
шестидеся́тый [she-stee-dye-syá-ti]	sixtieth
семидеся́тый [sye-mee-dye-syá-ti]	seventieth
восьмидеся́тый [vasy-mee-dye-syá-ti]	eightieth
девяно́стый [dye-vee-nó-sti]	ninetieth
со́тый	hundredth

All these forms are adjectives. All except **тре́тий** have the same endings as **но́вый** or **молодо́й** (see 7.4).

17.2 Telling the time

'What time is it?' **Кото́рый час?** (lit. 'Which hour?')
You may also hear: **Ско́лько вре́мени?** (lit. 'How much of time?') (**вре́мени** is gen of **вре́мя** (n) 'time'.)

Exact hours use the word **час** 'hour' for 'o'clock':

It is one o'clock.	**Час.** ('(It is) hour') (lit. <u>оди́н</u> **час** but оди́н is always omitted)
It is 2, 3, 4 o'clock.	**Два, три, четы́ре часа́.** (gen sing after 2, 3, 4 – see 9.3)
It is six o'clock.	**Шесть часо́в.** (gen pl after 5 and upwards – see 9.3)

Between the full hour and half past, you need the ordinal (adjective) form of the numbers, because the hour from twelve to one is called in Russian 'the first hour' (**пе́рвый час**), one to two is 'the second hour' (**второ́й час**), two to three o'clock is 'the third hour' (**тре́тий час**) and so on. You also need the word **мину́та** 'minute', which becomes **мину́ты** (gen sing) after 2, 3, and 4, and **мину́т** (gen pl) after other numbers (see 9.3). 'Five past one' is lit. 'five minutes of the second hour (gen)':

Пять мину́т второ́го [fta-ró-va].
   It is five past one.

Сейча́с пятна́дцать мину́т тре́тьего.
   It is now a quarter past two. (fifteen minutes of the third)

Два́дцать две мину́ты пя́того.
It is twenty-two minutes past four.

'half' is **полови́на:**

Полови́на оди́ннадцатого.
It is half past ten. (lit. 'half of the eleventh [hour]')

Сейча́с полови́на тре́тьего.
It is now half past two. ('half of the third')

<u>Work out the following times in Russian, covering the answers on the right:</u>

10 minutes past four	**де́сять мину́т пя́того**
25 minutes past ten	**два́дцать пять мину́т оди́ннадцатого**
22 minutes past eleven	**два́дцать две мину́ты двена́дцатого**

From the half hour to the following hour ('ten to six' etc.) Russian uses the preposition **без** 'without' + gen (9.4, 10.5):

It is ten to six.	**Без десяти́ шесть.**
It is twenty-five to one.	**Без двадцати́ пяти́ час.**
It is three minutes to twelve.	**Без трёх мину́т двена́дцать.**

You will see from the examples that Russian numbers have case endings just as nouns do (table 7). The nom + acc forms of all numbers except **оди́н** (see 9.2) are the same, but the genitive forms are as follows:

Nom	*Gen*	
два	**двух** [dvooh]	
три	**трёх** [tryoh]	
четы́ре	**четырёх** [chye-ti-ryóh]	
пять	**пяти́** [pee-teé]	}
шесть	**шести́** [she-steé]	} These **-ь**
семь	**семи́** [sye-meé]	} numerals have
во́семь	**восьми́** [vasy-meé]	} the endings of
де́вять	**девяти́** [dye-vee-teé]	} soft sign
де́сять	**десяти́** [dye-see-teé]	} feminine
оди́ннадцать	**оди́ннадцати**	} nouns.
двена́дцать	**двена́дцати**	}
etc.	with **и** ending and stress on the stem (but **двадцати́**)	

197

Без десяти́ шесть is literally '(It is) without ten (gen) six'. That is, you name the following hour **шесть (часо́в)** and subtract the required numbers from it using **без** + gen.

NOTE As in English, if the number of minutes is not divisible by five the word 'minutes' (gen pl **мину́т**) must be inserted:

It is four minutes to eight.   **Без четырёх мину́т во́семь.**

From this example you will also see that the form of **мину́т** is gen plural, not singular, after the form of 'four' **четырёх**. So we must modify the rule given in 9.3: if 2, 3, or 4 is in the nom or acc, the following noun is gen sing, BUT if 2, 3 or 4 is itself in the gen, the following noun is in the gen plural.

Exercise 72

Work out the following times in Russian:

1   (It is) ten to two.

2   (It is) twenty to eleven.

3   (It is) a quarter (fifteen) to three.

4   (It is) three minutes to one (as in 'one o'clock' above).

5   (It is) one minute to twelve (NB **оди́н** has endings like **э́тот**).

6   (It is) half past five.

7   (It is) a quarter (fifteen minutes) past ten.

17.3 At a time

Answering the question 'When?' **Когда́?** Russians say:

at three o'clock **в три часа́** (at a full hour: just add **в**)
at half past two **в полови́не** (prep) **тре́тьего** ('in half of third')

'At ten past two' and 'At ten to three' use the same constructions as in the constructions for 'It is ten past/to two', i.e.:

Boris left at ten past ten.
    Бори́с уе́хал де́сять мину́т оди́ннадцатого.

Jane rang at ten to twelve.
    Джейн позвони́ла без десяти́ двена́дцать.

am/pm
To express am or pm, you can either use the 24-hour clock (formal style) with the words **час** and **мину́та** and **в** for 'at':

5.30 am   **пять часо́в три́дцать мину́т**
9.15 pm (21.15)   **два́дцать оди́н час пятна́дцать мину́т**

The train arrived at 11.37 pm.
    По́езд пришёл в два́дцать три часа́ три́дцать семь мину́т.

Or in spoken Russian this division of the day and night is used:

ночь	'night' midnight to 4 am:	3 am **три часа́ но́чи** ('3 of the night')
у́тро	'morning' 4 am to midday:	6 am **шесть часо́в утра́** ('6 of the morning')
день (Russian has no word for 'afternoon')	'day' midday to 6 pm.:	4 pm **четы́ре часа́ дня** ('4 of the day')
ве́чер	'evening' 6 pm to midnight:	11 pm **оди́ннадцать часо́в ве́чера** ('11 of the evening')

Exercise 73

Translate into Russian using **утра́, дня** *etc.:*

1 At 3 am (at three of the night)

2 At 6.30 pm (say 'half past six [of the seventh] of the evening')

3 At a quarter (use **пятна́дцать** 'fifteen') to four in the afternoon.

4 In Moscow it is one in the morning.

In <u>official</u> style you will hear the **час** and **мину́та** construction, e.g. on Russian radio stations:

Моско́вское вре́мя – два́дцать часо́в три́дцать мину́т.
  Moscow time [three hours ahead of London, eight ahead of New York] is 20.30 (8.30 pm).

'Twenty-three hundred hours' is **два́дцать три ноль-ноль.**

17.4 The date

First we need the names of the months. Note that they are all masculine, so the prepositional of all ends **-e** (e.g. **в январе́**) and the genitive is **-a** for **март** and **а́вгуст** and **-я** for all the others.

	Nom		*Gen*	
January	янва́рь	[yeen-váry]	января́	[yeen-va-ryá]
February	февра́ль	[fyev-rály]	февраля́	[fyev-ra-lyá]
March	март	[mart]	ма́рта	[már-ta]
April	апре́ль	[a-pryély]	апре́ля	[a-pryé-lya]
May	май	[may]	ма́я	[má-ya]
June	ию́нь	[ee-yoóny]	ию́ня	[ee-yoó-nya]
July	ию́ль	[ee-yoóly]	ию́ля	[ee-yoó-lya]
August	а́вгуст	[áv-goost]	а́вгуста	[áv-goo-sta]
September	сентя́брь	[syen-tyábry]	сентября́	[syen-tee-bryá]

October	октя́брь	[ak-tyábry]	октября́	[ak-tee-bryá]
November	ноя́брь	[na-yábry]	ноября́	[na-yee-bryá]
December	дека́брь	[dye-kábry]	декабря́	[dye-ka-bryá]

'What is the date today?' is **Како́е сего́дня число́?** ('What today (is) date?'). **число́** [chee-sló] literally means 'number'.

To give the answer, you need the ordinal numerals (see 17.1 above) in their <u>neuter</u> form, agreeing with the noun **число́**. The month is in the gen (like '<u>of</u> June', '<u>of</u> September').

Сего́дня деся́тое ма́рта. 'Today is the tenth of March.' (The word **число́** is always omitted, just as in English we omit the word 'day' in 'the tenth (day) of March'.)

'In + month' is **в** + prep: 'in January' **в январе́**.

'<u>On</u> + date' is the <u>genitive</u> (ending **-ого**) of the number adjective: **семна́дцатого октября́** 'on the seventeenth of October'.

Exercise 74

Translate:

1 За́втра четы́рнадцатое а́вгуста.

2 Два́дцать второ́е апре́ля – день рожде́ния Ле́нина.

3 Мы прие́дем два́дцать тре́тьего ию́ля.

4 We shall be in Moscow in December.

5 Today is the third of September.

6 Natasha's birthday is on the thirty-first of January.

17.5 The days of the week

Monday	понеде́льник ('after Sunday day' from the old word for 'Sunday' неде́ля 'not do day' which now means 'week')	
Tuesday	вто́рник [ftór-neek]	('second day')
Wednesday	среда́	('middle day')
Thursday	четве́рг [chyet-vyérk]	('fourth day')
Friday	пя́тница	('fifth day')
Saturday	суббо́та [soo-bó-ta]	('sabbath')
Sunday	воскресе́нье [vas-krye--syé-nyye]	('resurrection')

'On + day of the week' is в + acc:

on Wednesday	в сре́ду [fsryé-doo] (NB stress change)
on Thursday	в четве́рг [fchyet-vyérk]
on Tuesday	во вто́рник (о is added to в if the following word begins with two or more consonants of which the first is в or ф)

So 'on Friday the third of June' is в пя́тницу тре́тьего ию́ня.

17.6 Years

The year (e.g. 1988) in Russian is an ordinal numeral, i.e. the last figure has an adjective ending and the word 'year' год should always be added (in writing you can use the abbreviation г. after the figures):

'1988' is ты́сяча девятьсо́т во́семьдесят восьмо́й год 'thousand nine hundred eighty-eighth year' (usually written 1988 г.).

'In + year' is в + prep:

in 1988   в 1988 г.   to be read as в ты́сяча девятьсо́т во́семьдесят восьмо́м году́. -ом is the prepositional adjective ending. Году́ is the prep case of год.

In Russian it is normal to omit the century when it is obvious:

in 1948   в со́рок восьмо́м году́ (= 'in forty-eight')

If the month is included, use **в** + prep for the month and genitive for the year, i.e. Russians say 'in June of the 1948th year': **в ию́не (ты́сяча девятьсо́т) со́рок восьмо́го го́да.**

Exercise 75

Translate:

1   **В четве́рг двена́дцатого апре́ля ты́сяча девятьсо́т се́мьдесят тре́тьего го́да.**

2   **Ле́нин роди́лся в ты́сяча восемьсо́т семидеся́том году́.**

3   I will be there on Wednesday.

4   We were in Moscow in 1984.

17.7 'since'/'from' (с + gen), 'until' (до + gen), 'after' (по́сле + gen)

These three prepositions can be used with all the time and date words given in 17.2–17.6. Try these examples, covering the translations.

с пяти́ [gen] **часо́в**	since five o'clock
по́сле девяти́ (часо́в) ве́чера	after nine (o'clock) in the evening
до полови́ны тре́тьего	until half past two
Я бу́ду здесь до пя́того ма́я.	I shall be here until 5 May.
с во́семьдесят шесто́го го́да	since (19)86
по́сле тре́тьего ма́рта	after the third of March
до девяно́сто пя́того го́да	until (19)95

'from ... to' is **с ... до** (you will also meet **от ... до**):

The shop is open ('works') from 10 to 6.
   Магази́н рабо́тает с десяти́ часо́в до шести́ (часо́в).

17.8 Giving your age

The Russian for 'I am twenty' is literally 'To me (is) twenty', so you need the dat case (see 12.6 and 14.4 for the forms). Note that год 'year' has gen sing гóда (after 2, 3, 4) but gen pl лет (lit. 'summers', from лéто 'summer').

Скóлько вам (pol) лет? ⎫	How old are you? (lit. 'How
Скóлько тебé (fam) лет? ⎭	many to you of years?')
Мне двáдцать лет.	I am twenty.
Лéне шесть лет.	Lena is six.
Борúсу трúдцать одúн (год).	Boris is thirty-one (years old).

Make the past with бы́ло and the future with бýдет.

Лéне бы́ло шесть лет.	Lena was six.
Борúсу бýдет трúдцать одúн.	Boris will be thirty-one.

17.9 Vocabulary

прóшлый	last, previous
на прóшлой недéле	last week
пóздно [póz-na NB]	late
потомý что [pa-ta-moó-shta]	because
конферéнция	conference
знáчит [zná-cheet]	(common filler word like 'um'/'eh'; lit. '(it) means', 8.14)
уезжáть (i) (1) [oo-ye-zháty] я уезжáю, ты уезжáешь	to leave (by transport)
рóдина	homeland
на рóдину	to one's homeland
кон(é)ц [ka-nyéts]	end
побéда	victory
вы́йти зáмуж (p) (за + acc) [zá-moosh]	to marry (of a woman) (lit. to go out after a husband)
рáно	early
так-тáк	(another filler, like 'hmm')
порá (+ infin)	it is time (to do something)

жени́ться (i/p) (2) [zhe-nee-tsa]
я женю́сь, ты же́нишься
(на + prep)
начина́ться (i) (1)
фильм начина́ется [na-chee-
-ná-ye-tsa]

to marry (of a man) (to
take a wife)

to begin (intransitive)
the film begins

Exercise 76

Translate the conversation:

Boris's father talks to Jane

СИ: Здра́вствуйте, Джейн. Ка́жется, вы
познако́мились с мое́й жено́й на про́шлой неде́ле.
Меня́ зову́т Серге́й Ива́нович.

Дж: Здра́вствуйте, Серге́й Ива́нович. О́чень прия́тно.
Кла́ра Миха́йловна мне сказа́ла, что вы верну́лись
по́здно, потому́ что вы рабо́тали до восьми́ часо́в.

СИ: Да, обы́чно я прихожу́ домо́й в полови́не
седьмо́го, но в пя́тницу была́ конфере́нция ... Гм.
Вы давно́ в Москве́, Джейн?

Дж: С про́шлого сентября́.

СИ: А когда́ вы бы́ли в Москве́ пе́рвый раз?

Дж: В апре́ле се́мьдесят шесто́го го́да, когда́ я ещё
учи́лась в шко́ле. Я сра́зу полюби́ла и Росси́ю, и
ру́сских люде́й.

СИ: А когда́ вы уезжа́ете на ро́дину?

Дж: Я бу́ду рабо́тать здесь до конца́ ию́ля.

СИ: Прости́те, ско́лько вам лет, Джейн?

Дж: Два́дцать семь. Я родила́сь в шестьдеся́т пе́рвом
году́, в ма́е.

→

СИ: Бори́с мне сказа́л, что ваш день рожде́ния восьмо́го ма́я. А он роди́лся девя́того ма́я, в День Побе́ды. Зна́чит, два́дцать семь. Зна́чит, вы, наве́рно, ско́ро вы́йдете за́муж.

Дж: Что вы, Серге́й Ива́нович. Мне ещё ра́но. Моя́ ма́ма вы́шла за́муж, когда́ ей бы́ло три́дцать два го́да.

СИ: Так-та́к. А вам не ка́жется, что Бори́су уже́ пора́ жени́ться? Ему́ три́дцать оди́н.

Дж: Ну, э́то его́ де́ло. Кста́ти, где он? Я его́ жду с пяти́ часо́в. Мы идём в кино́. Фильм начина́ется без пятна́дцати семь.

Exercise 77

Say in Russian:

1 What time is it?

2 It's three o'clock.

3 Half past ten.

4 Ten to six.

5 Three minutes to two.

6 Eleven at night.

7 At half past one.

8 In 1950.

9 In January 1958.

10 On Monday 25 January 1988.

11 I work from ten in the morning until six in the evening.

12 How old are you (pol)?

13 I am 26.

14 How old is your wife?

15 My wife is 30.

Exercise 78

What is the date and time of the performance?

Chapter 18

- Conditional mood.
- Comparative.
- The remaining case endings (dative and prepositional plural).

18.1 Conditional sentences with 'would' (бы)

Look at these examples:

Джейн позвони́ла Бори́су, когда́ она́ верну́лась в Москву́.
Jane rang Boris when she returned to Moscow.

Джейн позвони<u>ла</u> <u>бы</u> Бори́су, <u>е́сли бы</u> она́ верну<u>лась</u> в Москву́.
Jane <u>would</u> have rung Boris <u>if she had</u> returned to Moscow.

To make a 'would'-type conditional sentence from a non-conditional one, all you have to do is add **е́сли** ('if') **бы** [bi] and a second **бы** after the verb in the other clause (the consequence) and make both verbs past tense.

<u>Е́сли бы</u> я знал ру́сский язы́к (1st clause), я чита́<u>л бы</u> Достое́вского в оригина́ле. (2nd clause).
Lit. 'If would I knew Russian language, I read would Dostoyevsky in original.'

Since Russian has only one past tense, this sentence, depending on the context, could in English be either 'If I knew Russian, I would read Dostoyevsky in the original' or 'If I had known Russian, I would have read Dostoyevsky in the original.'

The rules for the choice of aspect are the same as in sentences without **бы**.

When I have money, I buy tickets to the theatre.
   Когда́ у меня́ есть де́ньги, я покупа́ю биле́ты в теа́тр.

If I had money now, I would buy tickets to the theatre.
   Éсли бы у меня́ сейча́с бы́ли де́ньги, я купи́л (p) **бы биле́ты в теа́тр.**

If I had money, I would buy [frequently] tickets to the theatre.
   Éсли бы у меня́ бы́ли де́ньги, я покупа́л (i) **бы биле́ты в теа́тр.**

You can also use the conditional in polite requests, as in English:

Я хоте́л бы пойти́ в рестора́н.
   I would like ('would want') to go to a restaurant.

and in conditional sentences without an 'if' clause:

Бы́ло бы лу́чше ('better') **пойти́ в кино́.**
   It would be (*or* would have been) better to go to the cinema.

Exercise 79

Say in Russian:

1   If Jane had known (i), she would have telephoned (p).

2   If I lived (i) in Moscow, I would speak (i) Russian.

3   I would like to meet (get to know) (p) your sister.

4   If you (pol) were a woman, you would understand (i).

18.2 чтобы

The particle **бы** combines with **что** ('that') to form the conjunction **чтобы** which is used with the verb **хотéть** (6.5) when someone wants somebody else to do something:

I want you to come at six.
Я хочý, чтóбы вы пришлú в шесть часóв. (lit. 'I want that you came at six').

Boris wants Jane to phone him.
Борúс хóчет, чтóбы Джейн емý позвонúла.

NOTE As in the **бы** 'would' construction in 18.1, the verb after **чтóбы** is always <u>past tense</u> in form (never present or future).

Exercise 80

Say in Russian:

1   I want him to know.

2   We want Boris to come (p) tomorrow.

3   They don't want us to wait (i).

чтóбы can also be used with an infinitive to mean 'in order to':

Чтóбы купúть билéты, нáдо позвонúть по этому телефóну.
In order to buy tickets it is necessary to ring this phone number.

18.3 Comparative of adjectives and adverbs

Here are some common comparatives:

better	лу́чше [loó-che NB]	→	хоро́ший
cheaper	деше́вле [dye-shé-vlye]		деше́вый cheap
easier	ле́гче [lyéh-chye NB]		лёгкий easy
larger	бо́льше [bóly-she]		большо́й
less	ме́ньше [myény-she]		ма́ленький
longer	длинне́е [dlee-nyé-ye]		дли́нный long
more	бо́льше [bóly-she]		большо́й
more beautiful	краси́вее [kra-seé--vye-ye]		краси́вый
more difficult	трудне́е [trood-nyé-ye]		тру́дный
more expensive	доро́же [da-ró-zhe]		дорого́й
more interesting	интере́снее [...-ryé--snye-ye]		интере́сный
more often	ча́ще [chá-shshye]		ча́сто
nicer	прия́тнее [pree-yát--nye-ye]		прия́тный
quicker	быстре́е [bi-stryé-ye]		бы́стрый
slower	ме́дленнее [myé-dlye--nye-ye]		ме́дленный
smaller	ме́ньше [myény-she]		ма́ленький
worse	ху́же [hoó-zhe]		плохо́й bad

These are also the comparatives of the equivalent adverbs ending in -o (хорошо́ well, бы́стро quickly etc.).

All these forms are indeclinable. Since many of these comparatives are very irregular in formation, it is better simply to learn them as new vocabulary items. They are used like this:

Э́то бы́ло бы лу́чше.
That would be better.

Э́тот фильм бу́дет интере́снее.
This film will be more interesting.

Москва́ краси́вее.
Moscow is more beautiful.

If you want to say 'than', use **чем** [chyem]:

Э́та су́мка деше́вле?
Is this bag cheaper?

Э́та су́мка деше́вле, чем кра́сная?
Is this bag cheaper than the red one?

In colloquial Russian, instead of **чем** the gen is preferred:

Э́та су́мка деше́вле кра́сной? (gen adj)
Is this bag cheaper than (lit. 'of') the red one?

Ру́сский язы́к трудне́е, чем япо́нский?
Is Russian more difficult than Japanese?

Нет, ру́сский ле́гче япо́нского.
No, Russian is easier than Japanese.

Э́тот фильм бу́дет интере́снее того́ фи́льма, кото́рый вы смотре́ли вчера́ *or* **интере́снее, чем тот фильм ...**
This film will be more interesting than the (that) one you saw yesterday.

NOTE **тот** 'that' can be used when you want to contrast 'that' with 'this' **э́тот** – for its declension see table 4.

18.4 Formation of comparatives

Learn the common ones above and note these general points:

(a) if the adjective/adverb ends **-ный/-но, -лый/-ло, -рый/ -ро** or **-вый/-во**, replace the **-ый/-о** with **-ее** (often stressed **-е́е**), e.g. **интере́снее, холодне́е** 'colder'.
(b) most other adjectives have a change of last consonant and the ending **-е: лёгкий: ле́гче** 'easy: easier'.
(c) some common adjectives have unpredictable comparatives, as in English: e.g. **хоро́ший: лу́чше** 'good: better' and **плохо́й: ху́же** 'bad: worse'.
(d) you can also form the comparative by simply placing the word **бо́лее** [bó-lye-ye] 'more' (which is another form of the comparative of **большо́й**) before the adjective/adverb:

Кни́га бо́лее интере́сная, чем фильм.
    The book is more interesting than the film.

In this construction, the adjective form is the same as if **бо́лее** was not present (**Кни́га интере́сная.** 'The book is interesting') and for 'than' only **чем** can be used (<u>not</u> the gen).

NOTE The differences between the **-e/-ee** comparative (18.3) and the construction with **бо́лее** are as follows:

(a) if the comparative is followed by the noun it qualifies ('a more interesting book'), the **бо́лее** form is used:

   I want to buy a more interesting book.
   Я хочу́ купи́ть бо́лее интере́сную кни́гу.

(b) if the construction is of the type 'something is/was/will be/would be + comparative adj' with <u>no</u> following noun, the **-e/-ee** form is <u>preferred</u>, particularly in spoken Russian:

   This wine is cheaper.
   Э́то вино́ деше́вле (rather than **бо́лее деше́вое**).

<u>However</u>, since the **бо́лее** construction is easier, foreigners often prefer to use it. It is not wrong to say **Э́то вино́ бо́лее деше́вое** (instead of **Э́то вино́ деше́вле**). If the comparative you want to use is not in the list above, simply use **бо́лее** with the adjective.

18.5 'much' with comparatives

'Much' is **намно́го** (literary) or **гора́здо** (colloquial):

Э́та кни́га гора́здо доро́же.
    This book is much more expensive.

Кни́га намно́го интере́снее фи́льма (*or*, **чем фильм**).
    The book is much more interesting than the film.

18.6 'less' (ме́нее)

'Less' is **ме́нее** [myé-nye-ye], placed before the adj/adverb:

Э́та кни́га ме́нее интере́сная, чем фильм.
This book is less interesting than the film.

Сего́дня ме́нее хо́лодно.
It's less cold today.

18.7 Superlative ('most interesting', 'largest' etc.)

In Russian, simply place the word **са́мый** [sá-mi], which declines like **но́вый**, in front of the adjective:

са́мая интере́сная кни́га
the most interesting book

Он хо́чет купи́ть са́мую дешёвую во́дку.
He wants to buy the cheapest vodka.

NOTE There is a special adj **лу́чший** [loó-chi NB] meaning 'best':

Э́то лу́чшая гости́ница.
This is the best hotel.

18.8 'more' (бо́льше) and 'less'/'fewer' (ме́ньше)

In quantity constructions **бо́льше** and **ме́ньше** behave like quantity words (9.7) and take the genitive.

We need more money.	**Нам ну́жно бо́льше де́нег** (gen). (lit. 'more of money')
There is less room here.	**Здесь ме́ньше ме́ста.** (lit. 'less of place')

Exercise 81

Say in Russian:

1 This hotel is better.

2 Russian is more difficult than English.

3 In Tula we spoke Russian more often.

4 Boris has less money than Jane has.

5 Which vodka is cheaper?

6 This film is the most interesting.

18.9 'a little faster'

In spoken Russian, the **-e/-ee** indeclinable comparatives (18.3) are often prefixed with **по-** (meaning 'a little'): **побыстрée** [pa-bi-stryé-ye] 'a little faster', **почáще** [pa-chá-shshye] 'a little more often'. The **по-** often shows politeness rather than littleness.

Приходи́те к нам почáще.	Do come and see us more often (lit. 'Come to us a little more often').
Побыстрée!	Please hurry up! (lit. 'A bit faster!')
Я хочý купи́ть биле́т подеше́вле.	I would like a somewhat cheaper ticket (lit. 'I want to buy a ticket (which is) a little cheaper.')

Exercise 82

Say in Russian:

1   St. Petersburg is more beautiful than Moscow, but Moscow is more interesting.

2   This room is worse than the first one.

3   Perhaps it would be better to telephone (p).

4   This seat (place) will be better.

5   Which town is the most interesting?

6   The other hotel is much better.

7   Hurry up (quicker), please!

18.10 Dative and prepositional plural of nouns

These are our last two noun endings and the rarest ones. They are straightforward. <u>All</u> dat plurals end either **-ам** or **-ям**. Simply remove the **и** from the end of the inst plural (16.5):

де́вушкам to the girls   **бра́тьям** to the brothers

The three nouns with irregular inst plural endings (**-ьми́**) have the regular ending **-ям** in the dat:

де́тям to the children

The prepositional plural is **-ах** or **-ях**. Simply replace the **м** of the dat plural with **x**:

о де́вушках about the girls

о бра́тьях   about the brothers

о де́тях   about the children

18.11 Dative and prepositional plural of adjectives

The adjective endings are:
-ым (но́в<u>ым</u>) or -им (ру́сск<u>им</u>, хоро́ш<u>им</u>) for the dat pl
-ых (но́в<u>ых</u>) or -их (ру́сск<u>их</u>, хоро́ш<u>их</u>) for the prep pl

NOTE The dat pl = the m/n inst sing and the prep pl = the gen pl:

э́т<u>им</u> ста́р<u>ым</u> лю́дям (dat)	to these old people
в ста́р<u>ых</u> ру́сск<u>их</u> города́х (prep)	in old Russian towns
на краси́в<u>ых</u> моско́вск<u>их</u> у́лицах (prep)	in attractive Moscow streets

---

Exercise 83

Add the correct plural endings and translate:

1 Я бу́ду писа́ть пи́сьма сво́___ но́в___ ру́сск ___ друзь___.

2 Я говори́л о сво́___ но́в___ ру́сск___ друзь___.

3 Мно́гие иностра́нцы же́нятся на ру́сск___ де́вушк___.

4 Мы бы́ли в э́т___ город___.

18.12 Vocabulary

ти́ше (comp of ти́хий 'quiet')	quieter
вы пра́вы	you are right (set phrase)
обе́дать (i) (1)	to dine, have a meal
я обе́даю, ты обе́даешь	
нра́виться (i) (2) (+ dat of person)	to please
мне нра́вится Ната́ша	I like Natasha ('to me pleases Natasha')
стиль (m)	style

капстрана́ (капиталисти́ческая страна́)	capitalist country
что́бы [shtó-bi]	(in order) to
охо́тно	willingly
грани́ца	border
за грани́цу	abroad ('over the border')
расчёт [ra-shshyót]	calculation
по расчёту	based on calculation
действи́тельно	really, indeed
план	plan
скры́тный	secretive
религио́зный	religious
це́рк(о)вь (f)	church
да́же	even
дружи́ть (i) (2) с + inst	to be friendly with
я дружу́, ты дру́жишь они́ дру́жат (8.4)	
свяще́нник	priest
безусло́вно	undoubtedly
у́мный	intelligent
умне́е	more intelligent
встреча́твся (i) (1)	to meet (with), see someone
я встреча́юсь, ты встреча́ешься	
официа́нтка (gen pl официа́нток)	waitress
наконе́ц	at last
подходи́ть (i) (2) (к + dat)	to come up (to)
я подхожу́, ты подхо́дишь	
принести́ (p) (1B)	to bring
я принесу́, ты принесёшь	
пе́рвое (n adj)	first (course) (soup)
борщ	beetroot soup
второ́е (n adj)	second (course) (main course)
шашлы́к	kebab, pieces of meat on a skewer
спу́тница	(female) companion
котле́ты по-ки́евски	Chicken Kiev
бефстро́ганов	Beef Stroganoff
вку́сный	tasty
заку́ски (pl of заку́ска)	hors d'oeuvre
икра́	caviare

гриб	mushroom
сметáна	sour cream
прекрáсно	fine, splendid
пóрция	portion
трéтье (n adj)	third (course) (dessert)
морóженое (n adj)	ice cream
чай	tea
варéнье	jam
возражáть (i) (1)	to object

18.13 CONVERSATION

Sergey Ivanovich and Tatyana Nikolayevna meet for a
meal in the International (**«Междунарóдная»**) Hotel in
Moscow's International Trade Centre (**Междунарóдный
торгóвый центр**) on the Krasnopresnenskaya
(**Краснопрéсненская**) Embankment of the Moscow-River
(**Москвá-рекá**). The hotel, built for the 1980 Olympics,
marked the arrival of the West in Moscow, with a huge
atrium, fountains, artificial trees and glass-sided lifts.

СИ: Здесь тúше, чем в другúх москóвских ресторáнах.

ТН: Вы прáвы, Сергéй Ивáнович [ee-vá-nich], но
гостúница Метропóль красúвее. Éсли бы я былá
инострáнным турúстом, я хотéла бы жить в
стáрой гостúнице. И я обéдала бы в такúх
ресторáнах, как Арáгви и Узбекистáн.

СИ: А мне бóльше нрáвится совремéнный стиль.
Я так хотéл бы поéхать в капстранý, чтóбы
посмотрéть, как там живýт в большúх городáх.
Но, навéрно, я никогдá не смогý поéхать.

ТН: А ваш Борúс поéдет? Кáжется, емý óчень
нрáвится эта англичáнка Джейн Óльдридж.

СИ: Так вы знáете об этом? Так-тáк. По-мóему, он
охóтно женúлся бы на ней.

ТН: Тóлько для тогó, чтóбы поéхать за гранúцу?

→

СИ: Не то́лько. Коне́чно, мы с жено́й не хоти́м, что́бы он жени́лся по расчёту, но нам ка́жется, что он действи́тельно лю́бит её.

ТН: Коне́чно, мно́гие ру́сские же́нятся на иностра́нках. А она́? Каки́е у неё пла́ны?

СИ: Как вам сказа́ть, Татья́на Никола́евна? Я её не совсе́м понима́ю. Англича́не таки́е скры́тные лю́ди. Кро́ме того́, мне ка́жется, что она́ о́чень религио́зный челове́к. Она́ ча́сто хо́дит в це́рковь, е́здит в Заго́рск, да́же дру́жит с одни́м свяще́нником там. Безусло́вно, она́ интере́снее и умне́е, чем Ната́ша, но Ната́ша симпати́чнее. Мы так хоте́ли, что́бы он жени́лся на Ната́ше, но тепе́рь он с ней почти́ не встреча́ется. А, вот официа́нтка, наконе́ц. Мы ждём уже́ два́дцать мину́т.

(Подхо́дит официа́нтка. *The waitress comes up.*)

Оф: Что принести́?

СИ: Пожа́луйста, на пе́рвое принеси́те нам борщ, пото́м на второ́е мне шашлы́к, а мое́й спу́тнице котле́ты по-ки́евски.

Оф: Возьми́те лу́чше бефстро́ганов. Он сего́дня вусне́е, чем шашлы́к. А заку́ски?

СИ: Гм. Икра́ есть?

Оф: Икры́ нет. Есть грибы́ в смета́не.

СИ: Прекра́сно. Две по́рции, пожа́луйста. А на тре́тье моро́женое и чай с варе́ньем.

Оф: Сейча́с принесу́.

ТН: Вы бы хоте́ли, что́бы ваш сын жени́лся на иностра́нке?

СИ: А вы бы хоте́ли, что́бы ва́ша дочь вы́шла за́муж за иностра́нца? Ва́ша Ни́на о́чень дру́жит с ми́стером Сми́том.

ТН: Я не возража́ла бы. Но они́ про́сто друзья́.

TRANSLATION

SI: It's quieter here than in other Moscow restaurants.

TN: You're right, Sergey Ivanovich, but the Metropol Hotel is more attractive. If I were a foreign tourist (inst after **быть**) I would want to live in an old hotel. And I would dine in such restaurants as the Aragvi (Georgian) and the Uzbekistan (Central Asian cooking).

SI: I like the modern style more. I would like so much to go to a capitalist country to see what life is like there in the big cities. But I'll probably never be able to go.

TN: But will your son Boris go? He seems to be very interested in that English girl Jane Aldridge.

SI: So you know about that. Hmm-hmm. I think he would willingly marry her.

TN: Just in order to go abroad?

SI: Not just for that. Of course my wife and I don't want him to make a marriage of convenience, but it seems to us that he really does love her.

TN: Of course, many Russian men marry foreigners. And what about her? What are her plans?

SI: What can I say, Tatyana Nikolayevna? I don't really understand her. The British ('English') are so secretive. It also seems to me that she's a very religious person. She often goes to church and to Zagorsk and she even has a friend who's a priest there. Undoubtedly she is more interesting and intelligent than Natasha, but Natasha is nicer. We were so keen that he should marry Natasha, but now he hardly sees her at all. Ah, there's the waitress at last. We've been waiting for twenty minutes.

W: What (am I) to bring?

SI: We'd like beetroot soup for the first course, then for the main course I'll have a kebab and my companion will have Chicken Kiev.

W: You'd do better to have (lit. 'take better') the Beef Stroganoff. It's better than the kebab today. What about hors d'oeuvre?

SI: Hm. Is there any caviare?

W: No. There are mushrooms in sour cream.

SI: Splendid. Two portions please. And for dessert (we'll have) ice cream and tea with jam.

W: I'll bring (things) straightaway.

TN: Would you want your son to marry a foreigner?

SI: And would you want your daughter to marry one? Your Nina is very friendly with Mr Smith.

TN: I wouldn't object. But they are simply friends.

Chapter 19

We have now covered the basic grammar and vocabulary
you will need for reading, comprehension and simple
conversations in the kinds of situations you might have
to deal with when visiting Russia. Now we can tackle
some more complex communication skills you may need
for certain types of everyday activity.
- Filling in forms.
- Writing notes and letters.
- Telephoning.

19.1 Writing English names in Russian letters

You should know the basic principles for transcribing
English words into Russian, if only to make sure that
Russians know what you are called. The main point is that
English names are transcribed according to their
pronunciation, not according to the letters. (By contrast,
Russian words are spelt in English according to the letters,
not the pronunciation: **Горбачёв** pronounced [gar-ba-chyóf]
is transcribed 'Gorbachev'.) Thus a surname like Leigh is
transcribed **Ли** (not **Леигх**) because **Ли** is the closest
Russian equivalent of the sound of the word. The following
points may help:
(a) The Russian **ы** is never used to transcribe English i.
    By tradition **и** is used instead, so Nick is **Ник**.
(b) **x** is now used for h (not **г**, though **г** was the norm in the
    nineteenth century), so Harry is **Харри**.
(c) Double letters are represented by double letters even
    when no double sound is audible (Harry = **Харри**).
(d) th is **т**, so Thistlethwaite is **Тисльтуэйт**.

(e) э or е can be used for English e and short a: Benn can be either **Бэнн** or **Бенн**. Lamb can be either **Лэм** or **Лем** (Lamb could also be **Лам** if that is closer to your English pronunciation).

(f) The English article 'the', quite a problem for Russians to pronounce, is always omitted in transcription, so the *News of the World* is **«Ньюс оф уорлд»**.

(g) Russians tend to hear English l's as soft, so Liverpool is **Ливерпуль,** but use your own English pronunciation as a guide.

Mary Smith	**Мэри** or **Мери** or **Мэйри Смит**
John Dunn	**Джон Данн**
Bill Hetherington	**Билл** or **Билль Хэ**(or **е**)**тэ**(or **е**)**рингтон**
Elisabeth Wilson	**Элизабет** or **Элизабэт Уил**(**ь**)**сон**
The *Guardian*	**«Гардиан»**

Exercise 84

Write the following in Cyrillic (Russian) letters:

George;   Patricia;   Birmingham;
Brown;   Michael;   The Beatles

19.2 Addressing people in writing

If writing to a friend, you can use **Дорогóй/Дорогáя** 'Dear' as in English, followed by the short (diminutive) form of the first name (see 16.7):

Дорогáя Натáша!

You can also begin

Здрáвствуй, Натáша!

Suitable endings to the letter or note are **Целýю** ('I kiss' from **целовáть** (i) 'to kiss') or **Обнимáю** ('I embrace') or **До скóрого** [da-skó-ra-va] ('Until soon') or **До свидáния** ('Goodbye').

224

For more formal notes, to people you call **вы**, use

Уважа́емый/Уважа́емая (pl: **Уважа́емые**)

'Respected', followed by the full first name and patronymic (see 16.7) plus exclamation mark:

Уважа́емая Татья́на Никола́евна!

The ending repeats the respect

С уваже́нием ('Yours sincerely', lit. 'With respect')

NOTE In letters, all forms of the pronoun **вы** have a capital.

Examples:

> **Уважа́емый Михаи́л Алекса́ндрович!**
> **Извини́те меня́ за то, что я не смогу́ встре́титься с Ва́ми в пя́тницу. Я то́лько сего́дня узна́ла, что в пя́тницу для на́шей делега́ции устра́ивают прие́м в америка́нском посо́льстве. Сообщи́те, пожа́луйста, согла́сны ли Вы перенести́ на́шу встре́чу на суббо́ту, когда́ я бу́ду весь день в гости́нице.**
> **С уваже́нием,**
> **Уильхэльми́на Дж. Уа́тэрспун**

Dear Mikhail Aleksandrovich,
I'm sorry that I won't be able to meet you on Friday. I only learned today that there will be a reception for our delegation at the American Embassy on that day. Please let me know if you are willing to postpone our meeting to Saturday, when I shall be in the hotel all day.
Yours sincerely,
Wilhelmina J. Wutherspoon

> **Дорога́я Ната́ша!**
> **Приходи́ сего́дня по́сле шести́. Бу́ду це́лый ве́чер до́ма.**
> **Целу́ю,**
> **Ни́на**

Dear Natasha,
Come today after six. I'll be at home the whole evening.
Love (I kiss), Nina

Russian addresses begin with the country and end with the name of the recipient:

Росси́я	Russia
Москва́ 117292	(6-figure postcode [и́ндекс])
Профсою́зная у́лица	(street name)
д. 11, кв. 135	(д = дом 'building' кв = кварти́ра 'apartment')
Серге́еву Н.Н.	(-у is the dative ending '<u>to</u> Mr N.N. Sergeyev')

HANDWRITING NOTE

Russians write the figures 1, 4, 7, 9: ₁ ц ₹ ₉

Exercise 85

Translate into Russian:

Dear Mrs Pyetrova [her и́мя and о́тчество are Татья́на Никола́евна],
    Thank you for your invitation [приглаше́ние]. I accept [принима́ю] it with pleasure [с удово́льствием].
    Yours sincerely,
        Michael Smith

Dear Andryoosha [intimate form of Andrey]
    Please phone me this evening after six. My telephone in the hotel is 711-41-44.
    Love,
        Barbara

Dear Dr Sergeyev,
    I would like (хоте́л бы) to receive a copy (ко́пия) of the very interesting report (докла́д) which you read (p) at the conference (на конфере́нции) on Wednesday. My name (и́мя) and address (а́дрес) are Dr Trevor Blunt, 716, Hotel Ukraina, Moscow. In exchange (в обме́н) I enclose (прилага́ю) a copy of my report.
    Yours sincerely,
        Trevor Blunt

19.3 Filling in forms

Russian forms have three blanks for your name:
Ф(ами́лия), **Й(мя)**, **О(тчество)**. As a foreigner you can
leave the **О** space blank (with the risk that a Russian might
think you don't know who your father is), or construct
yourself an **о́тчество** by adding **-ович** or **-овна** to your
father's name (**Реджинальдович**, **Джоновна**), or write in
your middle name if you have one. Under **национа́льность**,
the Russians mean ethnic origin, so you write English
(**англи́йская**), Scottish (**шотла́ндская**), Welsh (**валли́йская**),
Irish (**ирла́ндская**) etc., and under **по́дданство** your citizenship British (**брита́нское**), American (**америка́нское**). All
citizens of the Russian Federation (Russia) have a
национа́льность (Russian, Ukrainian, Kalmyk, Korean,
Jewish or whatever). To describe their citizenship, one can
use the word **россия́нин** (man) or **россия́нка** (woman),
which means 'inhabitant of Russia'.

19.4 Telegrams

For urgent business Russians much prefer telegrams to
letters. To write in Russian telegraphese, delete all
prepositions but leave the case endings.

ARRIVING TULA WEDNESDAY 8.15PM TRAIN 23
COACH 9 STOP MEET ON PLATFORM

**ПРИЕЗЖА́Ю [В] ТУ́ЛУ [В] СРЕ́ДУ [В] 2015 ПО́ЕЗД 23
ВАГО́Н 9 ТЧК [= то́чка] ВСТРЕЧА́ЙТЕ [НА]
ПЛАТФО́РМЕ**

19.5 Understanding the spoken language

Even if you have mastered all the basic grammar and
vocabulary, do not be disheartened if you find that radio
and TV broadcasts can be difficult to follow and that your
ability to comprehend Russian spoken at normal speed is
well behind your ability to make sense of written texts.
Good aural comprehension may well require months of

practice and will depend on such factors as how good your hearing is and how well you know the subject being discussed.

So you will probably prefer written messages in Russian to telephoning in Russian, at least in the early stages. However, Russians prefer to do everyday business by phone, given that the mail has a reputation for slowness.

19.6 Telephone conversations

Despite the universal use of telephones, Russians tend to be abrupt. When answering a call, they say **Да!** or **Слу́шаю** ('I'm listening') or **Алло́!** ('Hello'), never anything informative such as their name or number. When you ring offices you will often find that if the person you want isn't there or your request can't be dealt with immediately, the phone is banged down without a **До свида́ния**. So learn the phrase

Не клади́те тру́бку, пожа́луйста!
[nye kla-dée-tye troo-koo, pa-zhál-sta!]
Don't hang up, please!

and don't omit to point out

Извини́те, я иностра́нец/иностра́нка/америка́нец/ англича́нка ...
Excuse me, I'm a foreigner/an American/British ...

which should get you more considerate treatment.

If you don't know who you're speaking to, say

Прости́те, с кем я говорю́?
Excuse me, with whom am I speaking?

If it's the name of the institution or the address which matters, ask

Э́то гости́ница?
Is that the hotel?

Э́то кварти́ра Достое́вских?
Is that the Dostoyevskys' flat?

If it is not the person you want who answers, the instruction is:

Позови́те, пожа́луйста, Ни́ну/господи́на Черне́нко/Серге́я Ива́новича/дире́ктора.
> Please call (i.e. may I speak to) Nina/Mr Chernenko/ Sergey Ivanovich (see 16.7 on names)/the director.

If the person isn't available, you may be asked if you wish to leave a message (**А что ему́/ей переда́ть?** 'Is there a message?' lit. 'What to transmit to him/her?'). You say:

Переда́йте ему́/ей, пожа́луйста, что звони́л(а) …
> Tell him/her that … rang (followed by any necessary details).

Practise the phrases

Говори́те ме́дленнее, пожа́луйста.
> Speak more slowly, please.

Повтори́те, пожа́луйста.
> Please repeat.

Извини́те, я не по́нял(а́).
> Excuse me, I haven't understood.

19.7 Vocabulary

институ́т	institute
биохи́мия	biochemistry
попа́сть (p) (1B) (past **попа́л**)	to get (somewhere)
я попаду́, ты попадёшь	
извини́те (imper)	excuse me
поговори́ть (p) (2)	to have a talk with
слу́шать (i) (1) + acc	to listen to
я слу́шаю, ты слу́шаешь	
беспоко́ить (+ acc)	to worry, trouble
я беспоко́ю, ты беспоко́ишь	(somebody)
возмо́жно	possible; it is possible
соедини́те (imper) (**меня́**)	connect (me)
к сожале́нию	unfortunately, I regret
де́ло	matter, piece of business
ли́чный	personal
нача́льник	boss, chief, head

отде́л	section, department
бу́дьте добры́	be so good (pol request) (set phrase)
слы́шно	(it is) audible
заста́ть (р) (1B)	to find, come upon
я заста́ну, ты заста́нешь	(a person)
не расслы́шать (р) (1)	to mishear, fail to make out
я не расслы́шал(а)	I didn't catch (that)
спра́вочное (бюро́)	enquiry (office)
абоне́нт	subscriber
отде́льный	separate
коммуна́льный	communal
назови́те (imper)	name
представи́тель (m)	representative
фи́рма	firm
дире́ктор (pl директора́)	director, head, manager
за́нят (m) (занята́ f, за́няты pl)	occupied, busy (participle – 20.7)

Exercise 86

Translate the conversations:

1 Wrong number

A: Алло́!

B: Э́то институ́т биохи́мии?

A: Нет, э́то кварти́ра. Вы не туда́ попа́ли.

B: Извини́те.

2 Jane seeks Boris

A: Слу́шаю.

B: Вас беспоко́ит учи́тельница из А́нглии Джейн О́льдридж. Е́сли возмо́жно, соедини́те меня́ с Бори́сом Серге́евичем.

A: К сожале́нию, его́ сейча́с нет. Вы по како́му де́лу звони́те?

B: По ли́чному. Прости́те, с кем я говорю́?

A: С нача́льником отде́ла. Вы меня́ хорошо́ понима́ете?

B: Спаси́бо, я всё понима́ю. Но бу́дьте добры́, говори́те ме́дленно, пло́хо слы́шно. Когда́ Бори́с Серге́евич вернётся?

A: Че́рез час, наве́рно. А что ему́ переда́ть?

B: Пожа́луйста, переда́йте ему́, что я бу́ду ждать его́ звонка́ до́ма до пяти́ часо́в. По́сле пяти́ он смо́жет меня́ заста́ть у мои́х друзе́й. Их телефо́н сто два́дцать три – во́семьдесят де́вять – ноль шесть.

A: Прости́те, я не расслы́шал. Во́семьдесят де́вять и́ли се́мьдесят де́вять?

B: Во́семьдесят де́вять.

A: Хорошо́. Я переда́м.

B: Спаси́бо. До свида́ния.

A: До свида́ния, мисс О́льдуитч.

3 Telephone directories are not common in Russia. If you know the person's three names and address, dial directory enquiries (09).

A: Спра́вочное, но́мер три́дцать четы́ре.

B: Да́йте, пожа́луйста, телефо́н абоне́нта в Москве́.

A: Отде́льная кварти́ра и́ли коммуна́льная?

B: Отде́льная.

A: Фами́лия?

B: Серге́ев.

A: И́мя, о́тчество?

B: Ива́н Никола́евич.

A: Назови́те у́лицу.

B: У́лица Паусто́вского.

A: Четы́реста два́дцать пять – три́дцать оди́н – ноль два.

B: Спаси́бо.

4 A business call

A: Да!

B: Э́то институ́т биохи́мии?

A: Да.

B: Здра́вствуйте. С ва́ми говори́т Майкл Смит. Я представи́тель англи́йской фи́рмы «Брок энд Парсонс». Позови́те, пожа́луйста, дире́ктора.

A: Извини́те, Серге́й Ива́нович сейча́с за́нят. Позвони́те че́рез час.

Chapter 20

- Reading Russian.
- Participles.
- 'Gerunds'.

20.1 Reading Russian

If you have mastered the basic Russian grammar and vocabulary of the previous nineteen chapters, you can begin to start puzzling your way through unsimplified Russian texts in books and journals. This last chapter contains some guidelines on how to proceed plus a number of grammatical structures you are unlikely to use yourself but which you will meet in written texts.

20.2 Dictionaries

First you will need a dictionary. The largest and best currently available is *The Oxford Russian–English and English–Russian Dictionary*, compiled by Falla, Wheeler, Unbegaun and Howlett. Also good is the *Penguin English–Russian and Russian–English Dictionary*, compiled by Ryan and Norman. If you want something compact to carry around with you, the *Pocket Oxford Russian–English English–Russian Dictionary*, by Coulson, Rankin, Thompson and Howlett, is excellent. To help you increase your vocabulary and your reading speed, there is the *Russian Learners' Dictionary*, compiled by Brown and published by Routledge, which gives the 10,000 commonest words of Russian in their order of frequency.

20.3 Problems to note when using your dictionary

(a) Irregular verbs: getting from **е́ду** to the infinitive **е́хать** 'to go, travel' can be a problem if your dictionary does not provide cross references. Learn the main irregular verbs as you meet them in this book and note that prefixed verbs behave in exactly the same way as the unprefixed verbs from which they are derived. For example, **уе́хать** 'to go away', **перее́хать** 'to go across', **вы́ехать** 'to drive <u>out</u>' and all the other prefixed forms of **е́хать** conjugate like **е́хать** i.e. with the stem **е́д-**.

(b) Fleeting vowels (see 8.13). If a noun is missing from the dictionary, try inserting **е** or **о** between the last two consonants, e.g. you come across the word **потолка́**, but there is no word **потолк** in the dictionary. Try inserting **о** or **е** and you will find **потол(о́)к** 'ceiling'; if there is a soft sign between the last two consonants, replace it with **е**, e.g. the form **владе́льца** is from **владе́л(е)ц** 'owner'.

20.4 Idioms

But the main problem in reading Russian with a dictionary is likely to be idioms. You may find all the words but still not understand the meaning of the phrase. This is particularly the case with such common words as **ещё, и, бы, так, как, же**. Large dictionaries will list the commoner idioms (e.g. **как бы не так** 'how would not so', meaning 'not likely'; **ещё бы** 'still would', corresponding to 'I'll say', 'you bet', 'indeed'). In those cases where your dictionary doesn't help, the only solution is to consult a qualified teacher or bilingual speaker.

20.5 Russian word order

You may have noticed in earlier chapters that the order of words in Russian sentences is much more flexible than in English.

For 'Andrey married Barbara' Russian can have **Андре́й жени́лся на Ба́рбаре/На Ба́рбаре жени́лся Андре́й/На Ба́рбаре Андре́й жени́лся** and three other permutations. The general rule for written Russian is that the main information (or emphasis) comes at the end of the sentence or clause. In **На Ба́рбаре жени́лся Андре́й** the stress is on <u>who</u> married her, an emphasis which we can achieve in English by using the complicated structure 'It was Andrey who married Barbara'. In **На Ба́рбаре Андре́й жени́лся** the effect of putting the verb after the object is akin to saying 'Andrey did marry Barbara'.

20.6 Participles and 'gerunds'

In bookish Russian (more rarely in spoken or everyday Russian) you will frequently come across six types of verb participle. You will need to know what these participles mean, but you will not need to <u>use</u> them in your own Russian, because there is always some way of avoiding them. Four of these forms are called <u>participles</u> (**прича́стия**) and two of them are traditionally known in English as '<u>gerunds</u>' or <u>verbal adverbs</u> (in Russian **дееприча́стия**).

20.7 Past passive participle from p verbs

This is the commonest of these six forms. It corresponds to the English participle form 'done' in 'The work was/has been/will be <u>done</u> by our engineer', or 'invited' in 'Jane was/has been/will be <u>invited</u>'. Typically the form ends in **-ан** or **-ен** with a gender/number ending to match the subject, so if you meet a verb (always perfective) with the ending **-ан, -ана, -ано, -аны, -ен, -ена, -ено** or **ены**, it is a participle corresponding to an English form of the verb ending -ed (-t) or -en (-n):

Рабо́та <u>сде́лана</u> (→ сде́лать 'to do'**)**
The work (is) <u>done</u>.

Э́то <u>запрещено́</u> (→ запрети́ть 'to forbid'**)**
That is forbidden.

Биле́ты бу́дут <u>ку́плены</u> за́втра (→ купи́ть 'to buy'**)**
The tickets will be <u>bought</u> tomorrow.

As the last example shows, the past passive participle is generally formed from the same stem as the **я** form of the verb, e.g. **я ку<u>пл</u>ю́** 'I shall buy.'

There is also a past participle ending **-т, -та, -то** or **-ты** for irregular verbs whose infinitive does not end **-ать** or **-ить**. They are easy to identify:

взят taken → **взять** to take

за́нят occupied → **заня́ть** to occupy
закры́т closed → **закры́ть** to close

Магази́ны бы́ли закры́ты.
The shops were closed.

These participles can be used as adjectives and placed in front of nouns, in which case they have **-ый** adjective endings (like **но́вый**) and the **-н** forms have an extra **н**:

запреще́нные кни́ги
forbidden books

If the person responsible for the action is mentioned, the person is in the instrumental case (16.1–16.6):

Рома́н «Война́ и мир» был напи́сан Толсты́м.
The novel 'War and Peace' was written <u>by</u> Tolstoy.

20.8 Present passive participle from i verbs

The least common of the participles is the pres passive participle, corresponding to English 'being V-ed' (V being any transitive verb), e.g. люби́мый 'being loved' ('beloved') from люби́ть 'to love' (this word can also mean 'favourite'); получа́емый 'being received, obtained' (from получа́ть (i) 'to receive, get').

These rare participles are formed from imperfective verbs by adding the adjective ending **-ый** to the **мы** form of the pres tense, e.g. **люби́м + ый**. If you read scientific Russian you will meet a few:

Результа́ты, получа́емые в таки́х усло́виях, сомни́тельны.
    Results (which are) obtained in such conditions are doubtful.

20.9 Present active participle from i verbs

This corresponds to English participles ending -ing as in 'The man reading the paper is my uncle'. It is easily recognized by its distinctive ending containing **-щ-**. The vowel before the **щ** is always **я, ю, а** or **у**, and after the **щ** comes an adjective ending.

чита́ющий reading → **чита́ть** to read
выпуска́ющий publishing → **выпуска́ть** to publish

В Росси́и есть изда́тельства, выпуска́ющие кни́ги на англи́йском языке́.
    In Russia there are publishing houses publishing (= which publish) books in English.

In everyday Russian this active participle is replaced by **кото́рый** 'who', 'which' (see 7.9) + the pres tense:

изда́тельства, выпуска́ющие = изда́тельства, кото́рые выпуска́ют
    publishing houses publishing = publishing houses which publish

20.10 Past active participles from i/p verbs

These have the distinctive ending **-вш-** + adj ending. They can be formed from both imperfective and perfective verbs. The imperfective ones translate as verb + ing (like the pres active):

чита́<u>вший</u> (i) reading (= who/which was reading)

Изда́тельства, выпуска́<u>вшие</u> **(i) таки́е кни́ги, бы́ли закры́ты.**
> Publishing houses producing (= which produced) such books were closed.

The perfective ones are translated with 'who/which' + past tense:

написа́вший (p)
> who/which wrote

Писа́тель, <u>написа́вший</u> **э́ту кни́гу, молодо́й инжене́р.**
> The writer <u>who wrote</u> this book is a young engineer.

Generally speaking, it is easy to find the infinitive from past active participles. Simply remove the **-вш-** + adjective ending and add **-ть** (**-ться** if the participle has a reflexive **-ся**).

Я зна́ю люде́й, прочита́вших э́ту кни́гу с удово́льствием.
> I know people (participle) this book with pleasure.

прочита́вших is from **прочита́** + **ть** i.e. 'to read' (p)

> I know people who (have) read this book with pleasure.

In everyday Russian, these participles are avoided by the use of **кото́рый** (see 7.9):

Я зна́ю люде́й, кото́рые прочита́ли э́ту кни́гу с удово́льствием.
> I know people who (have) read this book with pleasure.

20.11 Imperfective gerund (only from i verbs)

This 'gerund' is another kind of participle, which is equivalent to English '(while/when) VERB-ing'. It ends **-я** (**-ясь** if reflexive).

де́лая	(while/when) doing
говоря́	(while/when) speaking
зна́я	(while/when) knowing

Зна́я, что он здесь, мы реши́ли уйти́.
> Knowing that he is (= was) here, we decided to leave.

Чита́я газе́ту, она́ узна́ла, что вы́ставка откро́ется в сре́ду.
> When/while reading the newspaper, she learnt that the exhibition would open on Wednesday.

To find the infinitive, take off the **-я** and you have the present tense stem of the verb. As the name tells you, this 'gerund' is formed only from imperfective verbs; it describes an action in process when something else (described in the main clause) takes place.

20.12 Perfective gerunds from p verbs

This participle, normally ending **-в** (**-вшись** if reflexive) corresponds to English 'having (verb)-ed'.

прочита́в	having read
улыбну́вшись	having smiled

Прочита́в кни́гу, я верну́ла её дру́гу.
> Having read (= After reading/When I finished reading) the book, I returned it to my friend.

To find the infin, simply remove the **-в** (**-вшись**) and add **-ть** (**-ться**).

Exercise 87

Translate the following:

1 В институ́те мно́го студе́нтов, изуча́ющих англи́йский язы́к.

2 Инжене́ры, рабо́тающие на Кра́йнем Се́вере, получа́ют больши́е де́ньги.

3 Здесь у́чатся студе́нты, прие́хавшие из Аме́рики.

4 Что напи́сано на э́том биле́те?

5 Здесь за́нято.

6 Возвраща́ясь домо́й, Бори́с встре́тил ста́рого дру́га.

7 Прочита́в газе́ту, Ни́на дала́ её Ма́йку.

8 Получи́в письмо́ Андре́я, Ба́рбара сра́зу отве́тила на него́.

20.13 Vocabulary

предложе́ние	proposal, offer
поду́мать (p) (1) (i ду́мать)	to think (for a
я поду́маю, ты поду́маешь	short while)
отказа́ться (p) (1В)	to refuse
я откажу́сь, ты отка́жешься	
призна́ться (p) (1)	to admit
я призна́юсь, ты призна́ешься	
жизнь (f)	life
семе́йный	family (adj)
сча́стье	happiness
гла́вный	main
объясни́ть (p) (2)	to explain
я объясню́, ты объясни́шь	
помога́ть (i) (1) (+ dat)	to help (someone)
я помога́ю, ты помога́ешь	

оказа́ться (p) (1B)	to turn out to be
оказа́лось	it turned out
ока́жется	it will turn out
го́ре	grief, sorrow
с го́ря	from sorrow
удиви́ть (p) (2)	to surprise
я удивлю́, ты удиви́шь	
глу́пость (f)	stupidity, something stupid
ско́ро	soon
ко́нчиться (p) (2)	to finish, come to an end
разойти́сь (p) (1B like идти́)	to split up (the prefix раз- means dis- as in disperse)
мы разойдёмся	we shall split up
мы разошли́сь	we have split up
жа́ловаться (i) (1) (на + acc)	to complain (about)
я жа́луюсь, ты жа́луешься	
разгова́ривать (i)	to converse, talk
я разгова́риваю, ты разгова́риваешь	
вести́ (i) (1B)	to lead, conduct
я веду́, ты ведёшь	
себя́	self, oneself
вести́ себя́	to behave, conduct oneself
наха́льно	impudently
пожени́ться (p) (2)	to get married (of a couple)
изда́тельство	publishing house
«Ра́дуга»	'Rainbow'
выпуска́ть (i) (1)	to produce, issue, release
я выпуска́ю, ты выпуска́ешь	
продолжа́ть (i) (1)	to continue
я продолжа́ю, ты продолжа́ешь	
переговоры (m pl)	talks, negotiations
организа́ция	organization
мини́стр	minister (in the government)

You should now have a vocabulary of over 800 Russian words.

Exercise 88

Translate the reading text:

EPILOGUE

Через месяц после того вечера, когда Джейн
познакомилась с его отцом, Борис сделал ей
предложение. Подумав, она отказалась. Она
призналась, что Борис ей очень нравится, но сказала,
что выйти за него замуж она не может, потому что
в её жизни семейное счастье не главное. Ничего не
объяснив, она уехала из Москвы. Только через три
месяца Борис узнал, что она решила стать
священником в Америке. Там ей помогал её друг Марк.
Оказалось, что он стал священником уже давно.
С горя Борис женился на Наташе. Все были очень
удивлены. Нина сказала, что её подруга сделала
глупость, но что скоро всё кончится. Действительно,
Борис и Наташа разошлись через пять недель.
Наташа жаловалась, что муж всё время
разговаривает с иностранками и ведёт себя нахально.

А Барбара стала часто приезжать в Россию. Три
месяца назад они с Андреем поженились. Барбара
уже хорошо говорит по-русски. Она будет
работать в Москве в издательстве «Радуга»,
выпускающем книги на английском языке.

Майк и Нина продолжают дружить. Он часто
приезжает в Москву как представитель фирмы
«Брок энд Парсонс» и ведёт переговоры с
русскими организациями. Нина вышла замуж за
Виктора, друга Андрея, недавно у них родилась
дочь Елена. Лет через десять Нина станет
директором большого завода в Узбекистане и лет
через тридцать министром.

Поздравля́ем!

Key to exercises

CHAPTERS 1–20

1 Exercise 1: 1 da-cha 'country cottage'. 2 ho-ro-sho 'good', 'well'.
3 do-bro-ye oo-tro 'good morning'. 4 vla-dee-meer 'Vladimir'.
5 pa-styer-nak 'Pasternak'. 6 tsyen-traly-niy ko-mee-tyet
'Central Committee (of the Communist Party)'. 7 am-styer-dam
'Amsterdam'. 8 nyyoo-york 'New York'. 9 av-to-mo-beely 'car'.
10 poch-ta 'post office'. 11 pee-vo 'beer'. 12 soo-vye-neer 'souvenir'. 13 lye-neen 'Lenin'. 14 too-a-lyet 'toilet'. 15 a-e-ro-port
'airport'. 16 ko-fye 'coffee'. 17 kony-yak 'cognac', 'brandy'.
18 byoo-ro 'office'. 19 zhyen-shshee-na 'woman'. 20 chye-lo-
vye-ko-nye-na-veest-nee-chye-stvo 'misanthropy' (lit. 'man-
hating-ness').

Exercise 2: The drink is Pepsi-Cola [pyep-see ko-la].

2 Exercise 3: 1 spa-seé-ba (unstressed **o** is [a]). 2 vót-ka (д [d]
pronounced [t] before к [k]). 3 da-svee-dá-nee-ya (preposition
read as part of following word, so до [do] is read as an
unstressed syllable [da]). 4 peé-va 'beer' (unstressed **o** is [a]).
5 spoót-neek 'sputnik'. 6 af-ta-ma-beély 'car' (в [v] becomes [f]
before [t], unstressed **o** is [a]). 7 ma-shí-na 'car' (и [ee]
pronounced [i] after ш [sh]). 8 yosh 'hedgehog' (ж [zh]
pronounced [sh] at the end of a word). 9 rye-sta-rá-ni
'restaurants' (pronounce [ry] as one sound, unstressed **o** is [a]).
10 dzhín-si 'jeans' (и [ee] pronounced [i] after ж [zh]). 11 ba-reés
(unstressed **o** is [a]). 12 vla-deé-meer. 13 oó-tra 'morning'
(unstressed **o** is [a]). 14 tsary 'tsar'.

Exercise 4: Macleans (toothpaste), [ma-kleéns]. з devoiced to
[s] as in 2.9.

3 Exercise 5: 1 **Здра́вствуйте. Как вас зову́т?** [zdrá-stvooy-tye. kak vas za-voót?]. 2 **До́брое у́тро.** [dó-bra-ye oó-tra]. 3 **Меня́ зову́т ...** [mye-nyá za-voót ...]. 4 **Я не понима́ю.** [ya nye pa-nee-má-yoo]. 5 **Говори́те ме́дленно, пожа́луйста.** [ga-va-reé-tye myé-dlye-na, pa-zhál-sta].

Exercise 6: 1 [peesy-mó] 'letter' **оно́** [a-nó]. 2 [an-dryéy] 'Andrey' (Andrew) **он** [on]. 3 [maty] 'mother' **она́** [a-ná]. 4 [gó-rat] 'town/city' **он** [on]. 5 [vá-nya] 'Vanya' (fam form of 'Ivan') **он** [on].

Exercise 7: 1 [zdrá-stvooy-tye. mye-nyá za-voót neé-na] 'Hello. My name is Nina.' 2 [pa-zhál-sta, ga-va-reé-tye myé-dlye-na] 'Please speak slowly.' 3 [ya nye pa-nee-má-yoo] 'I don't understand.' 4 [gdye peesy-mó? vot a-nó] 'Where is the letter? There it is.' 5 [da, vot a-nó. spa-seé-ba] 'Yes, there it is. Thank you.'

Exercise 8: 1 **Как вас зову́т? Меня́ зову́т Андре́й.** [kak vas za-voót? mye-nyá za-voót an-dryéy]. 2 **Здра́вствуйте. Где такси́?** [zdrá-stvooy-tye. gdye tak-seé?]. 3 **Вот оно́** (= the taxi). **Спаси́бо.** [vot a-nó. spa-seé-ba]. 4 **Как вас зову́т? Меня́ зову́т Влади́мир?** [kak vas za-voót? mye-nyá za-voót vla-deé-meer].

Exercise 9: **Кторов** (m). **Анастасьева** (f). **Хромова** (f). **Ленникова** (f). **Титова** (f). **Зимин** (m). **Губанов** (m). **Яншин** (m). **Покровский** (m).

4 Exercise 10: **я рабо́таю** [ya ra-bó-ta-yoo], **ты рабо́таешь** [ti ra-bó-ta-yesh], **он/она́/оно́ рабо́тает** [on/a-ná/a-nó ra-bó-ta-yet], **мы рабо́таем** [mi ra-bó-ta-yem], **вы рабо́таете** [vi ra-bó-ta-ye-tye], **они́ рабо́тают** [a-neé ra-bó-ta-yoot].

Exercise 11: 1 – Do you know? – Yes, I know. 2 – Do you work/Are you working? – No, I don't work/I'm not working. 3 – Do you understand? – Yes, I understand. 4 – Is Boris working? – Yes, he's working. 5 – Where does Jane work? – She works in Liverpool. 6 – Vanya, do you know where Jane and Mark work? – No, I don't. 7 – I speak Russian. Boris speaks Russian. We speak Russian. – Yes, you speak Russian. 8 – Do Jane and Boris speak Russian? – Yes, they speak (it) well.

Exercise 12: 1 зна́ю [ya nye zná-yoo]. понима́ю [ya nye pa-nee-má-yoo]. 2 рабо́тает [on ra-bó-ta-yet vlón-da-nye], рабо́тают [a a-nee ra-bó-a-yoot vlee-vyer-poó-lye] 'He works in London and/but they work in Liverpool.' 3 понима́ешь [vá-nya, ti nye pa-nee-má-yesh]. 4 зна́ете [vi zná-ye-tye], рабо́таем [gdye mi ra-bó-ta-yem]. 5 говорю́ [ya ga-va-ryoó pa-roó-skee], говоря́т [a a-nee nye ga-va-ryát pa-roó-skee]. 6 говори́м [mi ga-va-reém pa-roó-skee ha-ra-shó].

Exercise 13: 1 Я не зна́ю. Я не понима́ю. [ya nye zná-yoo. ya nye pa-nee-má-yoo]. 2 Я зна́ю, и вы зна́ете. [ya zná-yoo, ee vi zná-ye-tye]. 3 Вы не понима́ете. [vi nye pa-nee-má-ye-tye]. 4 Я говорю́ по-ру́сски. [ya ga-va-ryoó pa-roó-skee]. 5 Джейн говори́т по-ру́сски хорошо́. [dzheyn ga-va-reét pa-roó-skee ha-ra-shó]. 6 Они́ не понима́ют. Они́ не говоря́т по-ру́сски. [a-nee nye pa-nee-má-yoot. a-nee nye ga-va-ryát pa-roó-skee].

Exercise 14: 1 Здра́вствуйте. Меня́ зову́т Джейн. [zdrá-stvooy-tye. mye-nyá za-voót dzheyn]. 2 Я англича́нка. [ya an-glee-chán-ka]. 3 Где Бори́с? (Я) не зна́ю? [gdye ba-reés? (ya) nye zná-yoo]. 4 Я не понима́ю. Говори́те ме́дленно, пожа́луйста. [ya nye pa-nee-má-yoo. ga-va-reé-tye myé-dlye-na, pa-zhál-sta]. 5 Они́ говоря́т по-ру́сски ме́дленно. [a-nee ga-va-ryát pa-roó-skee myé-dlye-na]. 6 Же́нщина не понима́ет. Она́ не говори́т по-ру́сски. [zhén-shshee-na nye pa-nee-má-yet. a-ná nye ga-va-reét pa-roó-skee]. 7 Вы рабо́таете ме́дленно. [vi ra-bó-ta-ye-tye myé-dlye-na]. 8 Где мой друг? Джейн зна́ет, где он. [gdye moy drook? dzheyn zná-yet, gdye on]. 9 Что э́то? Э́то письмо́. [shto é-ta? é-ta peesy-mó]. 10 Я не зна́ю, как вас зову́т. [ya nye zná-yoo, kak vas za-voót].

Exercise 15:   Boris: What is your name?
            Jane: Mark doesn't speak Russian.

5 **Exercise 16:** 1 Да, (я) говорю́ (по-ру́сски) [da, (ya) ga-va-ryoó (pa-roó-skee)]. 2 Да, (я) понима́ю. [da, (ya) pa-nee-má-yoo]. 3 Нет, (я) не зна́ю (, где он) [nyet, (ya) nye zná-yoo (, gdye on)]. 4 Да, (мы) зна́ем (, где она́ рабо́тает) [da, (mi) zná-yem (, gdye a-ná ra-bó-ta-yet)]. 5 Нет, (она́ рабо́тает) в Ливерпу́ле. [nyet, (a-ná ra-bó-ta-yet) vlee-vyer-poó-lye]. (Note: Parts in round brackets can be omitted in informal style.)

Exercise 17: 1 **Где она́?** [gdye a-ná?] 2 **Почему́ он рабо́тает ме́дленно?** [pa-chye-moó on ra-bó-ta-yet myé-dlye-na?]. 3 **Кто зна́ет, где Бори́с?** [kto zná-yet, gdye ba-reés?]. 4 **Что они́ говоря́т?** [shto a-neé ga-va-ryát?]. 5 **Когда́ они́ рабо́тают?** [kag-dá a-neé ra-bó-ta-yoot?].

Exercise 18: 1 Is Uncle Vanya in the town? **в го́роде** [vgó-ra-dye]. 2 Does he work in Moscow? **в Москве́** [vmask-vyé]. No, in St. Petersburg. **в Санкт-Петербу́рге** [fsankt-pye-tyer-boór-gye]. 3 My friend is in Liverpool. **в Ливерпу́ле** [vlee-vyer-poó-lye]. 4 They work/are working in Siberia. **в Сиби́ри** [fsee-beé-ree]. 5 Where is Jane? In Russia. **в Росси́и** [vra-sseé-ee].

Exercise 19: Note: rise-fall syllable underlined. 1 **Вы говори́те по-ру́сски?** [vi ga-va-reé-tye pa-roó-skee?]. 2 **Вы понима́ете?** [vi pa-nee-má-ye-tye?]. 3 **Вы (не) зна́ете, где Новосиби́рск?** [vi (nye) zná-ye-tye, gdye na-va-see-beérsk?]. 4 **Он ру́сский?** [on roó-skee?]. 5 **Вы живёте в Москве́?** [vi zhi-vyó-tye vmask-vyé?]. 6 **Где гости́ница?** [gdye ga-steé-nee-tsa?]. 7 **Кто зна́ет, где мой друг?** [kto zná-yet, gdye moy drook?]. 8 **Э́то гости́ница?** [é-ta ga-steé-nee-tsa?]. 9 **Они́ живу́т в Сиби́ри** [a-neé zhi-voót fsee-beé-ree]. 10 **Почему́ он рабо́тает в Ло́ндоне?** [pa-chye-moó on ra-bó-ta-yet vlón-da-nye?]. 11 **Мы в Росси́и.** [mi vra-sseé-ee]. 12 **Он говори́т по-ру́сски о́чень хорошо́.** [on ga-va-reét pa-roó-skee ó-chyeny ha-ra-shó]. 13 **Ты зна́ешь, кто э́то? Э́то Бори́с.** [ti zná-yesh, kto é-ta? é-ta ba-reés]. 14 **Вы Бори́с? О́чень прия́тно.** [vi bareés? ó-chyeny pree-yát-na]. 15 **Ба́рбара – америка́нка, а** (contrast) **Андре́й украи́нец.** [bár-ba-ra a-mye-ree-kán-ka, a an-dryéy oo-kra-eé-nyets]. 16 **Мы говори́м о ней, не о вас.** [mi ga-va-reém a-nyey, nye a-vas].

Exercise 20: Do you live in Moscow?

6 **Exercise 21:** 1 [on zná-yet mye-nyá]. 2 [vi pa-nee-má-ye-tye mye-nyá?]. 3 [kak vas za-voót?]. 4 [vi ha-ra-shó zná-ye-tye mask-voó?]. 5 [ya zná-yoo vá-nyoo]. 6 [mi zná-yem stoo-dyént-koo]. 7 [vi zná-ye-tye ba-reé-sa?]. 8 [a-neé zná-yoot (y)ee-zík]. 9 [brá-ta za-voót ee-ván]. 10 [mi pa-nee-má-yem oo-prazh-nyé-nee-ye].

Exercise 22: 1 Москву́. 2 вас. 3 дя́дю Ва́ню. 4 Влади́мира.
5 Сиби́рь. 6 Росси́ю. 7 меня́. 8 их. 9 же́нщину. 10 царя́ (m
person). 11 мать. (f soft-sign nouns don't change). 12 тебя́.

Exercise 23: 1 Его́ зову́т Ива́н. ('Him (they) call Ivan').
2 Вы зна́ете Бори́са и Влади́мира. (acc for masculine people).
3 Э́то Джейн. Вы зна́ете её or Вы её зна́ете. 4 Они́ понима́ют
письмо́? 5 Я вас не понима́ю or Я не понима́ю вас.

Exercise 24: 1 Куда́ вы е́дете? Мы е́дем в го́род. 2 Мы е́дем в
Росси́ю. 3 Она́ идёт в гости́ницу. 4 Они́ е́дут в Москву́. 5 Вы
идёте (пешко́м) и́ли е́дете?

7 **Exercise 25:** 1 ваш 'Is this your ticket?' 2 ва́ша? 'Where is your
book?' 3 на́ша 'I don't know where our hotel is.' 4 Её 'Her
mother is in Moscow.' 5 Твоё 'Your letter is here.'

Exercise 26: 1 Вы зна́ете (Ты зна́ешь) мою́ сестру́? 2 Я зна́ю
его́ мать. 3 Она́ зна́ет моего́ [ma-ye-vó] бра́та. 4 Он хо́чет
уви́деть ва́шего [vá-she-va] дру́га.

Exercise 27: 1 краси́вый. 2 симпати́чная ру́сская. 3 чи́стая.
4 друго́е ру́сское [droo-gó-ye roó-ska-ye]. 5 англи́йский
краси́вый.

Exercise 28: 1 но́вая 'There is the new hotel.' 2 но́вой 'We are
living (staying) in a/the new hotel.' 3 Кра́сная 'This/That is Red
Square.' 4 Кра́сную 'We love Red Square.' 5 ру́сский кни́жный
'This is a/the Russian bookshop.' 6 ру́сском кни́жном 'She
works in a/the Russian bookshop.' 7 ру́сский 'We love Russian.'
8 Ру́сское краси́вое 'The Russian word [pló-shshaty] "square"
is very beautiful.' 9 чи́стое 'The Moscow metro (The metro in
Moscow) is very clean.' 10 но́вую 'She is travelling/going to
her new job (work).' 11 но́вого америка́нского [nó-va-va
a-mye-ree-kán-ska-va] 'I know her new American friend.'
12 Англи́йскую 'The English teacher is called Miss Smith.'

Exercise 29: 1 на кото́рой (f sing prep). 2 кото́рая (f sing nom).
3 в кото́рый (m sing acc). 4 кото́рого (m sing, animate acc).

Exercise 30: 1 Я вас не понима́ю/я не понима́ю вас. Говори́те ме́дленно, пожа́луйста. 2 Он зна́ет англи́йский язы́к. 3 Я изуча́ю ру́сский язы́к. 4 Ната́ша идёт в кни́жный магази́н. 5 Ната́ша не хо́чет рабо́тать в кни́жном магази́не. 6 Мы идём на Кра́сную пло́щадь. 7 Джейн и Бори́с не хотя́т (6.4) идти́ (or е́хать) туда́. ('thither' – motion). 8 Когда́ вы е́дете в Аме́рику? 9 Их ба́бушка живёт в ру́сской дере́вне. 10 Вы говори́те по-ру́сски (not ру́сский язы́к with the verb говори́ть)? 11 Мою́ подру́гу (acc) зову́т Ни́на. 12 Ва́ша кварти́ра о́чень чи́стая. 13 Она́ не лю́бит твоего́ но́вого му́жа. [tva-ye-vó nó-va-va moó-zha]. 14 Я хочу́ уви́деть (моего́) ру́сского [(ma-ye-vó) roó-ska-va] дру́га Бори́са. (the ending of 'Boris' must be accusative, like the ending of 'friend'). 15 Мы лю́бим ру́сское вино́ и ру́сскую во́дку. 16 Где де́вушка, кото́рую зову́т Ни́на?

8 **Exercise 31:** 1 [a-ná lyoó-beet knee-gee] 2 [vi zná-ye-tye é-tee roó-skee-ye sla-vá?] 3 [a-mye-ree-kán-tsi lyoó-byat kra-seé-vi-ye ma-ga-zeé-ni] 4 [vmask-vyé yesty ga-steé-nee-tsi, rye-sta-rá-ni, moo-zyé-ee, pra-spyék-ti, pló-shsha-dee] 5 [vá-shi ([i] not [ee] after ш – see 2.7) brá-tyya (soft ty (2.6) followed by ya) seem-pa-teéch-ni-ye].

Exercise 32: 1 заво́ды 'factories'. 2 же́нщины 'women'. 3 англича́нки (8.4) 'Englishwomen'. 4 дя́ди 'uncles'. 5 музе́и 'museums'. 6 ба́бушки 'grandmothers'. 7 ста́нции 'stations'. 8 подру́ги (8.4) 'girlfriends'. 9 свида́ния 'meetings'. 10 учи́тельницы '(women) teachers'. 11 пло́щади 'squares'. 12 пи́сьма 'letters'.

Exercise 33: 1 краси́вые же́нщины 'beautiful women'. 2 мои́ ру́сские кни́ги 'my Russian books'. 3 америка́нские магази́ны 'American shops'. 4 но́вые у́лицы 'new streets'. 5 ва́ши кра́сные кни́ги 'your red books'. 6 други́е гости́ницы 'other (different) hotels'. 7 твои́ ста́рые друзья́ 'your old friends'.

Exercise 34: 1 хоро́ш<u>ее</u>. 2 хоро́ш<u>ей</u> <u>э</u>́т<u>ой</u>. 3 <u>э</u>́т<u>и</u>. 4 <u>э</u>́т<u>ом</u> хоро́ш<u>ие</u>. 5 <u>э</u>́т<u>у</u>.

Exercise 35:

A: Hello, Barbara. How are things? Where do you want to go today?

B: Hello, Andrey. Today I want to do some shopping. Would you show me the Moscow shops?

A: What kind of shops? What interests you? Books, records, souvenirs?

B: I'm interested in Russian books (lit. 'Me interest Russian books'). I often buy your books in Washington and New York. There are Russian bookshops there.

A: So Americans buy our books. That's interesting. But you're not only interested in books.

B: I have (lit. 'it is necessary') to buy presents. In a week's time I'm going home to America. My friends like Russian vodka.

A: Tourists usually buy such things in a 'Beriozka' store. In a 'Beriozka' there are very nice things, but there they take only foreign money – for example, British pounds and your American dollars. Let's go to the 'Beriozka' bookshop – that shop is on Kropotkinskaya Street – then to the 'Beriozka' in the Rossiya Hotel.

B: OK.

A: Wait a moment … Look.

B: What is it?

A: It's a present. Pasternak, my favourite poems. I know that you like Russian poetry.

B: You're very kind, Andrey.

[Barbara and Andrey are talking in 1988; since then, Beriozkas have been superseded by a wide range of new Western-style shops.]

Exercise 36: 1 Я хочу́ сде́лать поку́пки. 2 Здесь беру́т то́лько ру́сские де́ньги. 3 В э́том магази́не есть хоро́шие кни́ги/В э́том магази́не кни́ги хоро́шие ('In this shop the books are good' – Russians tend to prefer the second version, even though English speakers object that 'there are good books' doesn't imply that all the books are good). 4 Мои́ друзья́ живу́т на э́той у́лице. 5 Э́ти америка́нцы зна́ют, где на́ша гости́ница.

Exercise 36A: 'The Brothers Karamazov.' They (the three brothers Karamazov) are the sons (**сыновья́**) of Fyodor Pavlovich Karamazov.

9 **Exercise 37:** 1 1241. 2 332. 3 3506. 4 198.

Exercise 38: 1 сестры́ 'three sisters'. 2 фу́нта 'four pounds'. 3 пласти́нки '22 records'. 4 ста́нции 'three stations'. 5 трамва́я 'three trams'. 6 сло́ва '302 words'.

Exercise 39: 1 Де́сять рубле́й. 2 Мно́го рубле́й. 3 Не́сколько копе́ек. 4 Ма́ло де́нег. 5 Сто де́сять до́лларов.

Exercise 40: 1 три языка́. 2 Бори́са. 3 шесть до́лларов. 4 два́дцать одну́ буты́лку (acc) во́дки. 5 две́сти гра́ммов сы́ра. 6 мно́го америка́нцев. 7 Ско́лько ... Трина́дцать копе́ек. 8 две неде́ли.

Exercise 40A: 'The Three Sisters'. сестры́ is gen sing after три.

10 **Exercise 41:** 1 Пять рубле́й со́рок копе́ек. 2 Два́дцать четы́ре до́ллара. 3 Хлеб сто́ит трина́дцать копе́ек. 4 Ско́лько сто́ит кило(гра́мм) колбасы́? 5 Да́йте, пожа́луйста, пятьсо́т гра́ммов ма́сла. 6 Мно́го де́нег. 7 Пять ме́сяцев. 8 Три сестры́. 9 До свида́ния. 10 Де́сять яи́ц.

Exercise 42: 1 ру́сского 'Jane is a teacher of Russian.' 2 краси́вой молодо́й 'Do you know the name of the attractive young Englishwoman?' 3 хоро́ших ру́сских 'Ten good Russian friends.' 4 иностра́нных (gen pl adj after 2, 3, 4) 'I know three foreign languages.'

Exercise 43: 1 ва́шего ру́сского 'Where is your Russian friend's apartment?' 2 мои́х хоро́ших 'This is the house of my good friends.' 3 мое́й англи́йской 'My English friend's name is Jane.' 4 э́тих кра́сных 'We want to buy a kilo of these red apples.'

Exercise 44: *B:* Do you have a husband? *M:* I do. *B:* Do you have children? *M:* Yes, a daughter and two sons. *B:* Does your husband have (any) money? *M:* He does.

Exercise 45: 1 Здесь нет магази́на. 2 В буты́лке нет молока́. 3 У меня́ нет рубля́. 4 У меня́ нет одного́ до́ллара. 5 У меня́ нет до́лларов. 6 У них нет яи́ц. 7 У моего́ бра́та нет кварти́ры. 8 У меня́ нет но́вых книг.

Exercise 46: 1 Здра́вствуйте. Как вас зову́т? Меня́ зову́т Джейн. 2 Здра́вствуйте. Меня́ зову́т Бори́с (Я Бори́с). Вы америка́нка? 3 Нет, я англича́нка. Я учи́тельница. 4 Вы рабо́таете в Москве́? 5 Да, но я е́ду домо́й в А́нглию че́рез три ме́сяца. 6 Вы о́чень хорошо́ говори́те по-ру́сски и вы понима́ете всё. 7 Я понима́ю всё, когда́ вы говори́те ме́дленно. 8 Прости́те, куда́ вы идёте? 9 Я иду́ в ру́сский кни́жный магази́н. 10 Дава́йте пойдём вме́сте. Я о́чень люблю́ кни́жные магази́ны. 11 Хорошо́. Я ча́сто покупа́ю ру́сские кни́ги. Я люблю́ ру́сские стихи́ (ру́сскую поэ́зию). 12 Я люблю́ америка́нские кни́ги. Но на́ши магази́ны не о́чень хоро́шие. 13 Дава́йте пойдём в центр. На́до купи́ть пода́рки. 14 В э́том магази́не о́чень ма́ло иностра́нных книг. 15 У иностра́нцев есть до́ллары, поэ́тому они́ покупа́ют хоро́шее вино́. 16 У меня́ нет до́лларов. У вас то́же нет иностра́нных де́нег. 17 Я зна́ю э́тих америка́нцев. У них есть де́ньги. 18 Во́дка сто́ит два́дцать до́лларов, а кни́ги (сто́ят) два́дцать три до́ллара. 19 Вы покупа́ете э́ти буты́лки во́дки для (ва́шего) му́жа? 20 У меня́ нет му́жа, но у меня́ есть мно́го хоро́ших друзе́й.

11 **Exercise 47:** 1 **чита́л** 'Ivan read/was reading.' 2 **жи́ли** 'We lived/were living in Moscow.' 3 **говори́ли** 'Were you speaking/Did you speak Russian?' 4 **зна́ла** 'I knew you were English.' (lit. 'I knew you are English' – see 14.3). 5 **е́хал** 'He was going (travelling) to Moscow.' 6 **стоя́ли** 'Mike and Nina were standing in the queue (line).' 7 **понима́ли говори́ла** 'They didn't understand when I spoke/was speaking.'

Exercise 48: 1 У меня́ был оди́н до́ллар. 2 У меня́ не́ было до́ллара (gen). 3 В су́мке был килогра́мм колбасы́ (Put the place expression first unless you want to emphasize it. **Килогра́мм колбасы́ был в су́мке** is the equivalent of 'The kilo of sausage was in the bag'). 4 В магази́не не́ было колбасы́ (gen). 5 У нас бы́ли друзья́ в Москве́. 6 У нас не́ было друзе́й (gen pl) в Санкт-Петербу́рге. (The place expressions could come first in 5 and 6 if you want to stress 'friends').

Exercise 49: 1 **родила́сь** 'Her daughter was born in Moscow.'
2 **улыба́лись** 'Why were they smiling/did they smile?'
3 **одева́лась** 'She dressed well/attractively.' 4 **учи́лся (учи́лась)**
'I studied at this school' = 'I went to this school.'

Exercise 50: 1 **вы пи́шете.** 2 **они́ стоя́т.** 3 **мы смо́трим.** 4 **они́
де́лают.**

Exercise 51: 1 'Letters from Moscow take a long time.' 2 'Jane
went to America (and came back again).' 3 'Boris went to the
cinema (and came back again).' 4 'Boris and Jane are already
friends (using 'ti' to each other).' 5 'He waited for about thirty
minutes.'

12 **Exercise 52:** 1 **ку́пите** 'Will you buy this book?' 2 **сде́лаю** 'I'll
do it in a week's time.' 3 **пое́дет** 'He won't go to St. Petersburg.'
4 **поймёт** 'When will Jane understand (realize) that he loves
her?' 5 **ска́жет** 'She won't say that she doesn't love him.'

Exercise 53: 1 **Я чита́ю кни́гу.** 2 **Я прочита́ю э́ту кни́гу.**
3 **Почему́ он не отвеча́ет?** 4 **Он не отве́тит.** 5 **Вы позвони́те?**
6 **Да, я позвоню́.** 7 **Ба́рбара возвраща́ется в Москву́.** 8 **Когда́
Ба́рбара вернётся?** 9 **Когда́ они́ прие́дут?**

Exercise 54: 1 **мо́жем.** 2 **не мо́жет.** 3 **не могу́.** 4 **Вы смо́жете.**

Exercise 55: 1 **Он вам ска́жет (ска́жет вам** if stress on 'you').
2 **Я ей не скажу́ (не скажу́ ей** – stress on **ей).** 3 **Она́ звони́т
мне (мне звони́т).** 4 **Я позвоню́ им (им позвоню́).** 5 **Ни́на
(ему́) пока́зывает ему́ Кра́сную пло́щадь.** 6 **Они́ (нам)
пока́жут нам Москву́.**

Exercise 56: 1 **дам** 'I'll give you five roubles.' 2 **даду́т** 'They'll
give her money.' 3 **дашь** 'Who will you give this ticket to?'

13 **Exercise 57:** Barbara left (**уе́хала** – single completed event) for
America. Andrey wrote (**писа́л** – repeated action) to her every
week. He waited (**ждал** – unfinished action/state), but Barbara
neither wrote (**не писа́ла** – no action) nor called (**не звони́ла** –
no action). He looked very sad (**был** – state). But yesterday, when
he was writing (**писа́л** – unfinished action) her a letter, she
telephoned (**позвони́ла** – completed event with result, one of a

series of actions) from Washington and said (**сказа́ла** – completed event, one of a series) that she had received (**получи́ла** – completed event with result) his first letter and had long ago answered (**отве́тила** – completed action) it.

'Haven't you received (**не получи́л** = have you failed to receive what you should have received) my letter?' she asked (**спроси́ла** – completed action).

'No,' he answered (**отве́тил** – completed action).

Her letter was on its way (**шло** – process, duration) (letters go on foot [**идти́**] in Russian!) a very long time, three weeks. It arrived (**пришло́** – completed action) today. (**пришло́** is the neuter past of **прийти́** 'to arrive on foot', a prefixed form of **идти́** whose past is **шёл, шла, шло, шли** – see 11.3). (Note: Although it is something of an oversimplification to say that perfective means 'completed action', that 'rule-of-thumb' gives a general idea of how the choice of aspect is made.)

Exercise 58: 1 **чита́ла** (i) – stress on process, no mention of completion. 2 **прочита́ла** (p) – I finished the book. 3 **звони́л** (i) repeated (habitual) action. 4 **верну́лся** (p), **чита́ла** (i) – the completed event of returning took place while the reading was in process (unfinished). 5 **купи́ла** (p), **верну́лась** (p), **дала́** (p) – sequence of three completed actions. 6 **открыва́ла** (i) – habitual, repeated action. 7 **не приходи́ла** (i), **не звони́ла** (i) – imperfectives used with **не** ('not'), meaning simply that the actions didn't take place. Perfectives with **не** would imply failure to carry out the actions (i.e. that Jane had said she would come or ring but failed to keep her promise). 8 **написа́ла** (p) When an action is repeated a specified number of times (three in this case) it is treated as a single event and the perfective is used. 9 **покупа́ли** (i) habitual action, repeated an unspecified number of times. 10 **купи́ли** (p) single completed action. 11 **говори́л** (i) process, no mention of completion. 12 **сказа́л** (p) single completed event. 13 **понима́ли** (i) **говори́ла** (i) habitual. 14 **по́няли** (p) single completed event with result; **говори́т** (i) present tense, always imperfective.

Exercise 59: 1 **Мы покупа́ли** (i – process, uncompleted) **кни́ги.** 2 **Я (ей) писа́л(а)** (i – repeated action) **ей ка́ждую неде́лю.** 3 **Я прие́хал(а)** (p) **в Москву́, пое́хал(а)** (p) **в гости́ницу, пото́м позвони́л(а)** (p) **ему́.** (sequence of completed actions). 4 **Я хочу́ купи́ть** (p – you want to complete the act of buying) **э́ту кни́гу.**

5 **Вы написа́ли/Ты написа́л(а)** (p – you want to know if the writing is completed) **письмо́?**

Exercise 60:
> *M:* Hi, Nina, what's new (lit. 'what have you of new [gen]?')?
> *N:* I've bought (p) a cat, or to be precise, a tomcat.
> *M:* Really? And I thought (i) that Russians didn't (lit. 'don't') like animals.
> *N:* On the contrary. All my friends have either a cat or a dog.
> *M:* What have you called (p) your cat?
> *N:* Liverpool.
> *M:* Pardon, I didn't get (p) that. What ('How') did you say (p)?
> *N:* I said (p) 'Liverpool'. Why did you smile (p)?
> *M:* But don't you think it's funny? Who thought up (p) that name?
> *N:* There's nothing funny about it. We called (p) him that after a very handsome cat which recently won (p) first prize at a Moscow exhibition.
> *M:* Jane will be pleased (p) when she finds out (p) (lit. 'will find out'). I think Liverpool is her home town.
> *N:* She found out (p) yesterday, when she visited me. She fell in love (p) with him immediately.
> *M:* So now she loves both Liverpool [place] and Liverpool [animal]. By the way, about Jane. I wanted to ask (p) you when she came (p) to Moscow.
> *N:* She came (p) about six months [number and noun reversed to mean 'about'] ago. She was offered (p) work in a school.
> *M:* Where did she work (i) (What did she do) in England?
> *N:* She taught (i) Russian in Liverpool. She'll go back (p) there in about eight or nine weeks [if the number has a preposition, in the 'approximately' construction the noun is put in front of the preposition].
> *M:* Why did she decide she wanted (p) to live (i) (lit. 'Why did she want (p) to live') and work (i) in Moscow?
> *N:* Moscow is interesting. Many foreigners are very fond of Russian people. Also Jane loves Russian.
> *M:* I think you're wrong. I think she was bored in Liverpool. Perhaps she's in love with someone here.
> *N:* Nonsense! She's a very serious girl.

254

14 **Exercise 61:** *N:* Tomorrow I shall be at Natasha's. Will you come? There will be dancing (We shall be dancing). *M:* Of course I'll come. (And) will Jane be there? *N:* She said that she would be in Zagorsk all day. When she gets back (returns) to Moscow, she will call. *M:* What will she be doing in Zagorsk? *N:* She said she wanted to go to the monastery. *M:* What about Boris? *N:* He said he would definitely come.

Exercise 62: 1 За́втра мы бу́дем рабо́тать (i). 2 Он бу́дет жить (i) в гости́нице. 3 Когда́ придёт (p) по́езд? 4 Когда́ мы прие́дем (p 'shall arrive') в Москву́, мы пое́дем (p) в гости́ницу «Интури́ст» 5 Е́сли вы ему́ дади́те (p 'will give') (ему́) пять до́лларов, он вам даст (p) кни́гу.

Exercise 63: 1 Мне хо́лодно. 2 Ва́шему/Твоему́ дру́гу ску́чно? 3 Нам на́до идти́/е́хать. 4 Вам/Тебе́ на́до говори́ть по-ру́сски. 5 Мне на́до бы́ло говори́ть по-ру́сски. 6 Им на́до бы́ло рабо́тать. 7 Ей на́до бу́дет говори́ть ме́дленно. 8 На́до взять такси́. 9 Мо́жно (нам) спроси́ть, ско́лько вы зараба́тываете? 10 Здесь нельзя́ кури́ть or Нельзя́ кури́ть здесь (emphasizing 'here'). 11 Нельзя́ бы́ло/Невозмо́жно бы́ло найти́ (p used after words meaning 'it's impossible') такси́. 12 В Москве́ бы́ло хо́лодно. 13 (Мне) мо́жно (мне) кури́ть? 14 (Мне) мо́жно (мне) откры́ть окно́? 15 (Мне) мо́жно (мне) купи́ть э́ту кни́гу? 16 Мо́жно спроси́ть, где вы купи́ли э́тот план го́рода?

Exercise 64: No smoking here (lit. 'By us [in our place] [they] do not smoke', 'Here one does not smoke'). Happy birthday (with handwriting form of д).

15 **Exercise 65:** 1 Come to us tomorrow = Come and see us tomorrow (invitation). 2 Tell me please where the cash desk/ticket office is here = Could you tell me where the cash desk/ticket office is? (request). 3 Don't worry (negative command), she will certainly phone (I'm sure she'll phone). 4 Please help me to find my friend/Could you help me to find my friend? (request). 5 Call us tomorrow (command).

Exercise 66: 1 Да́й(те) мне э́ти кни́ги, пожа́луйста. 2 Покажи́ мне фотогра́фии, пожа́луйста. 3 Принеси́те мне ко́фе, пожа́луйста. 4 Скажи́те (нам), пожа́луйста, где живёт А́нна Ива́новна? 5 Пожа́луйста, помоги́те. Я не зна́ю, где моя́ гости́ница. 6 Не уходи́(те). 7 Сади́тесь/Сади́сь (, пожа́луйста). 8 Пожа́луйста, купи́(те) мне «Пра́вду». 9 Бу́дьте здоро́вы (pol/pl). (The fam forms are Будь здоро́в (m)/Будь здоро́ва (f) – special adjective forms in these fixed phrases.) 10 Дава́й(те) вы́пьем за её здоро́вье.

Exercise 67: 1 Улыбни́тесь/Улыбни́сь. 2 Пойми́(те). 3 Сде́лай(те). 4 Верни́тесь/Верни́сь. 5 Не задава́й(те).

Exercise 68: 1 Вы́йди(те) из магази́на. 2 Поверни́(те) напра́во. 3 Иди́(те) пря́мо, пото́м поверни́(те) нале́во. 4 Поезжа́й(те) на метро́ до ста́нции «Кита́й-го́род». 5 Найди́(те) вы́ход на пло́щадь. 6 Иди́(те) пря́мо по Кита́йскому проспе́кту. 7 Спра́ва вы уви́дите/ты уви́дишь гости́ницу «Росси́я».

16 **Exercise 69:** 1 Я писа́л(а) карандашо́м. 2 Он с на́ми. 3 Она́ рабо́тает ве́чером/Ве́чером она́ рабо́тает (if stress on <u>works</u>). 4 Ме́жду гости́ницей и пло́щадью. 5 Она́ ста́ла учи́тельницей.

Exercise 70: 1 'Tomorrow there will be a meeting with our new (female) teacher' на́шей но́вой учи́тельницей. 2 'Meet (become acquainted with) my Russian friends' мои́ми ру́сскими друзья́ми. 3 'Many Russian women have become good engineers' хоро́шими инжене́рами. 4 'Will you go with the children to the cinema?' детьми́. 5 'Did you speak to (with) these people?' э́тими людьми́.

Exercise 71: *K:* Hello. *S:* Hello (How are you). *K:* Allow (me) to introduce myself. My (sur)name is Kuznetsov. *S:* Pleased to meet you. My name is Michael Smith. What are your first name and patronymic? *K:* Boris Petrovich. *S:* Hello, Boris Petrovich. *K:* How are you, Mr Smith? Meet my wife. This is Natalya Aleksandrovna. And this is my daughter Lena. *S:* How are you, Natalya Aleksandrovna? Hello, Lena. How old are you? *L:* Hello. I'm six.

Exercise 71A: Влади́мир. Андре́й. Алекса́ндр. Васи́лий. Пётр. Л(е)в. – a difficult one because of the fleeting vowel, which is replaced by a soft sign. Note Лев Толсто́й (Lev Tolstoy), gen Льва Толсто́го. Илья́ – a rare type of masculine name; the patronymics from names ending -а or -я have no -ов-/-ев-.

17 **Exercise 72:** 1 Без десяти́ два. 2 Без двадцати́ оди́ннадцать. 3 Без пятна́дцати три. 4 Без трёх мину́т час. 5 Без одно́й мину́ты двена́дцать. 6 Полови́на шесто́го. 7 Пятна́дцать мину́т оди́ннадцатого.

Exercise 73: 1 В три часа́ но́чи. 2 В полови́не седьмо́го ве́чера. 3 Без пятна́дцати четы́ре дня. 4 В Москве́ час но́чи.

Exercise 74: 1 'Tomorrow is the fourteenth of August.' 2 'The twenty-second of April is Lenin's birthday.' 3 'We shall arrive on the twenty-third of July.' 4 Мы бу́дем в Москве́ в декабре́. 5 Сего́дня тре́тье (exceptional adj) сентября́. 6 День рожде́ния Ната́ши три́дцать пе́рвого января́.

Exercise 75: 1 On Thursday the twelfth of April 1973. 2 Lenin was born in 1870. 3 Я бу́ду там в сре́ду. 4 Мы бы́ли в Москве́ в (ты́сяча девятьсо́т) во́семьдесят четвёртом году́.

Exercise 76: *SI:* Hello, Jane. I think you met my wife last week. I'm Sergey Ivanovich. *J:* How are you, Sergey Ivanovich. I'm pleased to meet you. Klara Mikhaylovna told me that you came back late because you worked until eight. *SI:* Yes, usually I come home at half past six but on Friday there was a conference … Let's see. Have you been in Moscow long (lit. 'You since long in Moscow'), Jane? *J:* Since last September. *SI:* And when were you first in Moscow? *J:* In April 1976 when I was still at school. I immediately fell in love with Russia and Russian people. *SI:* And when are you going home ('to your homeland')? *J:* I shall be working here until the end of July. *SI:* Excuse me, how old are you, Jane? *J:* Twenty-seven. I was born in 1961, in May. *SI:* Boris told me that your birthday was (on) the eighth of May. Now he was born on the ninth of May, on Victory Day [every year on 9 May Russia celebrates the end of the war against Fascist Germany]. Let's see. Twenty-seven … Hmm. You'll be getting married soon, no doubt. *J:* Don't say

that, Sergey Ivanovich! I'm not ready yet ('to me it is still early').
My mother got married when she was thirty-two. *SI:* Hmm, yes.
But don't you think that it's time Boris got married? He's thirty-
one. *J:* Well, that's up to him. Incidentally, where is he? I've been
waiting (present tense in Russian) for him since five o'clock.
We're going to the cinema. The film begins at a quarter to seven.

Exercise 77: 1 Кото́рый час? (Ско́лько вре́мени?). 2 Три часа́.
3 Полови́на оди́ннадцатого. 4 Без десяти́ шесть. 5 Без трёх
мину́т два. 6 Оди́ннадцать часо́в ве́чера. 7 В полови́не
второ́го. 8 В ты́сяча девятьсо́т пятидеся́том году́. 9 В январе́
ты́сяча девятьсо́т пятьдеся́т восьмо́го го́да. 10 В понеде́льник
два́дцать пя́того января́ ты́сяча девятьсо́т во́семьдесят
восьмо́го го́да. 11 Я рабо́таю с десяти́ часо́в утра́ до шести́
часо́в ве́чера. 12 Ско́лько вам лет? 13 Мне два́дцать шесть
(лет). 14 Ско́лько лет ва́шей жене́? 15 Мое́й жене́ три́дцать
лет.

Exercise 78: 4 April 1987, starting at 7 p.m.

18 **Exercise 79:** 1 Е́сли бы Джейн зна́ла, она́ позвони́ла бы.
2 Е́сли бы я жил(а́) в Москве́, я говори́л(а) бы по-ру́сски.
3 Я бы хоте́л(а) познако́миться с ва́шей/твое́й сестро́й.
4 Е́сли бы вы бы́ли же́нщиной (inst after быть), вы понима́ли
бы.

Exercise 80: 1 Я хочу́, что́бы он знал. 2 Мы хоти́м, что́бы
Бори́с пришёл/прие́хал за́втра. 3 Они́ не хотя́т, что́бы
мы жда́ли.

Exercise 81: 1 Э́та гости́ница лу́чше. 2 Ру́сский язы́к трудне́е
англи́йского/бо́лее тру́дный, чем англи́йский язы́к. 3 В Ту́ле
мы говори́ли по-ру́сски ча́ще. 4 У Бори́са ме́ньше де́нег, чем
у Джейн. 5 Кака́я во́дка деше́вле? 6 Э́тот фильм са́мый
интере́сный.

Exercise 82: 1 Санкт-Петербу́рг краси́вее Москвы́/бо́лее
краси́вый, чем Москва́, но Москва́ интере́снее. 2 Э́та
ко́мната ху́же, чем пе́рвая. 3 Мо́жет быть, бы́ло бы лу́чше
позвони́ть. 4 Э́то ме́сто бу́дет лу́чше. 5 Како́й го́род са́мый
интере́сный? 6 Друга́я гости́ница намно́го (гора́здо) лу́чше.
7 (По)быстре́е, пожа́луйста!

Exercise 83: 1 свои́м но́вым ру́сским друзья́м 'I shall write a letter to own (= my) new Russian friends.' 2 о свои́х но́вых ру́сских друзья́х 'I was talking about my new Russian friends.' 3 на ру́сских де́вушках 'Many foreigners marry Russian girls.' 4 в э́тих города́х 'We were in these towns/ cities.'

19 Exercise 84: Джордж; Патриша; Бирмингем (standard spelling)/Бирмингэм/Бирминхам; Браун; Майкл (Майкль); Битлз (standard spelling).

Exercise 85:   Уважа́емая Татья́на Никола́евна!
    Спаси́бо за приглаше́ние. Я принима́ю его́ с удово́льствием.
    С уваже́нием,
                    Майкл Смит

        Дорого́й Андрю́ша!
    Пожа́луйста, позвони́ сего́дня ве́чером по́сле шести́
(часо́в). Мой телефо́н в гости́нице 711-41-44.
        Целу́ю,
                    Ба́рбара

        Уважа́емый до́ктор Серге́ев!
    Я хоте́л бы получи́ть ко́пию о́чень интере́сного докла́да,
кото́рый Вы прочита́ли на конфере́нции в сре́ду. Мое́ и́мя и
а́дрес: Москва́, гости́ница Украи́на, 716, д-р Трэ́вор Блант
(or, in the dative д-ру Трэ́вору Бла́нту). В обме́н я прилага́ю
ко́пию моего́ докла́да.
        С уваже́нием,
                    Трэ́вор Блант

Exercise 86: 1 *A:* Hello! *B:* Is that the biochemistry institute?
A: No, this is a (private) flat. You've got the wrong number.
B: I'm sorry.

2 *A:* Hello. *B:* Excuse me for troubling you (lit. 'you troubles a teacher'). I'm Jane Aldridge, a teacher from England. I'd like to speak to (If possible, connect me with) Boris Sergeyevich.
A: I'm sorry, he's out at the moment. Why do you need to speak to him? (On what matter are you ringing?) *B:* On a personal matter. Excuse me, who am I speaking to? *A:* The section head. Can you understand me all right? *B:* Thank you, I understand everything. But please speak slowly, it's a bad line

(lit. 'badly audible'). When will Boris Sergeyevich return? *A:* In an hour, probably. Do you want to leave a message? *B:* Would you tell him that I shall wait for him to ring me at home until five o'clock? After five he'll be able to find me at my friends' place. Their telephone is 123-89-06. *A:* I'm sorry, I didn't catch that. 89 or 79? *B:* 89. *A:* All right. I'll tell him. *B:* Thank you. Goodbye. *A:* Goodbye, Miss Oldwitch.

3 *A:* (Directory) enquiries, (assistant) number 34. *B:* Please give me the number of a Moscow subscriber. *A:* Separate [one family] or communal [with several families] flat? *B:* Separate.
A: Surname? *B:* Sergeyev. *A:* First name, patronymic? *B:* Ivan Nikolayevich. *A:* Name the street. *B:* Paustovsky Street.
A: 425-31-02. *B:* Thank you.

4 *A:* Yes! *B:* Is that the biochemistry institute? *A:* Yes. *B:* Good morning/Hello. This is Michael Smith representing the British firm 'Brock and Parsons'. May I speak to the director?
A: I'm sorry. He's busy at the moment. Ring back in an hour.

20 **Exercise 87:** 1 'In the institute there are many students <u>studying</u> (**изучáющих** is the gen pl of the present active participle from **изучáть** (i) 'to study' **я изучáю, ты изучáешь**) English.'
2 'Engineers <u>working</u> (**рабóтающие** is the nom pl of the present active participle from **рабóтать** 'to work') in the Far North earn ('receive') a lot of (big) money.' 3 'Here study students <u>who have come</u> (**приéхавшие** is the nom pl of the past active participle from **приéхать** (p) 'to arrive, come') from America.'
4 'What <u>is written</u> on this ticket?' **напи́сано** is the n sing past passive participle from **написáть** (p) 'to write'. 5 'Here is occupied' = 'This place <u>is occupied</u> (taken)' **зáнято** is the n sing past passive participle from **заня́ть** 'to occupy'. 6 '(While) <u>returning</u> (**Возвращáясь** is the imperfective gerund from **возвращáться** (i) 'to return' **я возвращáюсь, ты возвращáешься**) home, Boris met an old friend.' 7 '<u>Having read</u> (= after she had read) (**Прочитáв** is the perfective gerund from **прочитáть** (p) 'to read') the newspaper, Nina gave it to Mike.' 8 '<u>Having received</u> (= When she received) (**Получи́в** is the perfective gerund from **получи́ть** (p) 'to receive') Andrey's letter, Barbara answered it immediately.'

Exercise 88: A month after the (that) evening when Jane met (became acquainted with) his father, Boris proposed to her. After thinking for a while (perfective gerund 20.12) she refused. She admitted that she liked Boris very much (that Boris to her very pleases), but she said that she could not (cannot) marry him because in her life family happiness was (is) not (the) main (thing). Without explaining anything (Having explained nothing – perfective gerund) she left Moscow. Only three months later did Boris learn (find out) that she had decided to become a priest in America. Her friend Mark was helping her there. It turned out that he had become a priest long ago (became a priest already long ago). Feeling sad, Boris married Natasha. Everybody was very surprised (past passive participle 20.7). Nina said that her friend had made a bad mistake but that it would all soon be over. Indeed, Boris and Natasha split up five weeks later: Natasha complained that her husband was (is) always (all the time) talking to foreign women and behaving badly.

As for Barbara, she started to make frequent visits to Russia. Three months ago she and Andrey (they with Andrey) got married. Barbara already speaks good Russian. She will be working in Moscow for the Raduga ('Rainbow') publishing house which produces (present active participle 20.9) books in English.

Mike and Nina are still friends. He often comes to Moscow as a representative of Brock and Parsons and conducts negotiations with Russian organizations. Nina married Victor, Andrey's friend, and recently they had a daughter Yelena. In about ten years' time (inversion of лет and дéсять means approximation) Nina will become manager of a large factory in Uzbekistan (formerly one of the Soviet Union's southern, Turkic republics) and in about thirty years (she will become) a government minister.

Mini-dictionary

Russian–English

For the order of Russian alphabet see 2.2. The numbers refer to section headings, not pages.

a! 9.8 ah! (surprise etc.)
a 4.3 and/but
a то 12.9 or else
абоне́нт 19.7 subscriber
а́вгуст 17.4 August
авто́бус 11.6 bus
автома́т 16.6 telephone callbox
алло́ 19.6 hello (on telephone)
Аме́рика 6.6 America
америка́нец 4.3 American (man)
америка́нка 4.3 American (woman)
америка́нский 7.4 American
англи́йский 7.4 English
англича́нин 4.3 Englishman
англича́нка 4.3 Englishwoman
А́нглия 6.6 England (Britain)
а́нгло-америка́нский 16.9 Anglo-American
апельси́н 9.8 orange
апре́ль (m) 17.4 April

ба́бушка 7.10 grandmother
бато́н 9.8 loaf
без + gen 9.8 10.5 without
безусло́вно 18.12 undoubtedly
бе́лый 10.12 white
Бере́зка 8.14 Beriozka, lit. 'little birch tree'
беспоко́ить i 19.7 to worry, trouble (somebody)
бефстро́ганов 18.12 Beef Stroganoff

биле́т 6.6 ticket
биохи́мия 19.7 biochemistry
бо́лее 18.4 more
бо́льше 9.8 18.3 more; larger
бо́льше не 12.9 no longer
большо́й 10.12 big, large
борщ 18.12 beetroot soup
брат 3.2 brother
брать i 8.14 12.2 to take
бу́ду 14.1 I'll/I will be (future of **быть**)
бу́дьте 15.6 be (pol/pl)
бу́дьте внима́тельны 15.6 be careful/pay attention
бу́дьте добры́ 19.7 be so good (polite request)
бу́лочка 9.8 bread roll
буты́лка 9.8 bottle
бы 18.1 (conditional particle) would, 'd
быстре́е 18.3 quicker
бы́стро 6.6 quickly
быть i 11.1 14.4 to be

в/во + prep 5.4 in
в/во + acc 6.4 to, into (place); at (time); on (day)
варе́нье 18.12 jam
Вашингто́н 5.10 Washington
ведь 11.9 you know
великоле́пный 13.6 magnificent
верне́е 13.6 more accurately, rather

верну́ть p 20.12 to return (something)
верну́ться p 12.3 to return
ве́село 14.10 (it is) merry
весна́ 16.2 spring
весно́й 16.2 in spring
вести́ i 20.13 to lead, conduct
весь 13.6; *table 4* all
ве́чер 14.10 evening
ве́чером 16.2 in the evening
вещь (f) 8.2 8.14 thing
взять p 12.2 to take
вид 12.9 expression, view
ви́деть i 11.8 to see
вино́ 7.10 wine
вку́сный 18.12 tasty
вме́сте 6.6 together
во 17.5 (see в)
во́дка 7.8 vodka
возвраща́ться i 12.3 to return, come back
возмо́жно 19.7 possible
возража́ть i 18.12 to object
возьми́те 9.8 take (pol/pl)
войти́ p 14.6 to enter
вокза́л 12.9 (main) station (terminus)
волнова́ться i 14.10 to worry
вопро́с 12.9 question
восемна́дцатый 17.1 eighteenth
восемна́дцать 9.1 eighteen
во́семь 9.1 eight
во́семьдесят 9.1 eighty
восемьсо́т 9.1 eight hundred
воскресе́нье 17.5 Sunday
восьмидеся́тый 17.1 eightieth
восьмо́й 17.1 eighth
вот 3.2 there (when pointing)
вот как! 13.6 ah!, so that's how it is!
вот почему́ 6.6 that's why
вре́мя 11.9 time
все 14.10 (pl of весь) everybody, all
всего́ 11.9 only
встре́тить p 12.3 to meet
встре́ча 16.6 meeting

встреча́ть i 12.3 to meet
встреча́ться i 18.12 to meet (with), see someone
всё 7.10 (see весь) all, everything
вто́рник 17.5 Tuesday
второ́е (n adj) 18.12 second (course) (main course)
второ́й 7.10 17.1 second
вход 15.6 entrance
выпуска́ть i 20.13 to produce, issue
вчера́ 13.6 yesterday
вы 4.6 you (pol/pl)
вы пра́вы 18.12 you are right
вы́йти p 15.6 to go out (on foot)
вы́йти за́муж 17.9 to marry (of a woman)
вы́пить p 14.10 to drink
вы́ставка 13.6 exhibition
вы́ход 15.6 exit

газе́та 20.11 newspaper
где 3.2 where
гла́вный 20.13 main
глу́пость (f) 20.13 stupidity
говори́ть i 4.8 to speak, say
год 17.6 17.8 year
гора́здо 18.5 much (with comparatives)
го́ре 20.13 grief
го́род 3.2 city/town
горя́чий 8.11 hot
господи́н 16.8 gentleman, Mr
госпожа́ 16.8 lady, Mrs
гости́ница 5.10 hotel
гостя́х 11.9
   быть в гостя́х to be visiting
грамм 9.8 gram(me)
грани́ца 18.12 border
гриб 18.12 mushroom
гро́мко 14.6 loudly
грузи́нский 10.12 Georgian
гру́стно 12.9 14.6 (it is) sad
гру́стный 12.9 sad

да 3.2 yes
дава́й 11.9 let's (fam)
дава́й потанцу́ем! 14.10 let's dance!
дава́йте 6.6 let's (pol/pl)
дава́йте пое́дем 6.6 let's go (by transport)
дава́йте пойдём 8.14 let's go
дава́ть i 12.8 to give
давно́ 12.9 long ago, since long ago
да́же 18.12 even
да́йте 9.8 give (pol/pl)
дать p 12.8 to give
да́ча 8.3 country cottage
два 9.1; *table* 7 two
двадца́тый 17.1 twentieth
два́дцать 9.1 twenty
двена́дцатый 17.1 twelfth
двена́дцать 9.1 twelve
две́сти 9.1 two hundred
де́вушка 7.10 10.12 girl, 'miss'
девяно́сто 9.1 ninety
девяно́стый 17.1 ninetieth
девятна́дцатый 17.1 nineteenth
девятна́дцать 9.1 nineteen
девя́тый 17.1 ninth
де́вять 9.1 nine
девятьсо́т 9.1 nine hundred
действи́тельно 18.12 really, indeed
дека́брь (m) 17.4 December
де́лать i 12.2 to do
делега́ция 19.2 delegation
де́ло 6.6 19.7 matter, thing, piece of business
день (m) 8.13 day
де́ньги 8.14 money
дере́вня 7.10 country, village
деся́тый 17.1 tenth
де́сять 9.1 ten
де́ти (pl) 10.12 16.2 children
деше́вле 18.3 cheaper
дешёвый 18.3 cheap
дире́ктор 19.7 director, head, manager
длинне́е 18.3 longer
дли́нный 18.3 long

для + gen 10.5 for
днём 16.2 in the afternoon
до + gen 15.6 17.7 as far as, until
до ско́рого 19.2 until soon
до́брый 8.14 kind, good
дово́лен 16.9 satisfied (m)
дово́льна 16.9 satisfied (f)
договори́лись 11.9 that's agreed
до́лго 11.9 for a long time
до́ллар 8.14 dollar
дом 8.6 house
до́ма 10.12 at home
домо́й 6.6 home (= to home), homewards
дорого́й 18.3 19.2 dear
доро́же 18.3 more expensive
доучи́ться p 13.6 to complete one's studies
дочь (f) 8.6 16.5 16.9 daughter
друг 4.3 friend/boyfriend
друг дру́га 11.9 each other
друго́й 7.4 different/other
дру́жба 6.6 friendship
дружи́ть i 18.12 to be friendly with
друзья́ 8.14 friends
ду́мать i 13.6 to think
дя́дя 3.2 uncle

его́ 7.1 his, its
её 7.1 her
е́здить i 11.9 to travel there and back; travel around
е́сли 12.9 if
есть 8.14 10.7 10.8 is/are (exists/exist)
е́хать i 6.3 to go (by transport), ride
ещё 10.12 yet, still

жа́ловаться i 20.13 to complain
жа́рко 14.7 14.10 (it is) hot
ждать i (+ acc) 11.9 to wait (for)
же 13.6 (emphasizes previous word)
жена́ 16.9 wife

жени́ться i/p 17.9 to marry (of a man)

же́нщина 3.2 woman

живо́тное (n adj) 13.6 animal

жизнь (f) 20.13 life

жить i 5.9 to live

за + acc 11.9 18.12 for (in return for), over

за + inst 16.2 behind

за грани́цу 18.12 abroad ('over the border')

забы́ть p 15.2 to forget

заво́д 5.10 factory

за́втра 12.9 tomorrow

задава́ть i 12.9 to set (a task), ask (a question)

зада́ть p 12.9 to set (a task), ask (a question)

заку́ски (pl) 18.12 hors d'oeuvre

заме́тить p 15.6 to notice

замеча́тельный 13.6 remarkable

занима́ться i 16.2 to occupy oneself with, study

за́нят 19.7 occupied, busy

записа́ть p 15.6 to note down

запрети́ть p 20.7 to forbid

зараба́тывать i 13.6 to earn

заста́ть p 19.7 to find, come upon (a person)

захоте́ть p 13.6 to want, conceive a desire

заче́м 6.6 for what purpose, why

звони́ть i 12.3 to ring, telephone

звон(о́)к 14.10 ring, telephone call

здесь 5.10 here

здоро́вье 14.10 health

здра́вствуйте 2.1 3.2 hello

зима́ 16.2 winter

зимо́й 16.2 in winter

знать i 4.7 to know

зна́чит 8.14 17.9 um, eh (hesitation), it means, so

зову́т 3.1 they call

и 4.3 10.8 and; too, also

игру́шка 10.12 toy

идти́ i 6.3 to go (on foot)

из + gen 10.5 out of

извини́те 19.7 excuse (me) (pol/pl)

изда́тельство 20.13 publishing house

изуча́ть i 7.10 to study

икра́ 18.12 caviare

и́ли 7.10 or

и́мя 7.10 name, first name

инжене́р 16.9 engineer

иностра́н(е)ц 9.8 foreigner (m)

иностра́нка 19.7 foreigner (f)

иностра́нный 8.14 foreign

институ́т 19.7 institute

интере́снее 18.3 more interesting

интере́сно 8.14 14.7 (it is) interesting

интере́сный 11.9 interesting

интересова́ть i 8.14 to interest

Интури́ст 5.11 Intourist

иска́ть i 15.6 to look for

исчеза́ть i 15.6 to disappear

их 7.1 their

ию́ль (m) 17.4 July

ию́нь (m) 17.4 June

к + dat 14.9 towards

к сожале́нию 19.7 unfortunately, I regret

ка́ждый 9.8 each, every

ка́жется 13.6 it seems

как 3.2 how

как дела́? 6.6 14.10 how are things?

как то́лько 15.6 as soon as

како́й 8.14 what, what kind of

Калифо́рния 13.6 California

капиталисти́ческий 8.12 capitalist

капстрана́ 18.12 capitalist country

каранда́ш 16.1 pencil

ка́рта 15.6 map

ка́сса 9.9 cashdesk

касси́р 9.9 cashier

кварти́ра 7.10 flat, apartment

кем (inst of **кто**) 16.9 by whom
кило́ 9.8 kilo
килогра́мм 9.8 kilogram
кино́ 11.9 cinema
кни́га 7.10 book
кни́жный 7.4 book
когда́ 5.3 when
колбаса́ 9.8 sausage (salami type)
коммуна́льный 19.7 communal
ко́мната 13.6 room
кон(е́)ц 17.9 end
коне́чно 5.10 of course
конфере́нция 17.9 conference
ко́нчиться p 20.13 to come to an
    end
копе́йка 9.1 kopeck
кот 7.10 tomcat
котле́ты по-ки́евски 18.12
    Chicken Kiev
кото́рый 7.9 who; which
ко́фе (m) 15.3 coffee
ко́шка 13.6 cat (female)
кра́йний 13.6 extreme
Кра́йний Се́вер 13.6 Far North
    (of Russia)
краси́вее 18.3 more beautiful
краси́вый 7.4 beautiful/handsome
кра́сный 7.4 red
кро́ме того́ 13.6 furthermore, also
кста́ти 13.6 by the way
кто 4.3 who
куда́ 6.4 6.6 where (motion),
    whither
купи́ть p 12.2 to buy
кури́ть i 14.6 to smoke

лёгкий 18.3 easy, light
ле́гче 18.3 easier, lighter
лежа́т 9.8 (they) lie
лет (gen pl of **год**) 17.8 (of)
    summers (= years)
ле́то 16.2 summer
ле́том 16.2 in summer
Ливерпу́ль (m) 4.3 Liverpool
литр 10.12 litre
ли́чный 19.7 personal

Ло́ндон 4.3 London
лу́чше 18.3 better
лу́чший 18.7 best
люби́мый 8.14 favourite
люби́ть i 6.6 11.8 to love, like
лю́ди 13.6 people

магази́н 6.6 shop, store
мада́м 16.8 madame
май 17.4 May
ма́ленький 10.12 small
ма́ло 9.7 few
ма́ма 11.9 mother, mum (fam)
ма́мочка 16.9 intimate form of
    'mother'
март 17.4 March
ма́сло 9.8 butter
матрёшка 10.12 matryoshka
    (wooden doll)
мать (f) 3.3d 8.6 mother
маши́на 16.9 machine, car
ме́дленнее 18.3 slower
ме́дленно 3.2 slowly
ме́дленный 18.3 slow
между + inst 16.2 between
междунаро́дный 18.13
    international
ме́нее 18.6 less
ме́ньше 18.3 smaller, less
ме́сто 18.8 place; space; seat
ме́сяц 6.6 month
метро́ 6.6 metro, underground,
    subway
мини́стр 20.13 government
    minister
мину́та 17.2 minute (noun)
мир 1.1 peace
мисс 16.8 Miss
ми́ссис 16.8 Mrs
ми́стер 16.8 Mr
мне́ние 14.9 opinion
мно́гие 13.6 many (people)
мно́го 9.7 9.8 many, much
мо́жет быть 12.9 perhaps, maybe
мо́жно 6.6 14.6 it is possible/
    permitted; one may

мой 4.3 7.1 my
молодо́й 7.4 young
молоко́ 9.8 milk
монасты́рь (m) ex. 61 monastery
мо́ре 16.4 sea
моро́женое (n adj) 18.12 ice cream
Москва́ 4.3 Moscow
москви́ч 5.10 Muscovite
моско́вский 8.14 Moscow (adj)
мочь i 12.4 to be able
муж 7.10 husband
музе́й 5.5 museum
му́зыка 10.12 music
мы 4.3 we

на + prep 5.4 on
на + acc 6.4 onto, to (a place), for (time)
наве́рно 6.6 probably
над + inst 16.2 above
на́до 8.14 14.6 it is necessary; one must
надое́сть p + dat 13.6 to bore
надо́лго 6.6 for a long time
наза́д 13.6 ago; back
назва́ть p 13.6 to call, give a name
назови́те 19.7 name (pol/pl)
найти́ p 15.6 to find
наконе́ц 18.12 at last
намно́го 18.5 much (with comparatives)
наоборо́т 13.6 on the contrary
написа́ть p 12.1 to write
напра́во 15.6 to the right
наприме́р 8.14 for example
наха́льно 20.13 impudently
находи́ться i 15.6 to find oneself, be located
нача́льник 19.7 boss, chief, head
начина́ться i 17.9 to begin (intransitive)
наш 7.1; table 6 our
не 3.2 4.9 not
не пра́вда ли? 16.9 isn't it?
неда́вно 13.6 recently
недалеко́ (indecl) 6.6 not far

неде́ля 6.6 week
недо́лго 11.9 not long
нельзя́ 14.6 14.10 (it is) not possible/not allowed; one must not
немно́го 5.10 a little
немно́жко 14.10 a little
не́сколько 9.7 11.9 a few
нет 3.2 10.9 no; there isn't/aren't
никогда́ не 12.9 never
ничего́ 6.6 13.6 not bad, all right; nothing
но 5.10 but
Новосиби́рск 5.10 Novosibirsk
но́вый 7.4 new
ноль (m) 17.3 zero
но́мер 19.7 number
ночь (f) 3.3 night
но́чью 16.2 during the night
ноя́брь (m) 17.4 November
нра́виться i + dat of person 18.12 to please
ну 11.9 well (to show hesitation)
ну́жно 14.6 (it is) necessary

о/об/обо + prep 5.4 about, concerning
обе́дать i 18.12 to dine, have a meal
обнима́ю 19.2 I embrace
обра́доваться p 13.6 to be pleased
обра́тно 6.6 back
объясни́ть p 20.13 to explain
обы́чно 8.14 usually
обы́чный 15.6 usual
обяза́тельно 12.9 definitely, without fail
одева́ться i 11.7 to get dressed
оди́н 9.1 9.2 12.9; table 7 one; alone
оди́ннадцатый 17.1 eleventh
оди́ннадцать 9.1 eleven
ожида́ть i 11.9 to expect
ой! 14.10 oh! (surprise)
оказа́ться p 20.13 to turn out
окно́ 13.6 window
око́нчить p 13.6 to graduate, finish

267

октя́брь (m) 17.4 October
он 3.2 4.6 he
она́ 3.2 4.6 she
они́ 4.3. 4.6 they
оно́ 3.2 4.6 it
опа́здывать i 11.9 to be late
опозда́ть p 12.9 to be late
опя́ть 7.10 again
организа́ция 20.13 organization
оригина́л 18.1 original
о́сень (f) 16.2 autumn
о́сенью 16.2 in autumn
осо́бенно 6.6 especially
остано́вка 15.6 stop
от + gen 9.4 from
отве́тить p 12.3 to answer, reply
отвеча́ть i 12.3 to answer, reply
отде́л 19.7 section, department
отде́льный 19.7 separate
оте́ц 8.13 father
отказа́ться p 20.13 to refuse
открыва́ть i 12.3 to open
откры́ть p 12.3 to open
о́тчество 16.9 patronymic
официа́нтка 18.12 waitress
охо́тно 18.12 willingly
о́чень 4.3 very
о́чередь (f) 9.8 queue, line
ошиба́ться i 13.6 to make a
    mistake

па́па 3.3 dad
пе́рвое (n adj) 18.12 first (course)
    (soup)
пе́рвый 7.10 17.1 first
перегово́ры (pl) 20.13 negotiations
пе́ред + inst 16.2 in front of
переда́ть p 19.6 to transmit
перее́хать p 13.6 to move house
перенести́ p 19.2 to transfer
пешко́м 6.3 6.6 on foot
пи́во 7.10 beer
писа́тель (m) 20.10 writer
писа́ть i 11.9 to write
письмо́ 3.2 letter
пить i 14.10 to drink

план ex. 63 18.12 map (of town),
    plan
пласти́нка 8.14 record
плати́ть i 13.6 to pay
пло́хо 19.7 badly
плохо́й 18.3 bad
пло́щадь (f) 7.10 square
по + dat 14.9 15.6 along
побе́да 17.9 victory
поверну́ть p 15.6 to turn
повтори́те p 19.6 repeat (pol/pl)
поговори́ть p 19.7 to have a talk
    with
пого́да 18.4 weather
под + inst 16.2 under
пода́р(о)к 8.13 present, gift
подожди́те мину́точку 8.14 wait
    a moment (pol/pl)
подру́га 7.10 (girl)friend
поду́мать p 20.13 to think
подходи́ть i 18.12 to come up (to)
по́езд 6.6 train
поезжа́йте 15.6 go (travel)
    (pol/pl)
пое́хать p 12.2 13.6 to go (by
    transport)
пожа́луйста 3.2 please; don't
    mention it
пожени́ться p 20.13 to get
    married (of a couple)
позво́лить p 12.9 to permit
позвони́ть p 12.3 to telephone
по́здно 17.9 late
поздравля́ть i (c + inst) 14.10 to
    congratulate (on)
познако́мить p 16.9 to introduce
познако́миться p 16.9 to become
    acquainted
познако́мьтесь p 16.9 meet;
    become acquainted (pol/pl)
позови́те p 19.6 19.7 call,
    summon (pol/pl)
пойти́ p 12.2 to go (on foot)
покажи́те 8.14 show (pol/pl)
показа́ть p 12.7 to show
пока́зывать i 12.7 to show

покупа́ть i 8.14 to buy
покупка 8.14 purchase
пол-ли́тра 10.12 half a litre
полови́на 17.2 half
получи́ть p 13.6 to receive
полюби́ть p + acc 13.6 to fall in
  love with
по-мо́ему 7.10 in my opinion,
  I think
помога́ть i 20.13 to help
понеде́льник 17.5 Monday
понима́ть i 4.7 12.2 to understand
понра́виться p 13.6 to please
поня́тно 9.8 (it is) comprehensible
поня́ть p 12.2 to understand
попада́ть i 15.6 to get (somewhere)
  (p попа́сть)
попа́сть p 19.7 to get (somewhere)
пора́ 17.9 it is time
по-ру́сски 4.3 in Russian
по́рция 18.12 portion
по́сле + gen 17.7 after
после́дний 15.6 last
посмотре́ть p 12.2 to watch
посмотри́те 8.14 look (pol/pl)
посо́льство 19.2 embassy
пото́м 6.6 next, then
потому́ что 17.9 because
поцелова́ть p 14.10 to kiss
почему́ 5.3 5.10 why
почти́ 10.12 almost
поэ́тому ex. 46 so, therefore
пра́вильно ex. 62 correct
предложе́ние 20.13 proposal
предложи́ть p 13.6 to offer
представи́тель (m) 19.7
  representative
предста́виться p 16.9 to introduce
  oneself
прекра́сно 18.12 fine, splendid
преподава́ть i 13.6 to teach
приве́т! 13.6 greeting, hi!
приду́мать p 13.6 to think up,
  invent
приезжа́ть i 12.3 to arrive
  (by transport)

прие́м 19.2 reception
прие́хать p 12.3 to arrive
  (by transport)
приз 13.6 prize
призна́ться p 20.13 to admit
прийти́ p 12.3 to arrive (on foot)
прила́в(о)к 15.6 counter
принести́ p 18.12 to bring
приро́да 13.6 nature
приходи́ть i 12.3 to arrive (on foot)
прия́тнее 18.3 nicer
прия́тно 5.10 pleasant(ly)
прия́тный 11.9 pleasant
продав(е́)ц 9.9 10.12 sales assistant
продолжа́ть i 20.13 to continue
прожи́ть p 13.6 (i жить) to live
  (for a specified period)
пройти́ p 15.2 to pass
проспе́кт 5.10 avenue
прости́ 12.9 excuse me, sorry (fam)
прости́те 5.10 excuse me, sorry
  (pol/pl)
про́сто 13.6 simply
профе́ссор 19.2 professor
прочита́ть p 12.3 to read
про́шлый 17.9 last, previous
пря́мо 15.6 straight, straight on
пятидеся́тый 17.1 fiftieth
пятна́дцатый 17.1 fifteenth
пятна́дцать 9.1 fifteen
пя́тница 17.5 Friday
пя́тый 17.1 fifth
пять 9.1 five
пятьдеся́т 9.1 fifty
пятьсо́т 9.1 five hundred

рабо́та 5.10 work
рабо́тать i 4.3 ex. 10 to work
ра́дуга 20.13 rainbow
раз 9.8 time
разгова́ривать i 20.13 to
  converse, talk
разойти́сь p 20.13 to split up
разреши́те 16.9 permit (pol/pl)
ра́но 17.9 early
рассказа́ть p 12.3 to tell, relate

расска́зывайте 11.9 tell (pol/pl)
расска́зывать i 12.3 to tell, relate
не рассл́ышать p 19.7 to mishear,
    fail to make out
расчёт 18.12 calculation
ребён(о)к 16.5 child
река́ 18.10 river
религио́зный 18.12 religious
рестора́н 1.1 ex. 31 restaurant
реши́ть p 13.6 to decide, solve
ро́дина 17.9 homeland
роди́тели (pl) 10.12 parents
роди́ться p 11.7 to be born
родно́й 6.6 native
рожде́ние 12.9 birth
рома́н 13.6 15.6 romance, love
    affair; novel
Росси́я 5.6 Russia
рубль (m) 3.3 rouble
ру́сская (f adj) 6.6 Russian woman
ру́сский 5.10 7.4 Russian (adj)

с + gen 17.7 from, since
с + inst 16.2 with
сади́ться i 15.2 to sit down
самолёт 11.9 aeroplane
са́мый 7.10 18.7 most
    (with adjectives)
са́хар 9.8 sugar
све́жий 8.11 fresh
свида́ние 3.3 meeting, rendezvous
свобо́дный 11.9 free
свой 13.6 own (belonging to the
    subject), my, his etc.
свяще́нник 18.12 priest
сда́ча 9.8 change (money returned)
сде́лать p 8.14 12.2 to do
себя́ 20.13 self
се́вер 13.6 north
сего́дня 8.14 today
седьмо́й 17.1 seventh
сейча́с 5.10 at the moment,
    (right) now
семе́йный 20.13 family (adj)
семидеся́тый 17.1 seventieth
семна́дцатый 17.1 seventeenth

семна́дцать 9.1 seventeen
семь 9.1 seven
се́мьдесят 9.1 seventy
семьсо́т 9.1 seven hundred
семья́ 16.4 family
сентя́брь (m) 17.4 September
серьёзный 13.6 serious
сестра́ 7.10 10.12 sister
Сиби́рь (f) 3.2 Siberia
симпати́чный 7.4 nice (of a person)
сказа́ть p 12.2 to say
ско́лько 9.7 how much, how many
ско́ро 20.13 soon
скры́тный 18.12 secretive
ску́чно 13.6 14.7 (it is) boring
ску́чный 16.9 boring
сла́дкий 7.10 sweet
сле́ва 15.6 on the left
сле́дующий 8.11 following, next
сли́шком 6.6 too (excessively)
слова́рь (m) 15.6 dictionary
сло́во 7.10 word
случи́ться p 13.6 to happen
слу́шать i 19.6 19.7 to listen to
сл́ышно 19.7 (it is) audible
смета́на 18.12 sour cream
смешно́ 13.6 (it's) funny
смешно́й 13.6 funny
смея́ться i 11.9 to laugh
смотре́ть i 8.14 11.9 12.2 to look,
    watch
смочь p 12.4 to be able
снача́ла 11.9 at first
сно́ва 11.9 again
соба́ка 13.6 dog
сове́тский 1.1 Soviet
совреме́нный 15.6 modern
совсе́м 10.12 completely, totally
согла́сен 16.9 (I) agree (m)
согла́сна 16 9 (I) agree (f)
соедини́те 19.7 connect (pol/pl)
сообщи́ть p 19.2 to inform
со́рок 9.1 forty
сороково́й 17.1 fortieth
со́тый 17.1 hundredth
сою́з 1.1 union

спаси́бо 3.2 thank you
спеши́ть i 12.9 to hurry
спра́ва 15.6 on the right
спра́вочное (бюро́) 19.7 enquiry
(office)
спроси́ть p 13.6 to ask
спу́тник 12.9 travelling companion
спу́тница 18.12 (female)
companion
сра́зу 13.6 immediately
среда́ 17.5 Wednesday
стака́н 9.3 (drinking) glass
ста́нция 6.6 (metro) station; small
railway station
ста́рый 7.10 old
стать p 16.2 16.9 to become; begin
стиль (m) 18.12 style
стихи́ (pl) 8.14 poetry, poem(s)
сто 9.1 hundred
сто́ить i 9.8 to cost
Столи́чная (f adj) 10.12
Stolichnaya ('Capital') vodka
стоя́ть i 9.8 to stand
страна́ 18.12 country
стра́нный 12.9 strange
стро́йка 13.6 construction site
студе́нтка 4.3 (female) student
суббо́та 17.5 Saturday
сувени́р 8.14 souvenir
су́мка 9.8 bag
сча́стье 20.13 happiness
счита́ть i 16.9 to count, consider
сын 8.6 son
сыр 9.8 cheese
сюрпри́з 11.9 surprise

так 14.6 so
тако́й 8.14 such
такси́ 3.2 taxi
так-та́к 17.9 hmm (hesitation)
там 5.10 there
твой 7.1 your (fam)
телеви́зор 13.2 13.6 television
телефо́н 15.2 telephone
тепе́рь 6.6 now
тепло́ 14.7 (it is) warm

ти́ше 18.12 quieter
това́рищ comrade
тогда́ 9.8 then (at that time); in
that case
то́же ex. 46 too
то́лько 7.10 only
торго́вый 18.13 trade (adj)
тот 18.3; table 4 that
трамва́й 5.5 tram
тре́тий 17.1 third
тре́тье (n adj) 18.12 third (course)
(dessert)
три 9.1 table 7 three
тридца́тый 17.1 thirtieth
три́дцать 9.1 thirty
трина́дцатый 17.1 thirteenth
трина́дцать 9.1 thirteen
три́ста 9.1 three hundred
тру́бка 19.6 receiver
труд 9.8 labour
трудне́е 18.3 more difficult
тру́дный 9.8 difficult
туда́ 6.4 there (motion)
тури́ст 8.14 tourist
ты 4.6 you (fam)
ты́сяча 9.1 thousand

у + gen 10.5 by, at
уважа́емый 19.2 respected
уваже́ние 19.2 respect
уви́деть p 12.2 to see
уговори́ть p 16.9 to persuade
у́г(о)л 15.6 corner
удиви́ть p 20.13 to surprise
уезжа́ть i 17.9 to leave
(by transport)
уе́хать p 12.9 to leave
(by transport)
уже́ 9.8 already
узна́ть p 13.6 to find out
украи́н(е)ц 5.10 Ukrainian (man)
у́лица 5.10 street
улыба́ться i 11.7 12.2 to smile
улыбну́ться p 12.2 to smile
у́мный 18.12 intelligent
университе́т 11.9 university

упражне́ние 5.6 exercise
успева́ть i 15.6 to have time to
устра́ивать i 19.2 to organize
у́тро 3.2 morning
у́тром 16.2 in the morning
учи́тель (m) 16.4 teacher
учи́тельница 4.3 (female) teacher
учи́ться i 11.9 to study

фами́лия 16.9 surname
февра́ль (m) 17.4 February
фильм 13.2 film
фи́рма 19.7 firm
фо́рма 9.8 form
фра́за 15.6 phrase
фунт 8.14 pound (money and
  weight)

хлеб 9.8 bread
ходи́ть i 11.9 to go (on foot); walk
  about
хо́лодно 13.6 14.6 (it is) cold
хоро́ший 8.11 good
хорошо́ 3.2 well, good, all right,
  OK
хоте́ть i 6.6 to want
ху́же 18.3 worse

царь (m) 3.3 tsar
целова́ть i 19.2 to kiss
це́лый 19.2 whole
цент 10.12 cent
центр 5.10 centre, city centre
це́рк(о)вь (f) 18.12 church

чай 18.12 tea
час 17.2 hour
ча́сто 8.14 often
ча́ще 18.3 more often
чек 9.9 receipt
челове́к 16.5 person
чем 18.3 than
че́рез + acc 6.6 after (with time
  words); through

честь (f) 13.6 honour
четве́рг 17.5 Thursday
четвёртый 17.1 fourth
четы́ре 9.1 table 7 four
четы́реста 9.1 four hundred
четы́рнадцатый 17.1 fourteenth
четы́рнадцать 9.1 fourteen
число́ 17.4 number, date
чи́стый 7.4 clean
чита́ть i 12.3 to read
что 4.3 what/that
что вы! 13.6 come now! don't be
  silly!
чтобы 18.2 18.12 (in order) to, so
  that

шампа́нское (n adj) 14.10
  (Russian) champagne
шашлы́к 18.12 kebab, pieces of
  meat on a skewer
шестидеся́тый 17.1 sixtieth
шестна́дцатый 17.1 sixteenth
шестна́дцать 9.1 sixteen
шесто́й 17.1 sixth
шесть 9.1 six
шестьдеся́т 9.1 sixty
шестьсо́т 9.1 six hundred
ши́ре 18.3 wider
шко́ла 16.9 school
шту́ка 10.12 thing

экземпля́р 10.12 copy (of book)
э́то 4.3 this (also used for 'that')
э́тот 8.12; table 4 this, that

я 3.2 4.6 I
я́блоко 9.8 apple
язы́к 5.10 language
яйцо́ 9.8 egg
янва́рь (m) 17.4 January
япо́нский 18.3 Japanese

Russian handwriting

Here are the handwritten forms of the Cyrillic letters:

А	а	Р	р
Б	б	С	с
В	в	Т	т
Г	г	У	у
Д	д	Ф	ф
Е	е	Х	х
Ё	ё	Ц	ц
Ж	ж	Ч	ч
З	з	Ш	ш
И	и	Щ	щ
Й	й	Ъ	ъ
К	к	Ы	ы
Л	л	Ь	ь
М	м	Э	э
Н	н	Ю	ю
О	о	Я	я
П	п		

Here are the two letters from 19.2 in handwritten form:

Уважаемый Михаил Александрович!
Извините меня за то, что я не смогу
встретиться с Вами в пятницу.
Я только сегодня узнала, что в пятницу
для нашей делегации устраивают
приём в американском посольстве.
Сообщите, пожалуйста, согласны ли
Вы перенести нашу встречу на субботу,
когда я буду весь день в гостинице.

С уважением,
Уильхэльмина Дж.
Уатэрспун

Дорогая Наташа!

Приходите сегодня после шести
Буду целый вечер дома.

Целую.
Ника.

Grammar tables

Declension

Gender 3.3

Cases: nominative (*N*) 4.2, accusative (*A*) 6.1, 6.2, animate *(anim)* accusative 6.2, 10.11, genitive (*G*) 9.4, dative (*D*) 12.7, instrumental (*I*) 16.1, 16.2, prepositional (*P*) 5.4

1 MASCULINE NOUNS

	ticket (6.6)		cat (7.10)	
	sing	*pl*	*sing*	*pl*
N	биле́т	биле́ты	кот	коты́
A	биле́т	биле́ты	кота́	кото́в
G	биле́та	биле́тов	кота́	кото́в
D	биле́ту	биле́там	коту́	кота́м
I	биле́том	биле́тами	кото́м	кота́ми
P	биле́те	биле́тах	коте́	кота́х

	dictionary (15.6)		museum (5.5)	
	sing	*pl*	*sing*	*pl*
N	слова́рь	словари́	музе́й	музе́и
A	слова́рь	словари́	музе́й	музе́и
G	словаря́	словаре́й	музе́я	музе́ев
D	словарю́	словаря́м	музе́ю	музе́ям
I	словарём	словаря́ми	музе́ем	музе́ями
P	словаре́	словаря́х	музе́е	музе́ях

2 FEMININE NOUNS

	newspaper (20.11)		dog (13.6)	
	sing	*pl*	*sing*	*pl*
N	газе́та	газе́ты	соба́ка	соба́ки
A	газе́ту	газе́ты	соба́ку	соба́к
G	газе́ты	газе́т	соба́ки	соба́к
D	газе́те	газе́там	соба́ке	соба́кам
I	газе́той	газе́тами	соба́кой	соба́ками
P	газе́те	газе́тах	соба́ке	соба́ках

	week (6.6)		square (7.10)		surname (16.9)	
	sing	*pl*	*sing*	*pl*	*sing*	*pl*
N	неде́ля	неде́ли	пло́щадь	пло́щади	фами́лия	фами́лии
A	неде́лю	неде́ли	пло́щадь	пло́щади	фами́лию	фами́лии
G	неде́ли	неде́ль	пло́щади	площаде́й	фами́лии	фами́лий
D	неде́ле	неде́лям	пло́щади	площадя́м	фами́лии	фами́лиям
I	неде́лей	неде́лями	пло́щадью	площадя́ми	фами́лией	фами́лиями
P	неде́ле	неде́лях	пло́щади	площадя́х	фами́лии	фами́лиях

3 NEUTER NOUNS

	matter (6.6)		exercise (5.6)		name (7.10)	
	sing	*pl*	*sing*	*pl*	*sing*	*pl*
N	де́ло	дела́	упражне́ние	упражне́ния	и́мя	имена́
A	де́ло	дела́	упражне́ние	упражне́ния	и́мя	имена́
G	де́ла	дел	упражне́ния	упражне́ний	и́мени	имён
D	де́лу	дела́м	упражне́нию	упражне́ниям	и́мени	имена́м
I	де́лом	дела́ми	упражне́нием	упражне́ниями	и́менем	имена́ми
P	де́ле	дела́х	упражне́нии	упражне́ниях	и́мени	имена́х

4 PRONOUNS (4.6)

	I	you	he	she	it	we	you	they	who	what
N	я	ты	он	она́	оно́	мы	вы	они́	кто	что
A	меня́	тебя́	его́	её	его́	нас	вас	их	кого́	что
G	меня́	тебя́	его́	её	его́	нас	вас	их	кого́	чего́
D	мне	тебе́	ему́	ей	ему́	нам	вам	им	кому́	чему́
I	мной	тобо́й	им	ей	им	на́ми	ва́ми	и́ми	кем	чем
P	мне	тебе́	нём	ней	нём	нас	вас	них	ком	чём

	this (8.12)				that (18.3)			
	m	*f*	*n*	*pl*	*m*	*f*	*n*	*pl*
N	э́тот	э́та	э́то	э́ти	тот	та	то	те
A	э́тот	э́ту	э́то	э́ти	тот	ту	то	те
A *anim*	э́того	э́ту	э́то	э́тих	того́	ту	то	тех
G	э́того	э́той	э́того	э́тих	того́	той	того́	тех
D	э́тому	э́той	э́тому	э́тим	тому́	той	тому́	тем
I	э́тим	э́той	э́тим	э́тими	тем	той	тем	те́ми
P	э́том	э́той	э́том	э́тих	том	той	том	тех

	all (13.6)			
	m	*f*	*n*	*pl*
N	весь	вся	всё	все
A	весь	всю	всё	все
A *anim*	всего́	всю	всё	всех
G	всего́	всей	всего́	всех
D	всему́	всей	всему́	всем
I	всем	всей	всем	все́ми
P	всём	всей	всём	всех

5 ADJECTIVES (7.4, 8.11)

	new (7.4)			
	m	*f*	*n*	*pl*
N	но́вый	но́вая	но́вое	но́вые
A	но́вый	но́вую	но́вое	но́вые
A *anim*	но́вого	но́вую	но́вое	но́вых
G	но́вого	но́вой	но́вого	но́вых
D	но́вому	но́вой	но́вому	но́вым
I	но́вым	но́вой	но́вым	но́выми
P	но́вом	но́вой	но́вом	но́вых

	Russian (7.4)			
	m	*f*	*n*	*pl*
N	ру́сский	ру́сская	ру́сское	ру́сские
A	ру́сский	ру́сскую	ру́сское	ру́сские
A *anim*	ру́сского	ру́сскую	ру́сское	ру́сских
G	ру́сского	ру́сской	ру́сского	ру́сских
D	ру́сскому	ру́сской	ру́сскому	ру́сским
I	ру́сским	ру́сской	ру́сским	ру́сскими
P	ру́сском	ру́сской	ру́сском	ру́сских

good (8.11)

	m	f	n	pl
N	хоро́ший	хоро́шая	хоро́шее	хоро́шие
A	хоро́ший	хоро́шую	хоро́шее	хоро́шие
A anim	хоро́шего	хоро́шую	хоро́шее	хоро́ших
G	хоро́шего	хоро́шей	хоро́шего	хоро́ших
D	хоро́шему	хоро́шей	хоро́шему	хоро́шим
I	хоро́шим	хоро́шей	хоро́шим	хоро́шими
P	хоро́шем	хоро́шей	хоро́шем	хоро́ших

last (15.6)

	m	f	n	pl
N	после́дний	после́дняя	после́днее	после́дние
A	после́дний	после́днюю	после́днее	после́дние
A anim	после́днего	после́днюю	после́днее	после́дних
G	после́днего	после́дней	после́днего	после́дних
D	после́днему	после́дней	после́днему	после́дним
I	после́дним	после́дней	после́дним	после́дними
P	после́днем	после́дней	после́днем	после́дних

6 POSSESSIVES (7.1)

my (same endings for **тво́й** 'your' and **сво́й** 'own' – 13.6)

	m	f	n	pl
N	мой	моя́	мое́	мои́
A	мой	мою́	мое́	мои́
A anim	моего́	мою́	мое́	мои́х
G	моего́	мое́й	моего́	мои́х
D	моему́	мое́й	моему́	мои́м
I	мои́м	мое́й	мои́м	мои́ми
P	мое́м	мое́й	мое́м	мои́х

our (same endings for **ваш** 'your')

	m	f	n	pl
N	наш	на́ша	на́ше	на́ши
A	наш	на́шу	на́ше	на́ши
A anim	на́шего	на́шу	на́ше	на́ших
G	на́шего	на́шей	на́шего	на́ших
D	на́шему	на́шей	на́шему	на́шим
I	на́шим	на́шей	на́шим	на́шими
P	на́шем	на́шей	на́шем	на́ших

7 NUMBERS (9.1, 9.2, 9.3, 17.2)

	one			two	
	m	*f*	*n*	*m/n*	*f*
N	оди́н	одна́	одно́	два	две
A	оди́н	одну́	одно́	два	две
A *anim*	одного́	одну́	одно́	двух	двух
G	одного́	одно́й	одного́	двух	двух
D	одному́	одно́й	одному́	двум	двум
I	одни́м	одно́й	одни́м	двумя́	двумя́
P	одно́м	одно́й	одно́м	двух	двух

	three	four	five	eight
	m/f/n	*m/f/n*	*m/f/n*	*m/f/n*
N	три	четы́ре	пять	во́семь
A	три	четы́ре	пять	во́семь
A *anim*	трёх	четырёх		
G	трёх	четырёх	пяти́	восьми́
D	трём	четырём	пяти́	восьми́
I	тремя́	четырьмя́	пятью	восемью́
P	трёх	четырёх	пяти́	восьми́

	twenty-six	forty	fifty	ninety
	m/f/n	*m/f/n*	*m/f/n*	*m/f/n*
N	два́дцать шесть	со́рок	пятьдеся́т	девяно́сто
A	два́дцать шесть	со́рок	пятьдеся́т	девяно́сто
G	двадцати́ шести́	сорока́	пяти́десяти	девяно́ста
D	двадцати́ шести́	сорока́	пяти́десяти	девяно́ста
I	двадцатью́ шестью́	сорока́	пятью́десятью	девяно́ста
P	двадцати́ шести́	сорока́	пяти́десяти	девяно́ста

	100	200	300
	m/f/n	*m/f/n*	*m/f/n*
N	сто	две́сти	три́ста
A	сто	две́сти	три́ста
G	ста	двухсо́т	трёхсо́т
D	ста	двумста́м	трёмста́м
I	ста	двумяста́ми	тремяста́ми
P	ста	двухста́х	трёхста́х

Conjugation

8 VERBS

aspects (perfective and imperfective) 12.1, 13.1, 13.2, 13.3, 13.4, 14.2, 15.3
conditional 18.1
future tense 12.1, 14.2
gerunds 20.11, 20.12
imperative 15.1, 15.2, 15.3, 15.4
infinitive 4.7
participles 20.6, 20.7, 20.8, 20.9, 20.10
past tense 11.1, 11.2, 11.3, 13.1, 13.3
present tense 4.7, 4.8, 5.9
reflexive 11.7

(a) **знать** (Type 1) imperfective 'to know'

	present	*past*	*future*	*imperative*
я	зна́ю	зна́л(а)	бу́ду знать	
ты	зна́ешь	зна́л(а)	бу́дешь знать	зна́й
он	зна́ет	знал	бу́дет знать	
она́	зна́ет	зна́ла	бу́дет знать	
оно́	зна́ет	зна́ло	бу́дет знать	
мы	зна́ем	зна́ли	бу́дем знать	
вы	зна́ете	зна́ли	бу́дете знать	зна́йте
они́	зна́ют	зна́ли	бу́дут знать	

pres active participle: **зна́ющий**
past active participle: **зна́вший**   *gerund:* **зна́я**

(b) **прочита́ть** (Type 1) perfective 'to read'

	past	*future*	*imperative*
я	прочита́л(а)	прочита́ю	
ты	прочита́л(а)	прочита́ешь	прочита́й
он	прочита́л	прочита́ет	
она́	прочита́ла	прочита́ет	
оно́	прочита́ло	прочита́ет	
мы	прочита́ли	прочита́ем	
вы	прочита́ли	прочита́ете	прочита́йте
они́	прочита́ли	прочита́ют	

past passive participle: **прочи́тан(ный)**
past active participle: **прочита́вший** *gerund:* **прочита́в**

(c) **говори́ть** (Type 2) imperfective 'to speak'

	present	past	future	imperative
я	говорю́	говори́л(а)	бу́ду говори́ть	
ты	говори́шь	говори́л(а)	бу́дешь говори́ть	говори́
он	говори́т	говори́л	бу́дет говори́ть	
она́	говори́т	говори́ла	бу́дет говори́ть	
оно́	говори́т	говори́ло	бу́дет говори́ть	
мы	говори́м	говори́ли	бу́дем говори́ть	
вы	говори́те	говори́ли	бу́дете говори́ть	говори́те
они́	говоря́т	говори́ли	бу́дут говори́ть	

pres active participle: **говоря́щий**
past active participle: **говори́вший**   *gerund:* **говоря́**

(d) **позвони́ть** (Type 2) perfective 'to telephone'

	past	future	imperative
я	позвони́л(а)	позвоню́	
ты	позвони́л(а)	позвони́шь	позвони́
он	позвони́л	позвони́т	
она́	позвони́ла	позвони́т	
оно́	позвони́ло	позвони́т	
мы	позвони́ли	позвони́м	
вы	позвони́ли	позвони́те	позвони́те
они́	позвони́ли	позвоня́т	

past active participle: **позвони́вший**
gerund: **позвони́в**

(e) **жить** (Type 1B) imperfective 'to live'

	present	past	future	imperative
я	живу́	жил(а́)	бу́ду жить	
ты	живёшь	жил(а́)	бу́дешь жить	живи́
он	живёт	жил	бу́дет жить	
она́	живёт	жила́	бу́дет жить	
оно́	живёт	жи́ло	бу́дет жить	
мы	живём	жи́ли	бу́дем жить	
вы	живёте	жи́ли	бу́дете жить	живи́те
они́	живу́т	жи́ли	бу́дут жить	

pres active participle: **живу́щий**
past active participle: **жи́вший**   *gerund:* **живя́**

(f) **написа́ть** (type 1B) perfective 'to write'

	past	*future*	*imperative*
я	написа́л(а)	напишу́	
ты	написа́л(а)	напи́шешь	напиши́
он	написа́л	напи́шет	
она́	написа́ла	напи́шет	
оно́	написа́ло	напи́шет	
мы	написа́ли	напи́шем	
вы	написа́ли	напи́шете	напиши́те
они́	написа́ли	напи́шут	

past active participle: **написа́вший**
past active participle: **напи́сан(ный)**   *gerund:* **написа́в**

281

Index

This index includes the abbreviations used in this book. The numbers refer to section headings, not pages.

The Russian alphabet in its dictionary order

1	А	а	a
2	Б	б	b
3	В	в	v
4	Г	г	g
5	Д	д	d
6	Е	е	ye as in yesterday
7	Ё	ё	yo as in yonder
8	Ж	ж	zh pronounced as the s in pleasure
9	З	з	z
10	И	и	ee as in meet (you may also hear yee)
11	Й	й	y as in boy
12	К	к	k
13	Л	л	l as in people
14	М	м	m
15	Н	н	n
16	О	о	o as in bottle
17	П	п	p
18	Р	р	r as in error (rolled as in Scots English)
19	С	с	s
20	Т	т	t
21	У	у	oo as in boot
22	Ф	ф	f
23	Х	х	h pronounced as the ch in Scots loch or German ach
24	Ц	ц	ts as in its
25	Ч	ч	ch as in check
26	Ш	ш	sh as in shall
27	Щ	щ	shsh as in Welsh sheep
28	Ъ	ъ	'hard sign', a very brief pause [-]
29	Ы	ы	approximately i as in bit
30	Ь	ь	'soft sign', a [y] sound which is always pronounced simultaneously with the preceding consonant, like the ny in canyon
31	Э	э	e as in fed
32	Ю	ю	yoo as in your
33	Я	я	ya as in yak

Picture Credits
Jacket: All special photography Demetrio Carrasco (including
Pushkin Fine Art Museum, Moscow top left and bottom of
spine) and Steve Gorton, except AA PHOTO LIBRARY: top centre;
MICHAEL JENNER: centre right; ELLEN ROONEY: main image.